The American Child

The American Child

*The Transformation of Childhood
Since World War II*

STEVEN MINTZ
PETER N. STEARNS

Oxford University Press is a department of the University of Oxford.
It furthers the University's objective of excellence in research, scholarship,
and education by publishing worldwide. Oxford is a registered trade mark of
Oxford University Press in the UK and in certain other countries.

Published in the United States of America by Oxford University Press
198 Madison Avenue, New York, NY 10016, United States of America.

© Oxford University Press 2025

All rights reserved. No part of this publication may be reproduced, stored in a retrieval system, transmitted, used for text and data mining, or used for training artificial intelligence, in any form or by any means, without the prior permission in writing of Oxford University Press, or as expressly permitted by law, by license or under terms agreed with the appropriate reprographics rights organization. Inquiries concerning reproduction outside the scope of the above should be sent to the Rights Department, Oxford University Press, at the address above.

You must not circulate this work in any other form
and you must impose this same condition on any acquirer.

CIP data is on file at the Library of Congress.

ISBN 9780197797082

DOI: 10.1093/9780197797112.001.0001

Printed by Marquis Book Printing, Canada

The manufacturer's authorized representative in the EU for product safety is
Oxford University Press España S.A. of Parque Empresarial San Fernando de Henares,
Avenida de Castilla, 2 – 28830 Madrid (www.oup.es/en or product.safety@oup.com).
OUP España S.A. also acts as importer into Spain of products made by the manufacturer.

Contents

Preface   vii

1. A New Childhood and New Problems   1
2. A Changing Childhood in Historical Perspective   8
3. The Fragile Child: A Theme in Contemporary Childhood   20
4. Diversity and Inequality in American Childhood Since World War II   47
5. More Schooling. Less Joy?   81
6. Children in a Changing Family   116
7. The Decline of Children's Play—and the New Alternatives   144
8. The Changing Face of Children's Culture   169
9. The New Neurodevelopmental, Emotional, and Behavioral Disorders of Childhood   196
10. Anxious Children   212
11. The Impact of the New Disorders   227
12. Facing Up to Contemporary Childhood   238

Endnotes   251
Suggestions for Further Reading   275
Index   279

Preface

Only by recognizing the many ways that American childhood has changed since the 1960s can we appreciate the challenges that today's children are dealing with—and also why American children may be trying to cope with a wider range of burdens than their counterparts in other affluent countries.

Contemporary American childhood must be explored as a distinctive experience, one that has taken shape over the past several decades. Only by appreciating the novelty of childhood today—from new forms of inequality to intensified schooling to shifts in adult perceptions—can we begin to discuss possible remedies for the problems involved.

Appreciating contemporary childhood as a new experience involves taking on several quite understandable distractions. Nostalgia is one. Many Americans regard the post-World War II decades as the golden age of American childhood—a time when childhood was more innocent and carefree and society as a whole more child-centered. While there are elements of truth in this vision, it is also deeply misleading. It overlooks the huge issues American children faced before the contemporary era, including racial segregation and massive gender disparities, as well as the thousands of children with disabilities who were barred from public school or confined to institutions. Nostalgia is a tempting approach to contemporary childhood, but it can hinder effective adaptation to the challenges children face today.

Shading off from nostalgia is a widespread tendency to overemphasize decline and deterioration—the declension distraction. Many of the changes that have redefined childhood are arguably good—improvements in opportunities for girls is one of the most obvious examples. Only by acknowledging the complexities of recent history, progress and problems alike, can we really work toward a better future.

Single-issue analysis is another common challenge, sometimes laced with a good bit of nostalgia—the oversimplification distraction. There has been a temptation in the twenty-first century to seize on one factor, such as the pandemic or the rise of social media, to account for the problems contemporary children confront. The approach is not entirely wrong—social media have affected children, though diversely—but it misleadingly ignores other factors, such as the rise of the work-oriented family, and it shortchanges longer-term shifts. As this book will show, if all too many children today are more troubled, less happy, and more burdened than their Baby Boom predecessors, this is the product of several decades in which the American approach to children has changed, with the adults involved often unaware of how much they were transforming the childhood experience.[1]

In the pages that follow, we will show how and why family life, schooling, and children's play have shifted since the 1950s, how new forms of inequality have stratified the experience of childhood in novel ways, and what these changes have meant for children's physical and psychological well-being and their overall development. And we will offer a number of practical, though demanding, solutions to the challenges contemporary children face. If we fail to innovate in the face of major change, we risk further damage to children themselves and, arguably, the nation's future.

Ultimately, the big issue centers on the importance of children and childhood. It is time to ask ourselves, as a society, whether we are losing the capacity to be child-friendly—long a bragging point in American discussions with foreign visitors. Today's parents certainly love their own kids, sometimes quite fiercely, but it is far less certain that Americans love children in general. And more and more of us are choosing not to have kids at all. Making childhood a greater national priority will not be easy. It involves addressing a range of developments that have taken shape over the past half century. Thinking about the meaning of child-friendliness, and what has happened to it, is a good way to start.

1
A New Childhood and New Problems

According to the annual UN-sponsored World Happiness Poll of 2024, American young people ranked sixtieth among the 144 nations surveyed. The annual report showed a major decline in the nation's overall happiness rankings, falling below the top twenty for the first time—entirely fueled by rising discontent among adults under thirty (only more favorable ratings by older folks prevented a more precipitous overall plunge). Experts evaluating the results talked, somewhat paradoxically, of a midlife crisis among people for whom adulthood was just beginning. Part of the problem undoubtedly stemmed from issues largely specific to young adults: housing costs, student debt, possibly worries about finding a romantic partner. But the growing tensions of contemporary childhood also factored in: many Americans were now entering adulthood on the heels of childhood experiences that themselves had been cutting into happiness for several decades. And while youth unhappiness showed up in some other advanced industrial countries (though not all), nowhere was it as pronounced as in the United States. From this angle as well, something was amiss in American childhood.

The recognition that American children are not doing well is not uniformly applicable: some, of various demographics and ages, seem to be doing fine, suggesting, among other things, some desirable political energy and greater tolerance for the future. But the levels of distress are high, most obviously given by increasingly ominous reports about mental health difficulties and social maladjustment, along with indications of growing loneliness.[1] The impact of growing inequality looms large as well, though children at many levels are encountering new challenges.

Worth noting as well is the fact that, according to a number of indicators, problems among American children, though not unique, are measurably more severe than those in otherwise comparable countries that have also experienced Covid and the impact of social media. A quick example: the percentage of children in the United States diagnosed with attention deficit hyperactivity disorder (ADHD) in the mid-2020s, at 11 percent following rapid recent increase, contrasts oddly with the 3.6 percent of their counterparts in Britain.[2]

American tensions are particularly startling, given measurable improvements in children's conditions in many respects over the past several decades. By the early twenty-first century, rates of smoking had markedly declined (though with some uptick in vaping). Teenage pregnancy dropped at least as sharply. School and college graduation rates continued to improve. Deaths in car accidents declined massively by the early twenty-first century, as did arrests for drunk driving: 36 percent down for young drivers since 1982.[3] Strikingly, teenage suicide rates, which had increased between 1975 and 1990, dropped noticeably by 2007, and while they then turned upward they remained well below 1990 levels.[4] Further, until Covid, even school violence was down—by 70 percent from the 1990s to 2013, according to one report, despite the distressing and highly publicized mass shootings.[5] Many commentators noted a heightened level of caution among many children and adolescents, which reduced many of the behavior problems that had seemed so troubling a few decades earlier. This was not, in other words, a generation out of control, and a number of welcome features deserve serious emphasis.

Changes in parenting contributed a variety of positives as well, though there were obvious complexities. By the 1990s parental time spent with children had increased, compared even with the halcyon 1950s; some of the worst stresses that had resulted from the entry of mothers into the workforce had been modified. The plight of "latchkey kids," a vivid issue in the 1980s, had receded. Parental commitment to children's happiness ran high as well: an early twenty-first-century poll showed 76 percent of American parents highlighting this as their primary goal.[6]

Accounting for bleak childhood indicators amid the many signs of parental commitment and a heightened sense of responsibility among children themselves is no easy task. This book is devoted to exploring the paradox by examining major patterns of change in American childhood over roughly the past seventy years. With deep awareness of the many and often growing diversities among American children, the book will probe a number of sources of new disruption, some of them predictable—like the new, though complex, signs of family instability—and others less familiar in this context, like the (probable) decline in the pleasure of attending school and the striking changes in patterns of children's play.

The Idea of Contemporary Childhood as a New Experience

The changes that differentiate the contemporary child from their mid-twentieth-century counterpart range from adult attitudes to specific changes in schooling and the use of free time. Both the relevant cultural framework and the ways children are pressed to organize their lives have shifted dramatically. A value system that romanticized children's innocence and sought to keep them separate from adult issues has progressively given way, though not without regrets, as children gain increasingly early and direct access to adult knowledge. A system that sought to combine some attention to schooling with an ideal of free, unregimented play, though particularly for boys, has largely yielded to more rigid arrangements combined with the growing influence of commercial culture. Children are still seen as deserving some entertainment, largely mediated by their elders, but emphasis on the importance of training for a challenging adulthood has measurably increased. Finally, the kinds of maladies that most deeply affect children and trouble the adults involved have shifted markedly—one of the most fundamental markers of change available. Evaluation of this final development is particularly challenging, but it includes awareness of the "psychologizing" of certain childhood characteristics.

Exploring a distinct kind of contemporary childhood as it has emerged over several decades sets an ambitious historical agenda. For the most part, the growing number of historians interested in childhood have either stayed away from the contemporary period, producing important findings about earlier patterns, or have assumed that contemporary developments largely extend innovations that began to take shape under the influence of the eighteenth-century Enlightenment and the industrial revolution of the nineteenth century. Links to these earlier precedents do exist, as we will see, but the level of change outweighs the continuities.[7] Despite a number of excellent surveys that extend into the later twentieth century, we lack a history of the contemporary.

For the many non-historians interested in childhood, whether as parents, scholars, or other observers, the focus on a new historical pattern, on the idea of a distinct contemporary childhood, offers both opportunity and challenge. The opportunity is to see the range of factors and symptoms that have made childhood today a measurably different experience, rather than centering on a list of unconnected developments. The challenge is twofold:

first, to increase the attention paid to a phase of life that may be somewhat taken for granted amid all the other pressing contemporary problems; and second, to realize that the troubles we do see among American children today cannot be captured by emphasizing one particular recent villain—social media, for instance. The issues range more widely and go back farther in time, which is why historical analysis is essential. Single-factor diagnosis—the oversimplification distraction—while capturing part of the problem, is off the mark and will not yield adequate solutions.

Contemporary children are not only somewhat different from their predecessors. They are also, on average, less joyful and more stressed. Childhood has moved away from the romantic simplifications of an earlier American middle class. It is increasingly psychologized and even pathologized, which is why, despite so many continued gains, a sense of concern is mounting and why so many children themselves report serious malaise.

The Common Targets

Historians of childhood are not alone in expressing concern about contemporary American children. A variety of experts and journalists regularly chime in, often with valuable data and insights, and the wider public is aware of many issues even aside from culture wars and disputes about what is happening with the nation's young. Understandably, attention often centers on two problem areas, both recent and both deeply troubling: the impact of the pandemic and the harmful effects of the rise of social media.

Children were among the pandemic's chief casualties, all the more because many American leaders initially seemed more concerned about other issues—like keeping the bars open—than what was happening to kids. Lockdowns severely disrupted children's formal education, resulting in significant and thus far durable learning loss. Test scores in all basic subjects dropped, erasing decades of improvement. Since schools also provide important social services, lockdowns also interrupted the provision of meals, vision and hearing testing, and monitoring children's well-being.[8]

Social development was set back, as lockdowns restricted children's physical activities and interactions with peers. Anxiety and stress increased. At the same time, social and economic divides widened, putting economically disadvantaged children further behind their privileged peers. Children who lost a parent or another relative were particularly at risk.

The pandemic is likely to have lingering effects on children's development, well-being, and opportunities. Prolonged uncertainty may contribute to lasting mental health issues, particularly anxiety and depression, in addition to the impact on educational achievement and social skills.[9]

For some children, the impact of social media intertwined with the pandemic in heightening loneliness and social disengagement. Well before 2020, children's screen time began to increase, whether the focus was TVs, cell phones, video games, or tablets and personal computers. Each adult generation since the 1970s has experienced a panic over the impact of new technologies on children, and while some of the earlier public fears were exaggerated, twenty-first-century concerns may be genuinely different.

The availability of social media accelerates the exposure to adult realities, as young children gain knowledge about transgender identities, sexual abuse, and other issues. It expands commercial influences, compared to the experience of Baby Boomers. While educational offerings like *Sesame Street* persist, animated shows and child-oriented fantasy fare are much more widely available, with specialized programming available virtually nonstop. "Influencers" gain far greater traction than the teenage icons of the mid-twentieth century. Above all, exposure to social media has reduced person-to-person interactions for many young people. It has introduced some children to new psychological challenges, to sometimes dangerous contacts with strangers, and to unrealistic standards of beauty and happiness that leave them deeply discontented with their own lives.[10]

Not surprisingly, a focus on the ongoing dislocations of the pandemic and the impact of new technologies often consumes most of the public space available for attention to children, along with culture war debates particularly about the schools. And there is no denying the importance of the issues or their probable durability. However, many of the crucial challenges facing children today cannot simply be pinned to the new crisis areas. In key cases, the pandemic and social media have intensified existing trends; in other cases they simply brought these issues to brighter light. To take one example: reports of girls' distress about body image is one of the problems legitimately discussed in the assessment of social media—but it goes back at least to the 1980s (particularly among white girls); the new media pick up the trend but do not cause it.[11]

This is why, despite the focus on recent dislocations, we clearly need a sense of American childhood's recent history. Putting the point simply: while we certainly should be trying to rein in the harmful effects of social media and remediating pandemic learning loss, dealing with these issues alone will not fix the problems of contemporary childhood. The problems are both broader, and a bit older, than this vital target alone.

In an 1858 speech, Abraham Lincoln said: "If we could first know where we are, and whither we are tending, we could then better judge what to do, and how to do it."[12] The advice is vital for the understanding of childhood now. We need to ask ourselves what childhood is like today as a result of changes over the past few decades, and not just one or two undeniably important jolts from the day before yesterday. A larger contemporary history, using but stepping beyond issues like Covid, has its own challenges, but it offers a vital perspective on the key issues in current American childhood.

Every item on the current child policy agenda—girls' self-esteem issues, boys' academic performance, social coping skills, anxiety, depression, and the apparent increase in the incidence of attention deficit and autism spectrum disorder—has a historical dimension that has largely escaped not only the general public but many policymakers and child savers. Providing this dimension includes pulling together some of the significant but dispersed findings of the experts themselves, but it offers wider perspectives as well. The result will measurably improve our grasp of what is going on and why—and may help fulfill the last part of Lincoln's plea as well, allowing us to better judge not only what is happening but what to do.

Conclusion

This is a study of childhood, where possible dealing directly with children's experiences but also with adult frameworks that surround children. Factors specific to childhood—like new kinds of inequality, the unprecedented decline of children as a percentage of the population, or the dramatic shifts in schooling—receive explicit attention. But it will also be clear that many of the issues of contemporary childhood relate deeply to changes in the adult world. Rising anxiety among children, for example, builds on similar changes among adults. Declining trust and optimism among many adults leads to growing concerns about the prospects of their offspring, as a new sense of caution and competition replaces belief in a future of rising opportunity. Contemporary childhood, arguably less separate from the adult world than modern childhood had been, inevitably introduces concerns about the state of American society more generally.[13]

The idea that contemporary children differ markedly from their Baby Boom counterparts risks touching base with an older tradition of worrying that the new crop of young people are not measuring up to past standards. This is not the point, and not only because there have been some measurable gains along the newer issues. What matters is not a facile story of declension or the impulse to identify a single villain, and certainly not children themselves. The challenge centers on exploring the wide range of developments that have been altering the experience of childhood for more than a half century, and then to reconsider the framework going forward. What has changed can change again, though the process may be difficult.

One final point: contemporary childhood involves a complicated interaction between attitudes and assumptions and measurable behaviors. In some respects, as we will see, value systems have changed particularly rapidly: hence, for example, a dramatically harsher judgment of young people who do not manage to graduate from high school—which was still the norm just eighty years ago. In other respects, less surprisingly, cultural assumptions have changed less swiftly than objective realities—as in the interactions between gender and childhood—which generates another set of challenges. Real differences between girls and boys have narrowed—as in sports—but older assumptions still count strongly. A history of the emergence of contemporary childhood may facilitate some rebalancing between realities and evaluations.

The notion of crisis has arguably become overused in the contemporary United States—while the menu varies by political perspective, it is very long. It may be unnecessary to add childhood to the list: again, there is great diversity and a variety of positive developments. But there is no question that problems run deep: if crisis may be overdoing it, urgency is not. It is vital, among all the pressing issues, to figure out how to give children a greater priority.

The American Child: The Transformation of Childhood Since World War II. Steven Mintz and Peter N. Stearns, Oxford University Press. © Oxford University Press 2025. DOI: 10.1093/9780197797112.003.0001

2

A Changing Childhood in Historical Perspective

The argument that the kind of childhood that has developed in the United States since the 1960s is a new condition may seem completely unsurprising—though many of the key novelties are not widely appreciated. Experts and popularizers have inundated us with generalizations about the differences among generations, from Gen X to Gen Z to the more amorphous millennials, as if every twenty years or so the characteristics of young people shift shapes. Many young people themselves are convinced that the advent of social media marks a huge dividing line between them and their counterparts in the past (though they do not necessarily know much about that past). More broadly, we live in a culture that tends to exaggerate novelty.

The notion of a somewhat longer and more complex process of change is less familiar, but it is central to understanding what childhood today is all about amid the sometimes exaggerated particulars about how one twenty-year age cohort differs from its predecessors. And it involves more than the undeniably important fact that children in the 2020s have cell phones and their predecessors did not.

At the same time, contemporary childhood builds on a set of major transformations that took shape over the previous century and a half, and while there is no need to rehearse the details of this process, some of the basic features remain essential. Modern childhood was in many ways redefined, compared to more traditional standards, and contemporary childhood is a further redefinition. The result, admittedly, may sound like a furniture store—from traditional to modern to contemporary—but it actually fits the process involved: change on top of change.

Contemporary childhood reshapes but also consolidates some of the features of the kind of childhood that had responded to the conditions of American industrial society. In some ways—schooling is a prime example—contemporary childhood is partly more of the same but with significantly new results. In other respects—for example, in play—current features are strikingly new but also enhance some minor themes in the industrial experience.[1]

The Modern Basics

By the 1950s, the basic contours of what can be described as modern childhood had been well established in the United States, the result of changes that had accumulated for many decades. Child labor, the subject of prolonged debate, had largely ended. Shockingly, it has reared its head again recently amid the stress of labor force disruptions and immigration quarrels. Some states, like Iowa and Arkansas, allow thirteen-year-olds to work long night shifts doing jobs like cleaning cutting machinery in chicken processing plants. The kids involved are, to be sure, from "other" families, not those of the employers or policymakers; still, it is a reminder that old habits die hard and that current attitudes to some children are not as benign as many Americans like to believe. Nevertheless, the fact remains that until recently the end of demanding child labor seemed to be a done deal aside from migrant farming. This had been achieved for most young children during the nineteenth century. Then a massive campaign early in the twentieth century, with more sweeping goals, reflected a crescendo of concern about children's well-being. Combined with the impact of the Great Depression, this finally resulted in legislation in the 1930s that banned children from most forms of work before the age of sixteen. Correspondingly, reliance on children as an economic asset clearly receded, and this may have freed up attention for other goals. This was a massive change in the nature and position of childhood, to which Americans are still assimilating in some ways.[2]

In turn, the role of schooling steadily expanded. Here too the nineteenth century saw solid gains at the primary level, at least outside the South. High school attendance then moved up steadily in the twentieth century, though, as we will see, graduation rates still lagged noticeably until the 1950s. Better enforcement of attendance and the wider introduction of grades early in the twentieth century already made schooling a more serious business.

Fundamental demographic changes affected children on yet another front. The per capita American birth rate started to decline from the late eighteenth century onward, beginning with the middle classes but gradually extending more widely and embracing even recent immigrants. By 1910, the average American family had 3.5 children, less than half the norm of a century before. Lower birth rates facilitated more parental attention to each child individually.[3]

From 1880 onward, lower birth rates were increasingly matched by a massive decline in children's mortality. In 1880 over 25 percent of all children born would perish before age five; by 1920, this figure was down to 5 percent and rapidly falling. By this point—as in other Western countries—the average family no longer had to expect one or more children to die, and children themselves would be less surrounded by expectations of death than ever before. The role of doctors and medical advice in children's lives correspondingly increased, and when children did die the result could seem far more agonizing than before; but the overall change was surely positive. Here were vital innovations in modern childhood that have largely persisted.

Patterns of discipline also eased somewhat, though there was great variety in the United States and a surprisingly high level of commitment to corporal punishment. Childrearing advice increasingly cautioned against spankings or even blatant shaming, urging parents to reconsider older disciplinary patterns.[4]

Symbolic commitments to children's happiness expanded. The idea of an annual birthday celebration, virtually unknown in the late eighteenth century, became increasingly common from the mid-nineteenth century onward, and even spread to schoolroom celebrations as teachers also sought new ways to appeal to their charges. This was capped, in the 1920s and 1930s, with the introduction and wide acceptance of the "Happy Birthday" jingle, surely one of the most widely recognized songs in modern American culture. Though it can be variously interpreted, a commitment to consumer pleasures spread as well. The first decade of the twentieth century saw a brief debate about providing consumer goods even for infants—in the form of such novelties as teddy bears, imitated from Germany—but the discussion quickly resolved in favor of giving children more things, and the United States became a world leader in toy production. Entertainment opportunities followed as well: the 1920s heralded the advent of the Disney company, explicitly devoted to providing happiness to young viewers.[5]

Well before 1950, in other words, American children, like their counterparts in other industrial societies, were less likely than ever before to be exploited at work, more likely to survive, more likely to be cared for by parents rather than siblings or servants, and more likely to be indulged with consumer items. Again, in contrast to traditional patterns, children were also more likely to have some government protection against undue work, toward the provision of education, against unsafe playgrounds, and toward some concern about nutritional adequacy. From the early twentieth century onward, the federal government regularly sponsored White House conferences about various aspects of childhood, and an active Children's Bureau sought to inform parents about best practices while also supporting other innovations, such as school lunches for needy students.[6]

Evaluation and the Challenge of Nostalgia

Even a brief summary of the characteristics of modern childhood raises several issues that affect the examination of more recent trends. In the first place, quite obviously, many basic modern features persist. Contemporary childhood reverts to some earlier patterns—undoing a nineteenth-century emphasis on childhood innocence, for example, in favor of more exposure to adult realities—but it retains key modern characteristics, including the massive aversion to children's deaths (though aversion does not always prompt remedial action, particularly for children of a different race). While the understanding that a key function of childhood involves formal education has been redefined, it was already set in motion. Changes are real, but they interact with the established backdrop.

Nostalgia offers a second link between the modern and the contemporary—a major distraction already noted. It can affect scholars as well as a wider public, where any falling away from the features of modern childhood is automatically suspect. Many historians have seen the changes that created modern childhood as a clear example of progress, against the liabilities of more traditional patterns. (There are not many defenders of the notion that traditional childhood was superior, though there has been some debate around the edges.) Thus, one authority, Lloyd deMause, writing in the 1970s, urged that "the history of childhood is a nightmare from which we have only begun to recover. The further back in history one goes, the lower the level of care, and the more likely children are to be killed, abandoned, beaten and sexually abused."[7] While this was an extreme statement, many scholars have seen the basic trends of modern childhood, not only the decline of child labor and earlier mortality levels but also the new emphasis on gentle parental care, in highly positive terms. This provides an academic twist to what many Americans more generally believe, looking back on childhood conditions by the mid-twentieth century in positive terms, bathing family life in a particularly warm glow but also waxing nostalgic about the simpler cultural fare available, or the charm of children's games.

This in turn restates one of the fundamental challenges in dealing with contemporary childhood, when contrasted with the impression of prior progress. Is the substantial redefinition of modern childhood also a story of troubling deterioration? Have decades of advance somehow turned to regression, tainting the gains that had been achieved by the 1950s? Can a book written by two non-children, both of whom enjoyed many aspects of their earlier childhoods before the contemporary era, avoid an emphasis on declension?

The troubles of the contemporary child are real, and (though partly because they are new) arguably harder to assimilate than the burdens children faced in the 1950s. It is far easier—to take an obvious example—to chart the diseases that children still regularly encountered in the early 1950s, from mumps to measles to polio (most of which were seriously troubling but no longer usually fatal), than to assess the rates and consequences of mental distress.

Yet the main point is to insist on the paradox presented by contemporary childhood, not the sore points alone. Many measurable gains have been registered in recent decades, at least aside from the Covid setbacks. Not only is physical health better, and a host of worries on that score reduced for adults and children alike, but other problems that seemed impossibly dire a half century ago, like teenage pregnancy, have eased immensely. Despite the huge current debates over gender issues, gender inequality in childhood has declined substantially—indeed the current debates in many ways reflect the change. Contemporary childhood presents a different basket of strengths and weaknesses from its modern counterpart, and too much nostalgia is simply misplaced.

And this leads to a final preliminary note about the modern patterns, which also serves as a starting point for the exploration of the contemporary: the patterns harbored their own complexities, which inevitably have affected later developments in their own right.

Inequality was a crucial feature of modern childhood: the most positive picture is a white, middle-class image that sidestepped the educational and health disadvantages faced by children of color or those who were simply poor. Substantial dependence on gender distinctions and stereotypes added its own complexity to the modern framework: girls and boys were assumed to be very different, and their treatment and opportunities varied accordingly.[8]

Further—even for some in the middle class—certain modern changes were double-edged in ways that may continue to complicate childhood today. Replacement of work exploitation by schooling was a vital change, but it could make it more difficult for some children to find a sense of purpose amid greater emphasis on classroom success, particularly as attendance was regularized after 1900. Schooling also increased age-grading among children, which could affect social contacts; and the decline in sibling numbers that accompanied lower birth rates might have similar effects. Child experts in the 1920s in fact emphasized tensions among siblings, in contrast to past assumptions of mutual support. Opportunity for play provided another crucial modern variable: while work did decline, adult supervision of children's activities actually expanded, in the interests of advancing educational preparation. On another front: exploitation of children as consumers was also already a concern in the first half of the twentieth century. Issues of this sort have become more prominent in contemporary childhood, but they are not brand new.[9] Finally, at least at some points, modern childhood in the United States created a number of new concerns. It was in the early 1950s, for example, that attention to the surge of juvenile delinquency reached unprecedented levels.

Modern patterns also raised fundamental questions about the purpose of having children in the first place. By the early twentieth century, and for many families well before this point, it was becoming clear that children had converted from being economic assets to liabilities. Improving methods of birth control, though limited by contemporary standards and bitterly contested, enhanced opportunities for adults to decide not only how many children to have but whether to have them at all. Questions about the purposes of children were not always easy to answer in the modern context, and they linger still.[10]

The basic point is clear. Any evaluation of American childhood today must reflect a complicated calculus about the ongoing impact of modern structures and issues. Contemporary childhood is different, and these differences are not always easy to evaluate, but it also builds on problems baked into many modern assumptions.

Turning Points

The transition from modern to contemporary childhood began to take shape in the 1950s and 1960s, not overnight and not based on any single big event. A number of specific factors contributed to change, from a rising divorce rate to new government mandates about education.

Beyond the specifics, however, it is possible to suggest a larger cluster of transformations that clearly set the stage. Just as modern childhood had been ushered in by new Enlightenment ideas about children plus the impact of industrial conditions and a declining birth rate, so its postmodern counterpart has reflected three or four major shifts—all taking shape well before the additional changes ushered in by social media or the pandemic. There are some clear reasons that contemporary childhood is different.

The first shift was cultural, centered on the increasing application of psychology in both expert and popular evaluations of children and the ways this gradually modified earlier, optimistic assumptions about the nature of the child. It was in the 1950s and 1960s, for example, that concerns about mental health in children began to intensify. They were not entirely new: the pioneering psychologist G. Stanley Hall had raised important issues in the late nineteenth century. More specifically, some discussion of what would later be called ADHD began in the early twentieth century, while psychologists involved with student services had also talked, though rather vaguely, about student needs as early as the 1930s. The first *Diagnostic and Statistical Manual* issued by American psychiatrists in 1952 made no mention of problems like ADHD, however, beyond a vague reference to "minimal brain dysfunction," while the introduction of the drug Ritalin in 1955 was initially aimed at adults. In 1957, however, researchers identified "hyperkinetic impulse disorder," and research on the use of psychoactive drugs for children was formally launched in 1958 (with Ritalin approved for use in children in 1961). In 1968 the second *DSM* edition formally recognized the hyperkinetic disorder, though the shift to "attention deficit disorder" occurred only with the 1980 version.

Roughly the same chronology applied to childhood depression, not seen as a disease category until the early 1970s despite scattered findings from the 1950s onward. By this juncture other kinds of work on children's potential psychiatric problems were advancing as well, including a battery of tests for anxiety that from this point onward were recurrently administered to college students and grade schoolers alike. Several scholars have identified the 1960s as the point at which the United States became a "therapeutic society," and the characterization clearly applies to children as well, though initially with no deep sense of crisis.[11]

The basic point is this: as childhood began to be increasingly psychologized, some of the Enlightenment/Romantic assumptions about childhood innocence and rationality encountered new complications or fell away entirely. This aspect of childhood became newly problematic. The issue went beyond adult perceptions, although these predominated in the later twentieth century. Children themselves ultimately picked up the therapeutic approach and its language. At least by the twenty-first century many young people, by middle school age if not before, were almost as ready as concerned adults to identify and label—and often overdiagnose—mental health issues in their peers or themselves. By the twenty-first century young people were even applying labels like Post Traumatic Stress Disorder (PTSD) to problems that were usually far less dire—watering down the concepts but reflecting a troubling tendency to claim mental distress. Here was one pillar of the new contemporary framework, emphasizing a partially new cultural approach to childhood on the part of adults and a new vantage point for children themselves.[12]

The second pillar of the redefinition of childhood, broadly comparable to the earlier impact of the Industrial Revolution, is more familiar still: the transformation of the economy toward greater emphasis on knowledge production and professional and service jobs that in turn required higher levels of education. Here too a sense of change began to emerge clearly by the 1950s and 1960s. Blue-collar labor did not disappear, but it shrank fairly steadily as a result of greater mechanization and global competition, and with this the calculus of many families, as well as national policy, had to change. A major redefinition of schooling was the most obvious result, again taking shape from the 1950s onward, but the new framework would impact play and other aspects of childhood as well. For many families, even some that seemed clearly successful, economic shifts made the future seem less secure or predictable in ways that could affect their handling of children. Here was the fundamental reason that childhood began to be reconsidered in terms of more focused preparation for adulthood.[13]

The third basic marker, not unrelated to the first two though emerging slightly later in time, centers on the end of the Baby Boom in 1964 and the onset of a level of demographic change that went well beyond what had occurred in earlier decades. Here too the first part of the story is familiar enough, but the ramifications have increasingly carried American society into new territory.

Increasing postwar affluence had led most married couples to interrupt the modern trend of birth rate reductions, while many middle-class families actually reversed course, averaging three or four children per household through the 1950s. Presumably part of the new momentum stemmed from the disruptions of the Depression and world war: many families were simply trying to compensate for past barriers. But there is no question that the baby boom reflected a deep enthusiasm for children, a belief that they should take priority over many other possible consumer goals. Some experts at the time contended that this was a durable American reorientation, noteworthy as well for being more robust than its counterparts in Europe.[14]

But the boom ended, and with it many of the motivations that had briefly sustained it. While initially the return to birth rate reduction merely restored a past trend, levels ultimately dropped well below any prior precedent, curtailing the number of children in society at large and in average neighborhoods, as well as individual families. In the nation as a whole, the percentage of children (eighteen and under) in the total population plummeted to 22 percent by 2020, by far the lowest in American history (contrasting with 36 percent at the height of the baby boom). Absolute numbers tell the same story: there were 1.2 million fewer children in the United States in 2021 than there had been just a decade before. Household data reflect the same pattern: today, a substantial majority of all households—61 percent—include no child, partly due to the increase of older adults but also reflecting the dramatic numerical decline of children. Concerns about birth rate decline normally focus on the implications for labor force size, but there are direct consequences for children themselves. While scarcity might in principle have increased the level of attention paid to children, it has clearly allowed many adults to concentrate on other issues and other groups.[15] And the average age of parents increased notably: for mothers, from twenty-one when the first child was born in 1970 to twenty-seven in 2000: for fathers, twenty-seven in 1970, thirty-one in 2020.[16] But the larger point was the sheer decline in children's numbers, which would affect many features of childhood. In families and neighborhoods, as well as society more broadly, the position of children was being redefined.

Other developments also contributed to change. From the 1960s onward, growing numbers of mothers entered the formal labor force. This could have a huge effect on childhood quite apart from the accompanying birth rate decline, amplifying other shifts in family life. Exposure to commercial media ramped up, with the growing fascination with television presenting kids with new influences in addition to simply taking up increasing chunks of time—even before the rise of the Internet. Here, the surge in advertisements directed at children, from 1981 onward, has played an increasingly important role in reshaping childhood.

The combination of factors was powerful. The increasing impulse to evaluate childhood in psychological terms, combined with the new imperatives for training and the declining numerical position of children at both local and national levels, ushered in a new framework, and these factors linked directly to the new sense of pressure at school and the escalating reports of mental distress. Schooling and reduced numbers of kids in a neighborhood, along with increased commercial pressures, combined to attack key forms of play. Novel signs of insecurity opened the door to new kinds of exploitation—as in the eagerness to convince ten-year-old girls that they must buy cosmetic products to make themselves more beautiful. Important modern characteristics remained, but most were substantially redefined and some were undone entirely by the interaction of the new factors that were shaping contemporary childhood.

It was also in these same decades that national policy focus began to shift away from a holistic interest in childhood to other issues. The last White House Conference on Children and Youth was held in 1971. The conferences had followed from a deep progressive belief in the power of policy to improve children's lives, with one held approximately every decade since the first gathering in 1909. The first conference had generated the Children's Bureau, devoted to "all matters pertaining to the welfare of children and child life among all classes of the people." Now, however, the initiative ended, just as the Children's Bureau itself was newly marginalized in a larger agency.

Efforts to revive a more general initiative, particularly under Barack Obama, simply fell flat, despite advocacy by the Child Welfare League that "it's time to again make children the focus of national debates and discussions." Partisan disagreements most obviously doomed the effort, leading one proponent to lament that failure followed from the "dysfunction of our times."[17] But White House conferences on other subjects continued to flourish, with a new tradition focused on issues among the elderly taking root from the 1960s onward—and effective lobbying groups to match. Children of course have never voted, but now the declining numbers both of children and of active parents, combined with greater work distractions for many parents and particularly for mothers, were changing the policy context.

The result was a diminution in the priority of children and children's issues, from the 1960s onward. To be sure, young people themselves mounted periodic efforts, such as the campaigns for gun control that followed school shootings—though with little success. Parents might organize too, particularly around school issues. On the whole, however, child advocacy groups tended to splinter into single-issue categories (from delinquency to school curricula to social media), rather than seeking to embrace the larger childhood experience. Nothing has galvanized attention to children in recent decades as the campaign against child labor once did. At the same time, the relative power of the relevant advocacy groups has steadily diminished, not only compared to the clout of other age sectors but even more to increasingly powerful corporate lobbies seeking free rein in their interactions with children. The success of the food industry in the 1980s, gaining new access in marketing sugared cereals and other treats, or the more recent capacity of the social media giants to escape significant regulation in their dealings with the young, are clear markers of a contemporary power balance that does not favor children's interests. While some new attention to children's rights has also informed more recent national dialogue, this has not really substituted for more systematic policy.

On a number of fronts, in fact, the status of childhood has measurably slipped, again raising questions about the "child friendliness" of the nation as a whole. Housing is a case in point. In 1980 a federal report revealed a growing problem: at least 25 percent of all landlords were denying access to families with children, and up to 50 percent tolerated only one child. In response, a 1988 Fair Housing Act prohibited discrimination against children—but not in units with a certain percentage of adults over fifty-five, a loophole many landlords and homeowners' associations quickly took advantage of, with labels of "Housing for Older Persons" keeping kids out save as occasional visitors. In the same vein, by the early twenty-first century children were more often evicted from rental units than any other age group: 12 percent of evictees were under the age of five. The investigator responsible for this report had assumed that the presence of kids might mitigate landlord zeal, but the opposite was the case. And no remedy has been forthcoming or even proposed, helping to explain why a distressing number of American children are homeless. Approval of other areas where children might be banned, such as some cruise trips, sections of trains, and even some restaurants has gained ground as well.[18]

Other question marks apply, depending in part on political persuasion. The nation stands literally alone in not having signed the International Convention on the Rights of the Child. It is unusual in allowing some children to be tried as adults for crimes, and possibly to sentences of life without parole. The United States is the only advanced industrial society where gun deaths loom large as a cause of child mortality (second on the list of all factors), because, despite some impassioned advocacy, other priorities take precedence. Even protection for young people against car accidents, though improving, lags behind patterns in Western Europe. Federal spending on children apart from schooling, never matching European levels in any event, has actually dropped at several points, though the pandemic introduced some new oscillations. The post-pandemic move in several states to eliminate many restrictions on child labor, even down to age thirteen, is another interesting straw in the wind. There are many challenges to the valuation of children in the contemporary world. It was a German word, *Kinderfeindlichkeit*, or hostility or indifference to children, that first picked up on the issue in 1979. But the contemporary question marks have become particularly intriguing in the United States, particularly in the policy domain.[19]

It took a while, in the nineteenth and early twentieth centuries, for American policymakers to wrap their heads around some of the key issues in modern childhood and to gain a new level of attention for children's issues: hence, for example, the belated if ultimately successful move against child labor. A comparable transition has yet to occur for childhood's contemporary counterpart, including addressing the slippage of children, collectively, on the list of national priorities. This adds to the need to assess how contemporary childhood has emerged and what the new patterns are. Restoring real child friendliness will be a complex process at best, but it depends on awareness of the many ways in which contemporary childhood has become a novel experience.

The American Child: The Transformation of Childhood Since World War II. Steven Mintz and Peter N. Stearns, Oxford University Press. © Oxford University Press 2025. DOI: 10.1093/9780197797112.003.0002

3

The Fragile Child

A Theme in Contemporary Childhood

The juiciest examples are extreme, but they reflect a larger shift in the concerns many parents have when it comes to their children. The father who always greets his fourth-grade daughter as she comes out from school, holding an extra coat in case she is chilly, for a five-minute walk home. The Florida couple who forbids their grade-school children from walking down a long driveway to get the mail, because at one point they will be out of sight. The mother who sneaks into school to watch her second-grade daughter, actually entering the classroom when another girl refuses to share a toy or when the teacher fails to give the daughter a top mark. The mother who sits in on her son's interview for a summer job and tries to answer the questions for him. Not to mention the many parents who do all or part of their offspring's homework. The parents who make the lives of soccer coaches and referees hell on the assumption the kids involved can't stand up for themselves.

Helicopter parenting, as it has developed since the 1960s in a large minority of American families,[1] involves a number of assumptions, but one of the most interesting, and arguably troubling, is the belief that kids are not very competent. Of course, the parents involved see the environment as menacing, whether the issue is an often-exaggerated fear of crime or a worry that the child cannot manage to get into a decent college, also often exaggerated. But alongside the concerns about the dangers of the wider world is the unstated feeling that kids cannot do much toward taking care of themselves physically, emotionally, psychologically, and sometimes even academically. They may be deeply loved, even viewed in terms of great hopes for the future. But right now they need a lot of help, including boosts to their fragile self-esteem. The attitude plays a measurable role in the experiences of, and reactions to, the contemporary child. And while the approach reflects a number of factors, it clearly expresses the application of the "psychological turn" to parental judgments of their offspring.

Most child study experts, and most historians dealing with American childhood into the contemporary period, believe deeply that the theme of childish vulnerability and incompetence has been considerably overdone, to the detriment of children (and probably parents) during recent decades.[2] As a 2023 report urges, "Children can often accomplish tasks at a much younger age than law, parents and caregivers in the United States believe."[3] And amid some renewed debate about relevant issues, advocates of what is called, rather bizarrely, "free-range parenting"[4] urge that children can probably take care of themselves in a park playground by the time they are six or seven, ride urban transportation once they approach their teens (as they once did), and maybe even visit colleges without parental escort. On the other hand, rising concerns about children's mental health over the past few years, with findings that well over half of all young people in certain categories, such as girls between ages thirteen and fifteen, are seriously troubled, bring the image of the fragile child into sharper focus than ever before. Parents are not the only agents in American society eager to insist that children need new levels of guidance and protection.

The widespread sense of children's vulnerability is all the more striking in that many earlier observers, commenting on trends through the middle decades of the twentieth century, highlighted a growing emphasis on the child's autonomy. Studies in Muncie, Indiana, in the 1920s, 1930s, and 1970s, most notably, showed a strong movement away from insistence on childish obedience toward a growing delight in demonstrations of independence and competence, with parents actively supporting the shift. Adults in the 1920s complained widely about how too many children seemed bent on having their own way—though there were significant differences by social class. This emphasis had already weakened somewhat by the 1930s—in part because of the growing role of school-based activities and more time spent away from home. By 1978 parental approval of traits like frankness, tolerance, and independence had increased markedly, while preference for obedience dropped from 45 percent of the parents surveyed to 17 percent. Studies in other American cities, such as Detroit, largely confirmed the trends, which in turn reflected the intervening advances in educational levels and major shifts in the evaluation of characteristics desirable for economic success.[5]

The interest in autonomy did not disappear thereafter: a number of child-rearing experts remain eager to provide advice on promoting an autonomous child. Nor was there a resurgence in an emphasis on purely traditional types of obedience. However, autonomy themes were widely overtaken by concerns about children's inadequacy and fragility, their need for active guidance and support, from parents most obviously but also from the growing variety of service providers in schools and colleges. Important new concerns set in, particularly from the 1960s onward, as part of the changing cultural framework that would shape many features of contemporary childhood.

In turn, the growing sense of children's vulnerability built on a blend of significant changes over the past half century, with some features beginning to reshape attitudes toward children even earlier, at least in the (largely white) middle classes. Contemporary trends, in other words, partly amplify previous reactions to developments in childhood—though the new features are vital as well. The resultant combination helps explain why the fragility theme has proved so hard to challenge, despite the abundance of commentary urging parents to loosen their grip, and why American anxieties about children seem to outpace those of other comparable societies.

Assessing the unstated tradition of a somewhat fragile child is not an easy task. Most obviously, children are not in fact fully competent, particularly amid the complexities of a modern urban society. As education has increasingly replaced child labor, most societies have widened the gap between childhood and adulthood. The issue is not whether there is a need for some protection and supervision, but rather the extent. Further, the argument that Americans have developed a particular penchant for emphasizing children's lack of competence is a comparative claim that needs further analysis. There is little question that, today, American helicopter parenting involves an unusual degree of nervousness about the child's ability to cope with the relevant environment. A number of studies provide some validation, and parents visiting the United States from other countries also comment, for example, about the unusual reluctance to let children travel on their own. Further, there are additional historical and contemporary data that support the comparative claim that many Americans seem particularly uncertain about children's competence, though there is more work to be done.[6]

There is no contention that all contemporary American parents assume considerable childish incompetence. Class divisions loom large: working-class parents rarely have the time to hover over their children as many of their middle-class counterparts do. Their children may be affected by the vulnerability theme—for example, through school and community efforts to regulate children's play and avoid types of even minor injuries that were once assumed to be a normal part of growing up—but their parental approach assumes greater autonomy. Even in the middle and upper classes, assumptions can be inconsistent. One has only to look at the flourishing industry of children's sports (for those families that can bear the expense), where massive practice and performance sessions are imposed on children with every assumption that they will thrive or at least survive (though under adult guidance). We also may believe that children are more competent drivers than is true in many other countries: the US age for a first driver's license is on the low side comparatively—sixteen on average, compared, for example, to seventeen (usually) in the UK and eighteen in China.

It is also obviously true that Americans vary greatly in their insistence on a protective approach. Many groups can be disconcertingly tolerant of abuses to other people's children, for example, in the acceptance of child labor among migrant agricultural workers or, now, other minority children, the sometimes barbaric treatment of child immigrants, or the shocking inability to deal with the impact of guns or food adulteration on children generally. In fact, the American approach to children overall involves some striking ambivalence, between excessive precaution and surprising nonchalance, and while the latter applies particularly to children of lower-class and minority groups it can show up within the middle classes as well.

Initial Components from the Nineteenth Century

The image of the child in the nineteenth century, conveyed, for example, in family manuals, was in many respects a sturdy one, very distant from the neediness of its helicoptered counterpart in the twenty-first century. Adults expressed a variety of concerns about children, of course, including the importance of guidance in establishing good habits as well as, increasingly, the need for some formal education. Child labor came in for comment, though surprisingly slowly by today's standards, in part because of wide acceptance of work for immigrant and rural children and, in some quarters, for enslaved children as well.[7] Attacks on excessive hours and safety hazards were compatible with ongoing assumptions that some work was acceptable and that, whether through employment or household help, children could and should pitch in. As Lydia Maria Child put it succinctly in the 1830s, criticizing what she saw as an inclination toward idleness, "a child can be useful at six."[8] Trade unions and other groups that sought restrictions on children's hours of work certainly believed that a child needed "time for recreation and mental cultivation"—but not a cessation of work altogether.[9]

Sturdiness was a clear feature of the kind of "boy culture" that emerged during the century, at various social levels. Boys routinely tested each other's courage and competitiveness, and new words like "sissy" designated the child who could not measure up.[10] The greater fragility of girls stood out in contrast but drew little concern given the mantle of domesticity.

A number of foreign observers frequently commented on American openness to the opinions of the young, finding children far more outspoken within the family than their counterparts in Europe. This certainly suggested that children were not only highly valued in nineteenth-century American society but that there was unusual confidence in their contributions.

However, a few other themes emerged by the middle of the nineteenth century, suggesting new complications that might later contribute to a fuller sense of childhood fragility. The most important was the unusual emphasis on childhood innocence in mainstream American Protestantism, an exaggerated counterthrust against the older idea of original sin. Childhood innocence was not an American invention: it followed from work by European educational theorists like Rousseau and Froebel. But whereas their implications applied mainly to school reform, the American version carried over strongly into family settings, becoming a standard emphasis in the most popular family manuals from the 1820s onward.

The notion of the innocent child formed part of the idealized picture of a happy family, but it carried with it a certain sense of vulnerability as well. Innocence could easily be sullied by clumsy adults, particularly those who used fear or anger in their treatment of young children. Thus, while innocent children had no intrinsic fear, they also had no real power of resistance. Their emotional tranquility depended on careful adult control of their environment, for the clumsy parent could easily "embitter the whole existence" of his or her offspring. As T. S. Arthur continued, "It is utterly impossible to calculate the evil" that fear or anger might cause the child, a theme that was sometimes highlighted by stories of children actually dying from the intrusion of negative emotions. Children should even be protected from too much exposure to gloomy aspects of death: hence a new emphasis on the certainty and joys of heaven. Lydia Maria Child again captured the new image of the beautiful but vulnerable child: "Infants come to us from heaven, with their little souls full of innocence and peace; and, as far as possible, a mother's influence should not interfere with the influence of angels."[11]

Children's innocence was also invoked against the old practice of using shame in discipline, part of the wider attack on shame that had been launched in the eighteenth century. Here was another emotion that might easily overwhelm the vulnerable child, another point emphasized in the new genre of family advice manuals. Children who became the "objects of ridicule or rebuke" could be seriously damaged, their "sensibilities tortured into obtuseness or misanthropy."[12] Discipline, where needed, must be imposed carefully, with "great gentleness and patience" given the vulnerability of the target. "Punishments which make the child ashamed should be avoided. A sense of degradation is not healthy for character." This new approach could even generate references to the importance of self-esteem, a theme that would be much more extensively embellished in the later twentieth century. The child who was criticized in front of others would experience "pain out of all proportion to the offense" and suffer a tragic loss of "self-respect."[13]

The new ideas, though increasingly pervasive in the standard types of child-rearing literature, were by definition hard to implement, and there is no claim that they were fully adopted even in principle by the most conscientious middle-class parents. Indeed, they suggested a clear ambivalence with continued expectations of work, at least in household tasks, and with the brasher qualities expected in boys. But they did introduce a new emphasis on emotional frailty as part of the increasingly popular image of the innocent child, a notion that would gain greater importance amid some of the new psychological ideas available in the twentieth century.

And even in the nineteenth century, concerns about children's vulnerability prompted one other note of caution, as childhood and schooling became increasingly intertwined in urban life. For although there was considerable acceptance of the importance of school and schoolwork, particularly by the middle classes, there was also an undercurrent of hesitancy, lest too much intensity harm children physically and psychologically. Discussion often focused disproportionately on girls (including mid-century discussion about possible damage to reproductive capacity from unnatural confinement and mental pressure), since they were generally held to be more fragile than boys amid the gendered assumptions of nineteenth-century culture; but there were some wider implications.

Posture problems came in for considerable comment, particularly in the final decades of the century. This was a rather specific focus, but it would spill over into other musings on whether children were up to their new role. Thus, a doctor in 1880 attacked school for its "injurious effects" on children, citing stress and sleep difficulties, along with distortion of the spine. The treatise claimed that 83–92 percent of all children were suffering from spinal cord deviation, and it urged a significant reduction in school hours. Several authorities more generally deplored "the abnormal captivity of school." Even at the end of the century, medical commentary continued to express concern: "with his introduction to school life, the child's physical troubles begin." Obviously schooling gained ground anyway, though many schools tried to respond with more formal physical education and even posture lessons. But the notion that extensive schooling might be an unnatural burden on children's strength provided an interesting counterpoint to the very real changes in children's lives. Here was another theme that would return in various forms during the twentieth century.[14]

Shifts in the Early Twentieth Century

Several developments from about 1900 onward significantly extended ideas about children's frailties. More intense schooling, as attendance requirements stiffened and grading gained ground, amplified anxieties in this category. The importance of the individual child was enhanced by declining birth and death rates, and while the "priceless" child was a source of admiration, this might also amplify a sense of risk. The revived and enhanced campaign against child labor, though it struck a number of chords, began for the first time to deploy the notion of the innocent child as an argument against the ardors of most forms of employment, in ways that might carry over into other tasks as well. But the most striking innovations came from the new findings of the rising science of psychology, which became an increasingly dominant feature in child-rearing manuals and which steadily uncovered further areas of concern. Indeed, the resulting advice in the early twentieth-century decades, while preserving the innocence theme, increasingly overshadowed it with the emphasis on the child's emotional inadequacy. Childhood fragility moved to a new level.

Pricelessness and Innocence

The idea of the child as "priceless" was demonstrated both in the increasing interest in buying insurance on children's lives and in expansive court settlements when a child was injured or killed, from the 1890s through the 1930s and beyond. In fact, the "priceless" label came from a case in law.[15] While pricelessness and vulnerability were not the same, they could clearly overlap in a growing interest in protection. The fact that child death rates were falling rapidly also meant that the loss of a child arguably became harder to contemplate than ever before—a paradox that rested in part on the concomitant reduction of the birth rate and that persists today. Certainly, there were more than enough news reports of child deaths or serious injuries—for example, as pedestrian accidents surged in the 1920s—to maintain edginess, despite the favorable demographic context. The interwar decades also saw the beginning of new safety movements that would ultimately make the United States, despite its libertarian image, one of the most cautious countries in identifying certain kinds of dangers to children, a really interesting and wide-reaching implementation of the idea of vulnerability. Indeed, the National Safety Council, formed in 1914, began to issue regular reports on dangers to children not only in the streets and on playgrounds but within the home as well, where the prevention of accidents became an increasingly urgent theme by the 1930s and 1940s—highlighting both children's vulnerability and the expanding responsibilities of parents.[16]

At the same time, the older theme of childish innocence gained new attention through the accelerating campaign against child labor from 1900 onward. While the employment of very young children had already dropped, young teenagers were still widely used, and in fact the percentage of children in the labor force was at an all-time high in the United States in the second decade of the twentieth century. But now an array of arguments was deployed not simply to reduce child labor but to end it altogether, at least in the cities and outside family-run shops. The new National Child Labor Committee, formed in 1904, extended the older message, backed by extensive evidence that included dramatic photographs. Children were being exposed to physical and moral hazards, with hours of work that in many cases prevented any effective education at least beyond the earliest grades. But these important arguments were increasingly enhanced by the more general sense that work deprived children of a "real" childhood, which is where the innocence factor came in. For example, Jane Addams, a passionate advocate, castigated labor obligations for children that were "wearing away their innocent young life." This was wrong in itself, and it produced people who in later life would be nothing but "tramps."[17]

The new campaign faced resistance, particularly in the South, from farmers and from parents who relied directly on children's work. It would take the unemployment of the 1930s to finally seal the deal, with significant national limitations enacted in 1938. In the meantime, however, the combination of practical arguments and the relevance of the image of easily damaged innocence persuaded a growing number of adults that work and childhood should not mix—at least for their own children. In the process—as in other industrial countries—new questions surfaced about the utility of the child and, at least with the American emphasis on delicate innocence, about the level of protection that must surround young people—about the capacity of young people to manage challenging tasks.

It was also in the decades after 1900 that the theme of innocence—but in this case, beleaguered innocence—began to feature in the recurrent parental campaigns against some of the commercial products aimed at children. Early targets were "penny dreadful" novels, comic books, and radio, with more to come later on in the form of even more comic books and television. Here was another problem more acute in the United States than in Europe, where commercialism was somewhat more restrained and where, at least with radio and television, government intervention was more consequential. American parental campaigns rarely won out, but they continued to draw attention to the need to protect innocent and defenseless children.[18]

The Onus of Homework

Many of the concerns involved in the growing objections to child labor spilled over into new discussions of school requirements. No wide objections to school itself persisted after 1900 as the posture debate faded, but there was growing attention to the impact of homework, where expert objections and parental anxiety often combined. Between 1900 and 1940 a variety of educational leaders urged the outright abolition of homework, and in fact the practice was outlawed or severely limited in a number of localities. The expert approach, fueled by the new assumptions of progressive education, centered not so much on homework per se as on its mindless, repetitive qualities. But for many parents and local politicians, it was the strain on children that really counted: "young and growing children should not be over-burdened with work." Clarence Dunsmoor, an educational administrator in New Rochelle, New York, captured the spirit of both types of concern around 1940 in arguing that tedious homework might "hurt the physical and mental health of children," causing "nervous instability." The movement ultimately died down, in part because the professionals moved from abolition to reform of content. But it did suggest—like the posture concerns of the late nineteenth century—an undercurrent of uncertainty about the compatibility of school requirements and the finite capacities of the innocent child.[19]

Psychological Findings and Popularization

Novel and widely publicized psychological findings added a different component to the uncertainties about a child's capacities, with a number of innovations that proved particularly important in extending the idea of childhood fragility. Here, in fact, were the origins of the larger cultural shift that would ultimately contribute more widely to the changes involved in contemporary childhood.

Not surprisingly, a core message of the rising science was that people needed a good bit of guidance in achieving proper mental and emotional balance, and children were a particularly tempting target—and their parents offered a particularly eager audience. American parents easily outstripped their counterparts in other countries in their enthusiasm for popularized expert advice, with child-rearing manuals filling substantial sections in bookstores and new outlets like *Parents Magazine* (founded in 1926) gaining subscribers. New research findings and claims did not undercut considerable faith in childish innocence, but they uncovered a darker side: children might indeed have been innocent, but they also suffered from a variety of emotional liabilities that required not only protection but redress. The fact was that, by themselves, many children were not capable of constructive emotional maturation. The new concerns in this category also applied, for the most part, across gender, reducing though not eliminating the female-male fragility divide. The steady acceleration in the production of popular child-rearing manuals capitalized on the growing appetite for greater guidance, the first of many steps in the commercial exploitation of growing parental concerns.

The focus centered especially on fear and grief, not now simply where innocent infants were concerned but for children more generally. Research by psychologist G. Stanley Hall and others, quickly brought to child-rearing manuals by popularizers like Alice Birney from the 1900s onward, showed that children harbored deep fears no matter how carefully they were treated by adults: it was inherent in the childhood experience and required both sympathy and care in response. Similar concerns now applied to childish encounters with the death of others, now seen as an experience that could be overwhelming, again demanding new levels of protection.[20]

The contrast with nineteenth-century thinking on children's emotions was explicit, particularly where fear was concerned. No longer, according to the most up-to-date advice, was it appropriate to urge boys to master childish fears by marshaling courage. The task was simply too great, and the pressure would simply make matters worse—urging a child to "buck up" would only magnify whatever fear was involved, pushing it to the "overwhelming" stage where it might "leave its mark for a long time."[21] Birney thus emphasized that a child might be afraid of animals or water or noise for no apparent reason, requiring sympathetic assistance not confrontation, and her approach became standard in ensuing decades.

Parental investment was essential, lest a fear be maintained for life—for "children do not appear to 'get used to' things they fear." "The important thing in dealing with a child's fear is not to force sudden contact with a dreaded object or situation."[22] Clearly, it was no longer enough for parents to avoid fear in discipline. Now, they were called on to organize elaborate strategies to help a child overcome the emotion. Sweet talk, bribes, and night lights might all be part of the often-demanding manipulation required to create an emotionally healthy child. Experts as different as John Watson and Benjamin Spock agreed that real investment might be required—buying a different house if road noises were too frightening (Watson), or delaying a long-planned trip if the child seemed anxious (Spock). The responsibilities of successful parenting measurably expanded, and with this the emphasis on the incapacity of the child. Childish innocence remained, but now it was embellished by insufficiency. The title of one new advice manual put the case clearly: "Big Problems on Little Shoulders."[23]

A similar combination of avoidance and manipulation was applied to children's jealousy, another area where the natural emotions of the young surpassed their ability to manage on their own. During the 1920s and 1930s, as "sibling rivalry" gained growing attention in manuals and parenting magazines, the need for adult intervention was held to be essential. Unchecked, a child's jealousy might permanently damage the personality, leading to later failure in relationships and even at work. Here was another emotional arena where children could simply not cope on their own, for unchecked emotions would "fester" (a favorite word) in ways that would damage children and possibly poison adulthood.[24]

On the same basis, though as part of a larger evaluation of nineteenth-century grief practice, children now must be shielded from death—another shift from practices just a few decades earlier that had provided children with explicit training in grief and mourning. (In the 1880s it had been possible to order mourning kits for dolls, complete with coffins, from mail-order stores like Sears Roebuck.) The word death itself should be replaced: it was in the 1920s that child-rearing manuals began to urge that children be told that a dead person had simply gone to sleep, passed, or was "through." As with fear more generally, avoidance was the best policy, and adults should be careful to shield the child from their own grief, showing "as little emotion as possible." Correspondingly, experts increasingly urged that the young be kept away from funerals altogether, for the encounter with potential emotional intensity would be too much to bear.[25]

Even on the positive side, parents were told that a child might need active assistance with certain emotional goals. The same decades that saw the new concern about negative emotions embraced growing attention to the importance of assuring happiness, though the theme had been introduced in the nineteenth century. But with this, a question: was the parental responsibility a matter of increasingly indulging a happy child—a pleasant task—or did it require explicit intervention against frequent sadness? Was this another area where many children were inherently deficient?[26]

The point is clear: psychological expertise was increasingly deployed to convince interested parents that children's emotional liabilities required active redress, expanding the gap between childhood and effective adulthood. The result was increasing reliance on the need to organize children—not only at school but also on the playground and in the home—and the emergence of another component in the construction of the fragile child.

Contemporary Themes: The Fuller Picture

Developments after World War II, and particularly after the Baby Boom with its resultant focus on the one or two offspring born to the average child-bearing family, added a number of crucial components that extended adults concerns and amplified some of the modern issues into the full-blown sense of anxious protectiveness that would inform helicopter parenting and a number of other children's services as well as regulatory outreach. This was the point when the earlier interplay between obedience and autonomy would shift into the worries about competence that would justify a rather different approach to the child. Growing concerns about vulnerabilities joined with the rising sense that preparation for adulthood was becoming considerably more demanding, as psychological assumptions encountered the challenge of the new service- and knowledge-oriented economy. Along with impressions that had already been established, the new combination resulted in a significant expansion of the emphasis on children's fragility—creating a major theme in contemporary American childhood and child-rearing.

New Factors

Three developments in the post-Baby Boom decades combined to move the needle regarding children's capabilities: a new surge of expert commentary and popularized advice that extended concerns about children's ability to cope; recognition of new and demanding expectations being placed on successful children; and the new set of fears about changes in the children's environment that exceeded their ability to respond on their own.

The Expert Component

While the role of psychological and medical expertise in defining children's problems had already surfaced earlier in the twentieth century, it clearly extended in the postwar decades as the cultural context for childhood shifted more decisively. Emphases shifted: some older problems, like sibling rivalry, receded somewhat. Dr. Benjamin Spock, the most popular new guide (with ultimately over 50 million copies sold of a book that went through seven editions after its first appearance in 1946), was at pains to take a more reassuring tone than that of many of his predecessors. But his book, already double the size of previous manuals at 500 pages in the first edition, steadily expanded to nearly 1,000 pages by the end of the century—suggesting a daunting list of potential childhood problems and deficiencies. Many parents who used the manual noted how it increased their sense of concern: there were so many ways that managing children might go wrong. This sense of an issue-filled childhood would be further intensified in the twenty-first century with the advent of website advice and a massive proliferation of parenting book options, well beyond the offerings of the Spock era. Particularly on the psychological side, the need to monitor children's development seemed to increase steadily.[27]

Key bases of expertise shifted as well. The increasing impact of neuroscience, for example, contributed to the further medicalization of concepts of childhood for an audience now attuned to learning about crucial deficiencies of the young. This involved both emphasis on the many things that could go wrong for a child in the vulnerable first development phase, from poverty to family discord, but also the striking finding that brain development continued into a person's twenties—an implicit suggestion that full competence was achieved even later than most people had imagined.[28]

Even orthodontists got into the act as a growing range of experts developed new knowledge and self-interest in urging the imperfections of uncorrected children. By the early twenty-first century growing numbers of middle-class parents were being convinced that their children needed braces because their natural teeth were inadequate for the perfect, Barbie-like smiles that would help assure a bright future. With over three and a half million kids outfitted at some point between ages six and eighteen, the American propensity to inflict braces was four times the rate in Europe, where only measurable dental malfunction seemed to require remediation (or in Japan, where irregular teeth might be seen as an attractive feature).[29]

Far more important was the growing literature, from the 1950s onward, calling attention to the variety of mental health problems and learning disabilities that could afflict children. Popularized findings on discoveries concerning ADHD or adolescent anxiety were increasingly influential on parents and teachers alike, building new concerns about the vulnerabilities of the child.[30]

The Expectations Component

More and more parents and other adult authorities also extended their emphasis on educational goals in defining a successful child. It became increasingly important for children to do well in school and, above all, aspire to go to college. Although actual rates of college attendance began to climb from the 1950s onward, parental aspirations changed even more dramatically: by 2012 a full 94 percent of all American parents of children under seventeen said that they "expected" their offspring to go to college—a figure that exceeded actual first-year student figures by a significant margin. This was, admittedly, a high point—figures dropped later—but it correctly suggested several decades of rising, if not always realistic, expectations.[31]

New educational goals also fed other efforts to bolster children's success, most notably by supporting childhood training in a wide variety of sports. By the twenty-first century, well over half of all children ages six to seventeen were taking part in organized sports of some sort, while almost a third participated in formal musical activities. Here were additional domains in which parental expectations could easily outstrip children's actual achievements, where children were called upon to do well in a host of adult-organized activities.[32]

The Fears Component

Many American parents became measurably more fearful about their children's safety from the 1970s onward. The ease with which the public accepted largely inaccurate stories about neighbors poisoning Halloween candy in the 1970s was a notorious case in point. "Trick or treat" traditions that had long offered children some latitude for an evening were quickly converted into parent-supervised parades in which trickery was removed and the treats carefully sorted. Quite literally, children were no longer competent to organize any part of Halloween on their own.[33] Vastly exaggerated fears of kidnappings, fed not only by stories in the media but by the pictures of abducted children featured on milk cartons (a practice that began in 1979) created yet another danger that, by definition, children could hardly be expected to manage.

Heightened anxieties about bullying were particularly revealing. This was an issue that had been discussed periodically since the mid-nineteenth century, but without a massive amount of trepidation. It was widely assumed that children, and particularly sturdy boys, should be encouraged to take care of themselves—and several children's stories provided examples. There is no question that a good bit of bullying did occur in schools, with boys teasing girls, boys razzing classmates who could not do certain exercises in gym class, accusations of homosexuality—and this was regarded as normal, fairly harmless, and not really an issue for adults to take in hand. This then changed. In the 1970s, concern ratcheted up, and the sheer volume of references to bullying began to soar. Psychologists devoted new attention to the problem, generating new methods of mitigation such as the Olweus Bully Prevention Program (imported from Norway). Stiffer laws were passed, while school authorities were newly pressed to intervene by regulations incorporated into No Child Left Behind legislation in 2001. By this point, to be sure, new dimensions of the problem were becoming clear, particularly when the motivation for the 1999 Columbine school shooting proved to be a reaction to bullying; subsequently, the phenomenon of cyberbullying and new kinds of bullying around issues of gender identity would further add to the thrust. While it is impossible to prove that bullying was increasing (indeed, reports suggested that physical bullying declined), there is no question that concern was mounting and that the phenomenon took on some novel forms. And the result measurably highlighted children's incompetence.

The new attitudes were not the province of parents and adult authorities alone. Child culture changed as well in revealing ways. While it would be delightful to have more documentation, there is every indication that children themselves, in the nineteenth and early twentieth centuries, assumed that bullying was something to be handled without adult intervention, either through action or endurance. But after the 1970s, with children more carefully instructed about the problem, the attitude changed. Now the responsible child, witnessing bullying, should immediately turn to an adult authority, most commonly a teacher; far fewer suggested more direct measures by peers. This was what all the growing volume of advice literature said, but more importantly, it was what kids themselves reported.

The new wisdom was simple enough. Bullying was a huge problem because so many sensitive children were vulnerable. It might easily yield to suicide. Adult intervention was essential, for asking children to deal with the problems themselves was simply beyond their capacity. Certainly, blaming a child for the inability to stand up to bullying was now intolerable; children's fragility was assumed. There is no need to contend that the enhanced attention now devoted to the bullying issue was entirely unwarranted; indeed, the whole point is that many Americans now became convinced that it was absolutely essential.[34] But it was striking that a problem area that had once largely been left to children now had to be removed from their control.

In 2018 a social psychologist and a journalist coined the term "safetyism." Their focus was on campus liberals who were using "trigger warnings" and outright limits on free speech to protect young people's sensitivities, and their work was criticized both on partisan grounds and because it arguably neglected the "precarity" that many young people were facing. Shorn of a specific political focus, however, safetyism is not a bad term to denote the elevation of certain kinds of protective concerns over all other goals and values. The safetyist approach, in turn, responded both to the sense of the many dangers surrounding the young and to their inability to cope. Earlier tolerance for the risks associated with considerable independence declined steadily, particularly affecting boyhood. The nervous insistence on bicycle helmets from the 1990s onward—far more extensive for children and adults alike than in bike-riding Holland—was one of the many areas where bumps and bruises (and, admittedly, occasional serious injury) were no longer acceptable.[35]

Overall, the combination of new expert concerns about children's deficiencies, new expectations that could see some children seem to fall short, and new threats that children appeared incapable of handling on their own was a powerful mix, propelling what had been subordinate themes into a larger reorientation that centered strongly on childhood fragility. But there was a host of quite practical developments that both reflected and promoted the sense of childhood fragility as well, taking shape in the same late twentieth-century decades. The menu here proved diverse, from early childhood on up, but it translated the new view of children in a number of domains, rounding out the picture of the vulnerable and less-competent child.

Protecting and Compensating: Reflecting the New Approach

In an intriguing innovation, new regulations in the 1970s required car drivers to stop when school buses were loading and unloading children—a measure unique to the United States and Canada (though Washington State bucked the tide). The underlying assumptions were that drivers could not be expected to behave prudently, that children were particularly valuable, and that children—even at high school age—were not really capable of taking care of themselves in the street.[36] In other respects, American safety measures clearly lagged, so the safety category must be handled with care: but the school bus symbolism was interesting.

Another trend was richer in implications: the average age for the introduction of toilet training rose steadily in the United States, easily outstripping patterns in Europe, Asia, and Africa where kids were expected to control themselves by age one or two. By the end of the twentieth century, most American parents counted themselves lucky if they achieved success by age three—an increase of over a full year since the late 1940s—and many did not try very hard before this point. The trend reflected small family size (though of course no smaller than in Europe), plus relative affluence, capable of affording the additional consumption of diapers. But the basic motivation centered on a real concern that pressing the child too early risked psychological damage—including the dreaded exposure to shame. American experts on the subject granted that children *could* learn by eighteen months but urged that many would not be "cognitively ready." Here was a pattern that both reflected a sense of psychological fragility and created yet another area where, in the adult mind, children—admittedly young children in this case—could not be expected to take care of themselves. In the process, a marker of toddlers' inferiority was maintained far longer than other societies would tolerate.[37]

Suburbanization and then further birth rate decline created yet another new area of childish vulnerability, particularly when confidence in the safety of using public transportation (or a bicycle) began to decline: the inability of children to get where they needed to be without help. Dependence on parental driving went up steadily, until the mid-high-school years. With fewer children in the neighborhood (thanks to the birth rate drop amid suburbanization) and with limited public transportation, assistance became essential even in finding people to play with. The problem was compounded by the unusually high rate of traffic deaths in the United States and, in some cases, gun violence: these domains, where the overall protection of children lagged, placed additional onus on protective parents. The term "play date," though introduced in the 1920s, began its steep ascent in the 1980s and 1990s. The resultant burdens on adults became increasingly obvious when more mothers entered the formal labor force—there was no question about the strain on parents—but the resultant vulnerability of children in adult eyes deserves attention as well. Even in basic play functions, kids needed help, particularly in the view of the growing band of nervously protective helicopter parents.[38] One result, which can be variously interpreted: when contemporary American children are polled about their parents, the latter score highest in the category "provides entertainment"; that would not have been the first choice in the mid-twentieth century, when kids could do more on their own.

On another front: expectations that children could be counted on for significant household chores declined markedly, for virtually all relevant age groups and for both genders (though more for boys than for girls). Some of this was virtually inevitable, as appliances took over many simple tasks (like dishwashing and drying) and as the lower birth rate reduced the need for in-family babysitting. More demanding schoolwork might also divert attention, on the part of parents and children alike.

Still, the changes were substantial, and they had broader implications. Between the 1970s and the 1990s, the percentage of high school students who said they did regular chores dropped by 50 percent (to about a quarter of the total), and at the same time reports of quarrels over chores essentially doubled (to about 50 percent of the children interviewed beyond grade-school age). Only one category of children could be counted on to contribute much at all in many American families: middle-school-aged kids with a single parent (but if the parent re-married, contributions dropped very quickly). Otherwise, children did very little, on average, on a regular basis, though girls put in a bit more time than boys did. At the least, here was another case in which the gap between childhood and adulthood widened. A domain for childhood competence receded, and with it the possibility of a growing sense of adult grievance might fester as well.

Equally interesting were reports of parents who simply admitted an increasing lack of patience with the pace and manner in which children did their work when they were called upon. "I mean, I could do it so much faster, it drives me mad sometimes." Ironically, as more mothers took jobs outside the home, the time and flexibility needed to introduce children to household chores—young children particularly—actually declined. Understandable assumptions about children's lack of competence clearly furthered their lack of competence. The contrast with the delight in young children's contributions in countries like Japan, with its popular TV documentation of what toddlers can do to help, was striking.[39]

Other venues where children had previously been able to demonstrate competence also trailed off. Scouting movements, with their carefully calibrated badges for various achievements, were in particularly steep decline. The drop in participation in organized religion removed another path—the proof of religious maturity—for at least some children. On the recreational side, opportunities that had blossomed earlier in the twentieth century, like building model planes and cars, working with chemistry or erector sets, or entering soap box competitions also trailed off—though the popularity of some newer toys, like Legos, might have provided some solace for younger children. And one key aspect of contemporary competence clearly bucked the trend: the innumerable occasions, by the 1990s and early twenty-first century, when children could prove their superiority over virtually any adult in dealing with computers. Further, many teenagers would add that computer games gave many an opportunity, in this case largely independent of adults, to gain and demonstrate skill. In other words, while occasions for demonstrating achievement and utility did grow sparser, there were some compensatory complexities.

Some of the tensions over competence spilled over into schoolwork as well, reprising the concerns about pressures on students that had first surfaced a century earlier. Concerns about competence may help explain the growing, and by comparative standards surprisingly large, number of hours American children had to spend in classrooms: learning could not be left to children alone. The same dynamic helps explain the erosion of many forms of unsupervised play, another key theme in contemporary American childhood. But rising concern about children's competence had more specific consequences as well. Reports of parents doing their children's homework and other school-linked tasks—to improve quality but also to sidestep the nuisance of tutoring children directly—date back at least to the 1920s. But the pattern intensified particularly from the 1960s onward, though there is no way to document precise rates. As with chores, many increasingly busy parents often found it easier and quicker to do the job directly. And the stakes measurably expanded, given the rapid increase in the percentage of middle-class kids who now expected (or were expected) to go to college and as a sense of competition mounted.

Case in point: in the 1950s the average college-bound high school senior applied to only one college; but by 1967, 26 percent were already applying to four or more, and by 2006 only 18 percent of all aspirants confined themselves to a single application. In some cases, of course, students took care of the added burdens themselves, but in many instances worried parents at least actively monitored the process and in some instances filled out key parts of the applications directly. Academic aspirations were mounting faster than a corresponding confidence in children's capacities, at least in some families—particularly among white upper-middle-class parents worried that their offspring's future, in the current competitive environment, might not match their own.[40]

The older anxieties about disparities between school demands and psychological health readily resurfaced in this environment, with the measurable expansion of testing and the growing complexity of homework, at least for many of the college-bound. Concerns about undue pressure helped fuel elements of helicopter parenting, with increasing parental interventions in schools and colleges alike. Schools themselves began to expand their awards roster, signaling out more types of achievements and multiplying the number of recipients of certain honors, like high school valedictorian, in an effort to reduce threats to children's self-esteem. Some episodes were particularly revealing, like a parental protest in Connecticut against teachers who marked up student essays with red pencil—the argument being that colored criticisms were somehow psychologically damaging. For many parents, the changing sense of responsibility—that the offspring should get into a "good" college—jarred with the nagging sense of children's special demands, their need for help and protection. (And for older children themselves the same equation helps explain the odd combination of rising expectations for good grades in college with a lack of confidence in their actual abilities).[41]

An intriguing series of moral panics heightened the atmosphere of protectiveness from another angle and in some cases added to anxiety about children's competence as well, particularly from the 1970s onward. This was when the inaccurate or greatly exaggerated stories of stranger kidnapping rates or Halloween mishaps seemed to require further parental intervention. Adult accompaniment on Halloween sorties became standard after 1981, a minor burden perhaps, but another case where children could no longer take care of themselves. Satanic cult scares in the 1970s and 1980s even raised concerns about the possibility that children—unable to resist brainwashing—might be drawn in. The range of essential protectiveness expanded.[42]

On yet another front: a new expansion of medical advice encouraged parents and a wider public increasingly to pathologize what had previously been seen as a normal range of childish traits. Thus the introspective or shy child might now be labeled autistic, the chubby child obese—often with yet another round of expert referrals enlisted to guide the child. As noted, even errant teeth must now be corralled by braces. Children needed guidance or correction in a growing array of areas.

Further, the postwar decades saw the troubling surge of explicit and widely publicized psychological evidence that many children were in considerable distress, beyond the previous emphasis on the support needed for their emotional maturation. The therapeutic approach to children expanded steadily from the 1950s onward, adding further dimensions to the idea of the fragile child and additional areas to the growing commitment to correction.

Evaluation is admittedly risky. The United States was hardly the only place where psychological concerns increased. And there is very real evidence that children's mental health was in fact deteriorating. Measurements of anxiety, for example—as anxiety tests began to be administered from the 1950s onward—showed that the average child in the 1990s was at least as anxious as counterparts a half century earlier who had been under active expert care.[43]

At the very least, however, the mounting sense of psychological vulnerability—exploding into widespread claims of a youth mental health crisis by the twenty-first century—measurably enhanced the theme of the needy child. For many parents, and certainly for many adults in the child and student care fields, the new signs of trouble resonated particularly in the United States because they played into the existing sense of special fragility.

Concern about ADHD again provides some intriguing evidence in what is, admittedly, a challenging comparative domain. There is no question that American researchers took the lead in this field from the 1950s onward or that many American adults—parents, counselors, and teachers alike— resonated to the diagnosis, particularly after the advent of Ritalin as a treatment in the later 1950s. Signs of particular concern range from comparatively high incidence rates—reflecting adult reports—to the fact that, in ensuing decades, Americans were utilizing half of all the relevant medications produced worldwide. By the later 1970s the United States was generating twenty times more diagnoses per child capita than the United Kingdom. Though this disparity would ultimately decline somewhat, its persistence today marks one of the challenges in evaluating the American version of post-modern childhood. Similar disparities apply to childhood depression, with American rates (currently listed as about 4.4 percent of the under-eighteen population) running at least 50 percent ahead of diagnoses in the United Kingdom. With all this, it is not clear that the "real" problem level was any worse in the United States than elsewhere: what was most obviously distinctive was the readiness to report and the eagerness to use the mental health label rather than other possible categories (such as "conduct disorder" in the United Kingdom). One virtually certain result was significant overdiagnosis in the United States, as experts and many parents and teachers veered toward expanding expectations that there were problems to be found.[44]

Similar comparative patterns apply to children's anxiety, where American diagnoses mounted and have continued to mount far more rapidly than those in many other countries (including the United Kingdom and Canada), especially before 2000. Again, the level of psychological research was unusually great in the United States, but the results found a particularly ready audience as well. There is the intriguing possibility that children's actual anxiety ran unusually high because American parents were particularly anxious about them, but the main point is the widespread willingness to acknowledge this additional sign of vulnerability. Where children were concerned, the growing acceptance of therapy in the United States built on an existing theme, while adding troubling particulars and expanding the definition of childhood fragility itself.[45]

Finally, in what has become an ongoing battleground over whose children are most fragile, the twenty-first-century version of the American culture wars highlighted additional areas in which adults, and some young people themselves, assumed that children were incompetent to handle crucial challenges. The belief that children must be shielded from certain kinds of reading material or that books themselves must be adjusted to take sensitivities into account opened another frontier in the needs for adult, and increasingly parental, intervention as against children's inability to work out tensions on their own. Though often contrived or manipulated, the asserted sense that there is a childhood innocence that must not be sullied by troubling words or histories added a new chapter to what by this point was a well-established theme, a new reason as well to revive the older concern that current schooling might not be good for fragile young people. While the culture wars opened huge battles over what children and young people needed to be protected *from*—from racist words or references on one side to any discussion of race at all on the other, to take one key example—both camps implicitly agreed that adult guidelines were essential to shield the delicate child. Safetyism, in this sense, proved to be nonpartisan.

* * *

As it has developed in the United States, the idea of some special childhood frailty has evoked protective and patronizing reactions alike, both affecting expectations about what children could and should be able to do. The theme has obviously intensified over time: it feeds the contemporary helicopter or parental interventionist impulse in new ways—though it remains worth repeating that the helicopter approach goes back somewhat further in the twentieth century than many imagine, beginning to emerge soon after the Baby Boom. Well-meaning professionals have also focused on real or imagined vulnerabilities, interacting with parental concerns. But the theme maintains some consistency as well, at several points over the past century or more shaping an adult approach to children—in families and beyond—somewhat different from comparable features in other countries.

The links to contemporary politics and implicit discussions of children's rights also demand attention. Both sides in the culture wars, though in different ways, have sought to mobilize arguments over children's fragility for their own purposes. Emphasis on vulnerabilities has enhanced an American tendency to assume that children's rights primarily involve protections *against* various threats—though there are important inconsistencies even here—or *for* adult-provided services like education. But the more complex notion that children also have rights of expression and action on their own account—rights to a degree of autonomy—has made particularly limited headway on American soil, and this too is reflected in current debates about transgender children, freedom of speech in schools, and other issues.[46]

The fragile child hypothesis, and particularly the claims for some degree of continuity over time, certainly warrants critical assessment—whether the focus is on families, policies, or children themselves. The comparative implications invite further evaluation. All industrial societies have experienced changes broadly similar to those in the United States, which everywhere have increased gaps between childhood and adulthood and raised new questions about what children should be expected to be able to do. The American variant, if such it is, operates within that common framework. But an unusual openness to the neediness of modern children, including the unusually eager reception of new information about children's problems and deficiencies and even their levels of mental distress, does seem arguably distinctive, even though most Americans remain unaware of their comparative standing.[47]

Most obviously, the fragile child hypothesis needs testing against other crucial themes in the evolution of American childhood. As noted, it is a predominantly middle-class and white indulgence, though it can spill over into the ways children in general are managed—as in the broad assumption, for example, that schoolchildren have few rights against adult authority. The role of race as well as class in defining children's treatment, particularly at the policy level, unquestionably commands attention, and it has considerably different implications from the idea of the fragile child. Indeed, as students of the childhood innocence argument have sometimes pointed out, race could be used to distort middle-class assumptions in order to take a more punitive approach to children who did not fit the innocence label.[48]

The theme of fragility has often operated alongside surprising unconcern about aspects of childhood that, in other societies, have commanded more urgent attention, and while some of this reflects American reliance on race and class distinctions, other inconsistencies factor in as well. Thus, the absence of explicit financial support for children in poor families, in contrast to every other Organization for Economic Co-operation and Development (OECD) member country, can be chalked up primarily to racism combined with aversion to extensive welfare programs: these children, and their families, must fend for themselves. But the continued, if debated, acceptance of an extraordinary gun culture—now the greatest source of childhood deaths in the United States, in marked contrast to peer nations—spills beyond poor and minority populations. Child protection here gives way to a larger cultural/political imperative, in this case the political delicacy of gun ownership. The same applies to the lack of other standard protections for children against vehicular accidents or adulterated foods, where American safety claims so often ring hollow and where rates of child harm rise well above those in other comparable countries. What may be particularly unusual in the American approach to childhood is the strange and ambivalent combination of protectiveness and nonchalance. The distinctive school bus ritual, with its exaggerated safety implications, must thus be combined, in comparative assessment, with the fact that vehicular death rates for American children, though improving, are twice as high as those as in other wealthy nations. At points, indeed, it seems likely that pious invocations of protectiveness deliberately distract from dealing with or even explicitly acknowledging some of the real hazards that American children face, hazards that are measurably greater than the norms in other industrial societies but where remediation would force encounters with powerful interest groups in the national society. An unproductive vicious circle is involved, with high levels of parental/child anxiety failing to address a number of the objective factors that make the American child less safe—with results that only increase anxiety.[49]

Admittedly, also, the fragile child theme harbors complexities in its own right. There is no question that it has sometimes been overdone. The frenzy about sibling rivalry in the 1920s and 1930s was based on faulty research and did finally die down somewhat. With largely good intentions, psychologists have at points exaggerated rates of ADHD or anxiety. Worried parents and concerned policemen have surely gone too far in trying to punish more independent-minded ("free-range") parents for letting their children play unsupervised in nearby parks or walk to a nearby grocery store. It is probably not good to let children off the hook for chores as often as is now the case.[50]

But this is not to insist that the fragility theme itself, and its various proponents, are fundamentally wrong. It is perfectly possible to emerge from a discussion of the fragile child with enthusiastic endorsement of the concept's basic validity: contemporary children are needy, as the mental health crisis or the rising concern about bullying so vividly demonstrate, and if this links to older findings about the vulnerabilities of innocence or the necessity of emotional guidance, so much the better. Current debates over the need to regulate social media thus clearly reflect yet another category of concern about children's ability to cope, but they may be absolutely essential even so. Identifying a persistent theme is not the same thing as determining what to do about it, and it is also true that adults in a number of other societies are picking up new concerns about issues such as young people's anxiety. There is a lot to be worried about concerning children in modern society, and evaluating the fragility theme is legitimately complicated.

The implications for children themselves warrant particular attention, notably with regard to schooling and leisure. Evaluations of helicopter parenting have particularly focused on young adults and the impact of delayed maturation and lack of experience with setbacks earlier in life, but there is room for more attention to childhood itself.[51] Clearly, protective restrictions on American children, whether through formal rules or nervous parental oversight, have significantly reduced independence of action, particularly during the past half century, as in the response to bullying. They play a measurable role in limiting opportunities for children to display, or gain a sense of, competence. Sports success offers an exception for a talented minority of kids, school achievement provides a channel for a somewhat larger group, and computer skills provide an outlet. But the range has narrowed as children encounter limited opportunities to accomplish many things on their own, often even at home. Many children profess an unusual reluctance to take up the apparatus of adulthood, whether the target is a demanding summer job or even getting a driver's license when legally allowed. Many entering college display an odd combination of high aspiration—expecting to get unrealistically high grades—but real uncertainty about how to move toward that goal. In other words, part of the fragile child motif has been internalized, with real impact on the ways many older children plan and operate.[52]

The same limitations may also help explain the surprising level of implicit docility plus risk aversion that has characterized American children for several decades—despite pervasive fictional imagery to the contrary, and despite the undeniable decline of explicit emphasis on obedience.[53] Children who, in contrast to previous generations, are newly hesitant about smoking or drinking or having sex or, in a growing number of cases, even driving are children who have picked up the insistence that their range of independent action should be limited. The results may be praised, but they harbor some nagging questions.

The overall evaluation of the theme of children's fragility, particularly as it has intensified over recent decades, suggests that it can be, and has been, easily overdone. Some rebalancing seems essential, for the sake of children and harassed parents alike. Here, of course, we merely add to comments already available about the stunting effects of helicopter parenting and the possible overreach of the therapeutic society. The historical angle, however, offers greater insistence on how deep the protective impulse runs in modern American parenting history, how long-standing it is, and how it has generated a combination of concern and beneficence that many American adults find demanding but comforting. Reassessment is arguably desirable but is clearly difficult, and a sense of the historical contours of the theme is essential to the process.

The American Child: The Transformation of Childhood Since World War II. Steven Mintz and Peter N. Stearns, Oxford University Press. © Oxford University Press 2025. DOI: 10.1093/9780197797112.003.0003

4

Diversity and Inequality in American Childhood Since World War II

A number of recent first-person accounts of childhood highlight the stark realities of diversity that have become such a crucial part of contemporary American society. These narratives humanize raw statistics and policy debates and illustrate how various aspects of a child's identity can influence their experiences, opportunities, and challenges from a very young age. They also show the complex and often novel ways that diversity and inequality intertwine in shaping American childhood.

The concept of intersectionality is crucial in understanding these first-person accounts. This concept refers to the way various forms of social stratification, such as race, ethnicity, class, immigrant status, and gender, intersect to create unique experiences of disadvantage or privilege. Not a new feature of American childhood, intersectionality took on new dimensions from the 1960s onward, as inequality deepened and the range of diversity expanded.

Despite the adversities stemming from these intersections, these narratives also illuminate the resilience and strength displayed by many young people. Faced with obstacles, many children develop coping strategies and resilience that enable them to overcome the challenges they encounter. This resilience is often nurtured by supportive relationships with parents, siblings, relatives, peers, teachers, and others who provide emotional support, mentorship, and resources that help children navigate their circumstances.

By offering insights into the lived experience of children at the intersections of race, immigrant status, gender, ethnicity, and class, these stories challenge us to consider the impact of inequality on young lives and underscore the importance of creating a more equitable society that honors the potential of each child.

Their Stories

Gritty, raw, intense, and unflinching, Rob Henderson's deeply disquieting coming-of-age memoir, *Troubled*, recounts the challenges he faced growing up in poverty and amid familial dysfunction. Born to a drug-addicted mother and a father he never met, Henderson recounts shuttling between ten different foster homes in California, where he suffered poverty, neglect, and abuse. His memoir describes the impact of domestic violence, divorce, and substance abuse, and how these shaped his worldview and sense of self. He discusses how he struggled with issues of identity and belonging, particularly as a biracial child, and the challenges he faced in finding acceptance in a society that tends to marginalize those who are different. But he also explains how he found solace and opportunity in education and how enlistment in the US Air Force and admission to Yale changed his life's trajectory.[1]

In her autobiography, *Becoming*, former First Lady Michelle Obama, born Michelle LaVaughn Robinson, chronicles her childhood on Chicago's South Side. Three generations of Robinsons lived in a house owned by an aunt and uncle, located in a poor, Black, working-class neighborhood on the wrong side of the tracks. She, her brother, her mother, and her father, a city water plant employee, lived in an attic apartment, and her bedroom, shared with her brother, comprised a carved out space in the family's living room. Her parents were strict and deeply religious, and they spanked her when she misbehaved. They placed a strong emphasis on education and enrolled her in the city's first magnet school, which challenged her identity and her ability to fit in. Neighborhood kids, who would ask her why she spoke like a white girl, would complain that she wasn't like them, while at school she had to adapt to an environment that treated her as an interloper.[2]

The novelist Samira Ahmed's *Love, Hate and Other Filters* provides a searing glimpse into what it's like to grow up half Muslim and half Hindu in small-town Illinois. The protagonist in this thinly veiled autobiographical novel must cope with Islamophobia, cultural clashes among peers, and her overly protective parents' rigid expectations. With vivid detail, the author describes the complexities of navigating American society with a South Asian identity, confronting stereotypes, and the struggle for acceptance while also celebrating her Indian heritage and religious faith.[3]

Born on the floor of her grandmother's house in a Jamaican slum, Staceyann Chin, later a poet, performance artist, and LBGTQ+ activist, was raised without a mother or father by her religiously devout but illiterate grandmother. Her memoir, *The Other Side of Paradise*, describes her struggle to deal with her abandonment by her mother, her uncertainty about who her father was, and the realities of growing up in extreme poverty. Especially powerful are her descriptions of the threats she faced from those who would exploit, hurt, and sexually abuse her, especially in light of her independence and refusal to conform to the dominant sexual norms. Her account also details the many challenges she faced in adjusting to life as an immigrant, first in Montreal and later in the United States.[4]

Born in Việt Nam three months before the end of the American War, Thi Bui and her family came to the United States in 1978 as part of the "boat people" wave of refugees. Her memoir, *The Best We Could Do*, describes the challenges and complexities of adapting to a new society while preserving one's heritage. The family's journey to escape the violence and oppression of their homeland is marked by trauma, loss, and uncertainty. Bui vividly portrays the hardships her parents endured, including the fear of persecution, the dangers of the journey by boat, and the challenges of resettling in a foreign land. The memoir sheds light on the challenges and hardships her family faced as her parents struggled to learn a new language and discovered that the skills and credentials they had acquired overseas were not accepted in the United States. As Bui grows up in American society, she grapples with the cultural and generational divide between herself and her parents and the complexities of navigating between two cultures. Despite the love and sacrifices her parents made for their children, Bui had to confront the scars of their past trauma and the emotional distance that sometimes exists between them. Throughout the memoir, Bui reflects on her own journey of assimilation and the pressures to conform to American culture and feels torn between her Vietnamese roots and her desire to accommodate to American society.[5]

Tell Me How It Ends: An Essay in Forty Questions by Valeria Luiselli offers a firsthand account of her experiences as a volunteer interpreter for undocumented Central American children seeking asylum in the United States. Through a series of forty questions posed to the children during their intake interviews, Luiselli sheds light on the harrowing journeys these young migrants undertook and the reasons behind their decision to leave their home countries in search of safety and opportunity. The book reveals the traumatic experiences these children have endured, including witnessing violence, experiencing abuse, and living in constant fear for their safety. The memoir also highlights the bureaucratic challenges and legal obstacles that child migrants encounter as they navigate the immigration system. In addition, the memoir addresses the emotional toll of family separation on child migrants, the challenges of reunifying with loved ones in the United States, and the struggles that children face in adjusting to life in a new country while longing for the families they left behind.[6]

Diversity and Inequality as Part of the New Childhood

Like any source of information, memoirs, interviews, and autobiographical fiction must be read critically and with caution. These retrospective accounts, colored by the authors' memories and narrative choices, are often littered with factual inaccuracies and conflations of events and individuals and influenced by later experiences and understandings. In addition, these portraits of childhood may not fully capture the broader context or experiences of others within their community, resulting in overgeneralizations or misunderstandings. Still, few sources of information are better able to convey the subjective experience of childhood or the complexities of growing up and coming of age, especially among those children who by the nature of their socioeconomic class, immigrant status, or racial and ethnic background live on American society's margins.

These recent accounts lay bare a number of the defining features of contemporary American childhood: its increasing diversity, due in part to immigration and differential birthrates, as well as the glaring realities of inequality along the intersections of race, class, and identity that shape the experiences of children of different backgrounds. These narratives highlight the stark contrasts between the middle-class ideal of childhood often portrayed in mainstream media and the varied, complex realities faced by many young people.

Diversity and inequality are, of course, not new. These have been hallmarks of American childhood since the colonial era. But today's diversity and inequalities differ significantly from those even in the 1950s and 1960s, generated by a variety of new demographic, educational, occupational, and socioeconomic factors. Contemporary childhood is profoundly shaped by the combination of new levels of immigration, a massive increase in economic inequality and its implications, and a set of gender disparities that has been redefined in complex ways.

A surge in immigration in recent decades has transformed the nation's demographic landscape, introducing far greater variety of cultural, linguistic, religious, and ethnic backgrounds into American childhood. This diversity has enriched American society, but it also presents challenges for immigrant children who must navigate cultural assimilation, language barriers, and often the psychological impact of migration and adjustment.

Widening disparities in income, wealth, education, and employment opportunities have also affected children in profound ways, influencing family structure, household dynamics, parent-child relationships, and child-rearing practices. Here too contemporary American childhood differs from its counterpart in much of the earlier twentieth century, because the gaps have widened and because they count for more in differentiating children's experiences and prospects. Economic resources, work demands, and cultural values all play a role in shaping family life across different social classes. These differences are not just about economic resources, they also involve social capital, parental expectations, and the stresses and challenges uniquely faced by families across different social strata. At the same time, gaps in education have especially significant implications for children's futures, including access to higher education and employment opportunities.

Economic pressures, work schedules, and job stability significantly impact family life, affecting the amount, nature, and quality of time parents can spend with their children. For instance, in more affluent families, there tends to be a greater focus on self-consciously fostering children's talents, leading to a more negotiated and dialogic relationship. These parents often view their children as projects to be developed, investing significant resources in their education and activities. In contrast, families in lower socioeconomic brackets experience more stress due to financial instability, leading, in many cases, to very different family dynamics, and at times resulting in increased conflict or tension. On the other hand, families with higher socioeconomic status often have access to resources that can stabilize the family unit, like the ability to afford childcare or engage in family activities that strengthen parent-child bonds.

Parenting styles and child-rearing practices often vary by social class, influenced by both cultural values and practical circumstances. Middle- and upper-class parents are more likely to adopt an "authoritative" parenting style, characterized by high responsiveness and high demands. These parents tend to emphasize the importance of cognitive development, preparing their children for competitive educational and career paths. In contrast, working-class parents tend to adopt approaches to child-rearing that involve more unstructured time, which allows them to play independently or with siblings and neighbors. These children have more autonomy in organizing their play and leisure activities, leading them to develop strong peer relationships and independence. This contrasts with the heavily scheduled lives of children from middle-class families, who are often enrolled in numerous extracurricular activities.

Also, communication styles in working-class families tend to be more directive, with parents issuing commands rather than engaging in negotiation. There is generally less verbal interaction between parents and children compared to middle-class families. Children raised in this context are often taught to respect authority and not to question adults. These differences are partly due to the practical realities of working-class lives, including dealing with multiple jobs or irregular hours, which can limit their ability to closely monitor and guide their children's activities and behavior. Furthermore, economic constraints may limit access to extracurricular opportunities, shaping a different set of priorities in child-rearing.

Intersectionality

Childhood diversity is inextricably connected to profound differences in social circumstances and access to resources and opportunities. As we all recognize, some children are more privileged than others, while others are more disadvantaged. To discuss diversity without reference to inequality is to fail to see how the former influences and reinforces the latter.

Intersectionality, a term coined by the law professor and critical race theorist Kimberlé Crenshaw in 1989, provides a framework for understanding how class, gender, ethnicity, race, and other social categories can reinforce social hierarchies and compound experiences of advantage and disadvantage. Intersectionality underscores the fact that each child's experience is shaped by a web of interconnected identities, each of which can influence their opportunities and challenges.

Applying the concept of intersectionality to American childhood reminds us that children's identity isn't defined by single characteristic, such as race or gender, but by various identities that work in tandem, resulting in distinctive sets of experiences. For instance, the challenges faced by low-income LGBTQ+ children of color differ from those of white middle-class LGBTQ+ children. Similarly, a child with a disability who is also a member of a marginalized ethnic group might face disadvantages due to both ableism and racism.

Recognizing intersectionality allows us to see differences within broader groups. Not all children from low-income families, for instance, have the same experiences. Factors like race, immigration status, neighborhood, and family structure can create a range of experiences within that broader category. In addition, the concept of intersectionality challenges singular narratives. It encourages us to question stereotypes associated with a particular group. For instance, not all Asian American children experience academic success, and to assume they do overlooks the varied experiences within this particular category.

Immigration and Racial Diversity

Today, the child age population is more diverse than any other portion of the US population. This diversity is a reflection of broader demographic shifts, including immigration and differential birth rates among various ethnic and racial groups.

In 1960, 86 percent of the US population under the age of eighteen was white and 14 percent was non-white. Most of the latter, 11 percent, were Black. At that time, less than 6 percent had an immigrant parent. In stark contrast, six decades later, the US Census reported that nearly 53 percent of those under the age of eighteen were children of color, with 15 percent non-Hispanic Black, 26 percent Hispanic, and 13.2 percent Black. In 2022, 26 percent of children under eighteen in the United States lived with at least one immigrant parent, up from 13 percent in 1990. A fifth of all Black children themselves are immigrants or the children of immigrants.[7]

While this nation's rich diversity can conjure up comforting and uplifting images of this nation as "a gorgeous mosaic of race and religious faith, of national origin and sexual orientation,"[8] and contribute to open-mindedness and empathy, diversity has often been accompanied by antipathy, ill will, and deep-seated inequalities. Any serious discussion of childhood diversity must take into account the complex dynamics, disparities, and discrimination that are a key aspect of this society's diverse world of childhood.

American childhood has always been diverse, and children's experiences have always been unequal. However, since the 1960s, the nature of childhood diversity has increased, and inequalities in children's lives have intensified as the demography of childhood has shifted, immigration has surged, class divisions have widened, parental education has grown more salient, and family structures and child-rearing practices have diverged.

The demographic shifts are the most obvious. As a result of immigration and differential birth rates among various demographic groups, the ethnic and racial composition of American childhood is far greater than it was during the early Cold War, when nearly nine out of ten children were non-Hispanic whites. The Immigration and Nationality Act of 1965, which abolished the national origins quota system favoring immigrants from northern and western Europe, opened the United States to immigrants from Asia, Latin America, Africa, and other regions. This led to a substantial increase in the diversity of the immigrant population, explaining why children of immigrants represent such a significant share of all children in the country.

Linguistic diversity is one outgrowth of the increase in children from non-English-speaking backgrounds, with over 21 percent of children speaking a language other than English at home. The United States' growing diversity has also led to a wider recognition of different cultural practices, traditions, and holidays and a push toward more inclusive representation in children's media, including television shows, movies, and books.

Variations in the birth rates of different racial and ethnic groups have also contributed to changes in the demographic makeup of American children. Latino and Asian populations in the United States have grown not only due to immigration but also because of higher birth rates compared to non-Hispanic whites. As a result of differential birth rates, the proportion of non-Hispanic white children in the US population has decreased, while the proportions of Latino, Asian, and multiracial children have risen. African American children's proportion has remained relatively stable but now forms part of a broader mosaic of American racial and ethnic diversity.

The shift in demographics has had far-reaching implications for the education system, which must adapt to the needs of a more diverse student population. This includes language support for English language learners and the adoption of culturally responsive teaching practices. Changing demographics also mean that children today are much more likely to interact with peers from diverse backgrounds, which can foster cross-cultural understanding and empathy but also presents challenges related to identity and belonging. Also, there's greater acknowledgment of multiracial identities. The ability to identify with more than one race on censuses and surveys reflects and supports this diversity, something that was not widely recognized in the 1960s. The growing visibility and, to a lesser extent, acceptance of diverse gender and sexual identities, including non-binary and transgender identities, has led to a growing awareness of gender variation, even among young children.

The Changing Nature of Childhood Inequality

As recently as 1970, it was possible to think of the United States as largely a middle-class society. With middle-income households accounting for over three-fifths (62 percent) of all families, society was far less economically stratified than it is today when, in stark contrast, only 42 percent of the population falls in the middle-income group.[9] In terms of financial resources, educational credentials, cultural attitudes, self-definition, and physical possessions this country was much more egalitarian than today's more class-conscious and economically, educationally, and culturally differentiated society.[10]

Since the early 1970s, when economic inequality began to intensify, differences in children's family lives, everyday experiences, and parents' child-rearing practices also widened. Particularly notable is the divergence between the lives of children from upper-middle-class backgrounds and those from lower-income families, with conditions in the now-diminished middle-income group falling somewhere in between.

Not surprisingly, children from upper-middle-class families generally grow up in environments marked by financial stability and access to a wealth of resources. Their homes are likely to be located in safer neighborhoods and their daily lives more insulated from the stresses of economic insecurity. In contrast, children from low-income families frequently experience instability in housing and food insecurity. Economic inequality is closely linked to educational disparities. Children from low-income families are more likely to attend under-resourced schools with fewer qualified teachers, extracurricular programs, and advanced courses, affecting their academic achievement and future prospects. They have less access to extracurricular and summer programs, because of cost constraints or because their parents cannot provide transportation or navigate the logistics due to long working hours or inflexible schedules.

Differences in child-rearing practices further accentuate the class divide. Parents from upper-middle-class families often engage in what sociologists call "concerted cultivation." This parenting style is characterized by actively fostering children's development and scheduling educational experiences, closely monitoring academic progress, and advocating for their children within educational systems. In contrast, parents from lower-income backgrounds might adopt a more "natural growth" approach, providing love and care but with less emphasis on structured activities and direct intervention in educational matters. While this approach fosters independence and resilience, it does not afford children the same level of academic support and enrichment.

Since the early 1970s, when inequalities in family income began to deepen, the United States has introduced a number of programs to supplement the income and support the welfare of lower-income families with children in order to mitigate the effects of poverty and ensure that children have access to the resources they need for healthy development. These include:

- TANF (Temporary Assistance for Needy Families), which provides financial assistance to families with children when the parents or other responsible relatives cannot provide for the family's basic needs.
- SNAP (Supplemental Nutrition Assistance Program), formerly known as food stamps, offering nutritional assistance.
- EITC (Earned Income Tax Credit), a refundable tax credit for low- to moderate-income working individuals and families to reduce tax burden, supplement wages, and encourage work.
- CTC (Child Tax Credit), to help offset the cost of raising children, based on family income and size.
- Medicaid, which offers health coverage to eligible low-income adults, children, pregnant women, elderly adults, and people with disabilities.
- CHIP (Children's Health Insurance Program), which provides health coverage to children in families with incomes too high to qualify for Medicaid but too low to afford private coverage.

- WIC (Special Supplemental Nutrition Program for Women, Infants, and Children), which provides federal grants to states for supplemental foods, health-care referrals, and nutrition education for low-income pregnant, breastfeeding, and non-breastfeeding postpartum women, and to infants and children up to age five who are found to be at nutritional risk.
- Housing Choice Voucher Program (Section 8), which assists very low-income families, the elderly, and the disabled to afford housing in the private market.
- Free and reduced-price school meals.

Yet despite significant increases in transfer payments, the United States remains a highly unequal society. Economic inequality among children is greater than among any other age group and worst among infants and very young children.

Although the proportion of children growing up in extreme poverty has declined, at any one time more than one in six young people under eighteen lives in poverty, from a low of 8.1 percent in Utah to a high of 27.7 percent in Mississippi. The number who experience a period of poverty during their childhood is far higher. According to the US Census Bureau, 44 percent of children experienced poverty for at least two consecutive months between 2013 and 2016.[11] At the other end of the spectrum, an upper-middle class has emerged with attributes definably different from the bulk of the population: income in the top 20–30 percent (though below the fabled "top one percent"), college or more advanced degrees, significant property assets, residence in a "desirable" neighborhood, and good social connections. While this group sometimes harbored real insecurities, the gap between it and the substantial minority in or near poverty has become yawningly wide.

The persistence of child poverty and the failure to significantly reduce class differences, despite marked increase in transfer payments, is due to several factors. These include the cost of living and child-rearing, which has risen faster than the increase in transfer payments, especially in high-cost areas; widening income inequality and the prevalence of low-wage jobs; insufficient coverage and gaps in assistance programs, as well as complex application processes and eligibility criteria that exclude families barely above the poverty line; and differences in how states allocate funds and determine eligibility.

Since the early 1970s, economic and educational inequalities in the United States have not only intensified but have become intertwined with other forms of social difference, leading to disparities in children's experiences and their future opportunities and compounding the challenges faced by children from marginalized or less affluent backgrounds. Most obviously, economic disparities often intersect with racial and ethnic inequalities due to historical and systemic discrimination. Children of color are more likely to experience poverty, attend less successful schools, and face barriers to health care and housing. These compounded disadvantages affect their educational outcomes, health, and future employment opportunities.

Residential segregation by race and income has led to concentrated areas of poverty, where children face compounded challenges, including limited access to quality education, higher exposure to environmental hazards, and fewer employment opportunities for the parents. An older view of a self-perpetuating culture of poverty, rooted in dysfunctional values and behaviors, has been superseded by a view of concentrated poverty as an ecosystem, which focuses on the systemic and structural factors that contribute to poverty and its persistence. This concept encompasses not just the lack of financial resources but also the interconnected issues that often accompany poverty, such as limited access to quality education, health care, employment opportunities, and stable housing, which reinforce one another and make it difficult for individuals and communities to break out of the poverty cycle. This approach, which emphasizes the impact of racist attitudes, household instability, inaccessibility to secure jobs, educational disparities, and the pervasiveness of stress and depression among impoverished parents, helps us better understand poverty's impact on children.

Economic inequality also manifests in geographic terms, with significant differences in resources and opportunities between urban, suburban, and rural areas. There are also regional disparities, with some parts of the country experiencing higher levels of poverty, unemployment, and social disinvestment, which can limit children's opportunities for advancement.

In addition, economic inequality intersects with changes in family structures. Single-parent families, which have become much more common since the 1950s, are significantly more likely to experience economic hardship. This can affect children's access to extracurricular activities, quality childcare, and other supports that enhance development and social mobility.

Meanwhile, disparities in access to quality early childhood education programs can have long-term effects on children's cognitive and social development, setting the stage for ongoing educational challenges. Ditto for attendance in high-poverty schools. Schools in high-poverty areas often face numerous challenges, including less experienced teachers and higher rates of student mobility. Children living in poverty are more likely to experience stress, food insecurity, and instability at home, which can adversely affect their cognitive development and ability to focus on schooling. Instability in school attendance, whether due to frequent moves, health issues, or other factors, disrupts students' learning processes and can lead to gaps in knowledge that are hard to overcome.

The digital divide has emerged as a new frontier of inequality, with disparities in access to technology and the Internet exacerbating differences in educational opportunities and outcomes. Children in economically disadvantaged households are much more likely to have limited access to computers and high-speed Internet, which are increasingly essential for learning.

The intersection of economic inequality with other forms of diversity since the 1950s has created new and complex disparities in American children's experiences and opportunities. Addressing these challenges will require policies and interventions that consider the interconnected nature of economic, racial, geographic, and familial factors influencing children's lives.

Inequality and Child-Rearing

Since World War II, the influence of socioeconomic class on childhood inequalities has intensified, with wealthier, better-educated parents adopting child-rearing practices distinct from those of lower-income, less-educated families, further entrenching disparities. The relationship between social class status, parental education, and child-rearing practices has become more tightly interwoven and has become a crucial mechanism through which economic and social inequalities are reproduced.

The increasing alignment of class status with child-rearing practices is both a cause and consequence of wider economic, educational, and social disparities. As economic inequality has widened, so too has the gap in resources that families can devote to their children's development.

These advantages set the stage for disparities in educational achievement and, later, in career success and earning potential.

Parental education plays a pivotal role in this dynamic, as inequalities in education gain increasing importance in the overall pattern of inequality in contemporary American life. Highly educated parents are more likely to engage in practices that promote the development of their children's skills and abilities. This includes reading intensively to children from an early age, providing intellectually stimulating environments, and fostering high expectations for educational attainment. These practices are linked to the concept of "concerted cultivation," where parents actively foster their child's talents and skills, navigating educational and extracurricular systems to their advantage. Such strategies are less prevalent or accessible among parents with lower levels of education, often due to constraints in time, resources, or knowledge about how to navigate these systems. As a result, over the last sixty years, the gap between children from wealthier families and their less affluent counterparts has significantly widened.[12]

Hypervigilance has become a defining characteristic among college-educated parents. They are eager to shield their offspring from a host of bad influences from peers, media, or drugs. The class and educational divide has rightly been described as a "rug rat race": as a competitive struggle by affluent, better-educated parents to ensure that their children will be successful academically, socially, and in other ways.

Let us be clear: It's not that less educated or poorer parents care less about their children's success, safety, or well-being; it's that they are less able to act on those aspirations. Not only do they have fewer material resources, time, or valuable personal connections, they have less firsthand knowledge about how to act strategically to advance their children's interests in the new climate of the post-industrial economy. In addition, these parents are less able to shield their children from potential roadblocks and to compensate with a "safety net" that might include psychological therapy, school accommodations, or access to tutors.

Wealthier parents are, of course, more likely to choose neighborhoods with resource-rich schools and low levels of crime and disorder. In addition, more affluent families are better able to grapple with childhood disabilities and with issues involving academic performance. These parents are also more likely to enroll them in high-quality nursery schools when they are young and in music classes and youth sports programs when they are older. Older children in this group have a wider variety of extracurricular activities and are more likely to go on college tours.

For all of its privileges and advantages, an upper-middle-class childhood spent with educated parents is not an unambiguous blessing. It often includes over-direction and demanding scheduling. Children also benefit from other qualities, including persistence, self-control, curiosity, conscientiousness, grit, and self-confidence, that are more likely to be instilled by giving children more household responsibilities or by encountering adversity and overcoming setbacks, failures, and disappointments.[13] One of the greatest challenges that this society faces if it is to live up to its democratic aspirations is to find ways to scale the kinds of opportunities that upper-middle-class children can take for granted—but also to reduce some of the liabilities of the overprotected segment.

At present, clearly, the advantages of wealth and levels of parental education are most easily measured. On average, children from affluent families outperform those from middle-class or poor families across multiple educational metrics. They receive higher grades and score better on standardized tests. These children also boast higher high school graduation rates and higher rates of college enrollment and completion. Children from more affluent families also tend to have higher educational and career expectations, both from themselves and from their parents. Their parents invest twice as much as their counterparts with less education. Parental expectations shape their children's goals, aspirations, and outcomes in life. In contrast, children from less affluent households, who lead less structured lives, may be more self-reliant and more resourceful.[14]

Interestingly, the growing disparities in academic achievement are not attributable to declining performance among middle-class, economically disadvantaged, or children of color. In fact, these groups have shown marked academic improvement over the past few decades. Instead, the disparity has expanded because children from more affluent backgrounds, who are also more likely to have well-educated parents, start their education with a significant advantage. Even before beginning kindergarten, these children have typically been exposed to a richer array of cognitively stimulating experiences. Their parents not only spend more overall time with them but also dedicate substantial effort to reading to them.

Even during the 1960s, better-educated and more affluent mothers devoted more time with their children, especially preschoolers, than did their less educated, less affluent counterparts. But the gap grew substantially during the twentieth century's last decade, even as many more mothers had entered the paid labor force. This class and educational divide has remained at a high level ever since.

A somewhat similar trend can be seen in breastfeeding. During the 1990s, college-educated mothers became much more likely to breastfeed, and the gap between them and their less well-educated counterparts widened substantially. That educational gap in breastfeeding narrowed somewhat during the early twenty-first century yet remains pronounced. Surveys of breastfeeding mothers found that they breastfed to enhance their baby's health and intelligence and to better bond with their child.

Precisely because more affluent parents have greater resources and, in many cases, more flexibility in their schedules, they can invest more time and money in their children. Their goal, as economists would put it, is to promote the development of their cognitive skills, enhance their noncognitive growth, and increase human capital. In contrast, families from lower socioeconomic backgrounds may struggle to provide these advantages due to financial constraints and limited access to resources.

At the same time, there has been a trend toward the resegregation of schools along class, racial, and ethnic lines, reversing the progress made toward educational integration during the 1950s and 1960s. This resegregation mirrors the socioeconomic and racial divides within society, leading to educational environments that are more homogeneous in terms of student backgrounds. Such segregation exacerbates class differences in childrearing and educational outcomes, contributing further to the impact of growing inequality in contemporary American childhood.[15]

Diverse Families

Growing economic inequality enhances, and is enhanced by, growing variety in family forms. The deep links between family structure and inequality require a preview here. In the mid-twentieth century, poverty was less linked to families organized around single parents or unmarried couples than is the case today, and the shift began soon after the 1950s—corresponding with the overall emergence of contemporary childhood.

One key shift, not necessarily correlated with inequality, was the virtually revolutionary change in women's work patterns. In 1960, 65 percent of all children lived with their married, biological parents, with a go-to-work dad and a stay-at-home mom. Now, less than one quarter (24 percent) of kids living in opposite-sex married-couple families have a full-time stay-at-home mom.[16]

But while considerable public concern attached to this shift, with some echoes still today, it was the decline of the two-parent household itself, with the decline of marriage and the rise of single parenthood, that ultimately drew the most attention. During the last decades of the twentieth century, there was intense concern that the decline of intact, two-biological-parent families would have disastrous consequences for children's well-being. Dire predictions abounded about the impact of divorce, single parenthood, unmarried cohabitation, or daycare on children. Almost all of the predicted consequences failed to materialize. Standardized test scores and high school graduation rates rose while rates of teenage pregnancy and juvenile delinquency fell. But that does not mean that changes in family form were without consequence.

The capacity of a family to provide a loving, caring, and supportive environment is not inherently determined by its structure. All families, irrespective of structure, can be loving, caring, and supportive or, conversely, dysfunctional, neglectful, or abusive. Families, whether headed by single parents, cohabiting couples, married couples, same-sex couples, or other configurations, have the potential to nurture and foster positive development in children. However, statistical and sociological research has highlighted that families led by single parents or cohabiting couples often face greater challenges, which is where inequality and poverty on the one hand link directly to family variety on the other in the contemporary period.

Single-parent families tend, on average, to be more vulnerable to layoffs, health emergencies, economic downturns, and evictions or other disruptions. In general, they tend to have less social support, both in terms of informal networks (like family and friends) and formal support (such as access to childcare services). Couples who are cohabiting tend to be less stable than those who are married, and frequent moves and changes in family composition can affect children's sense of security and attachment, potentially impacting their social and emotional development. Also, cohabiting couples may lack access to benefits (such as health insurance and Social Security) that are designed with married couples in mind and the legal protections that benefit married couples in times of crisis or separation.

It is important to note that while single-parent and cohabitating families face a variety of challenges, public policy can play a critical role in mitigating those problems. Economic support and access to affordable childcare, health care, and after-school programs can significantly enhance well-being for all families, regardless of their structure. At present, quite clearly, the social network in the United States has not compensated for the impact of growing inequality on family life, compounding this crucial trend.

Gender and Diversity

Some of the most striking transformations that have taken place in childhood since the 1950s involve gender. Traditional gender roles, with boys encouraged to be assertive and independent and girls steered toward nurturing roles and domestic skills, are less prevalent. While one must be wary of exaggerating the drift toward gender equality, there can be no doubt that parents are increasingly encouraging all children to explore a wide range of interests and activities, regardless of gender. Also, the meanings ascribed to gender differences have changed, with femaleness increasingly associated with agency and empowerment. While gendered marketing and stereotypes persist, there is increasing diversity in toys, media, and literature that challenge traditional gender norms.

Especially striking are girls' gains in education, with girls now outperforming boys not just in reading but in mathematics as well. Nor are sports regarded as a predominantly male domain with limited opportunities and social support for girls' athletic involvement. The passage of Title IX in 1972 significantly increased girls' participation in sports by prohibiting gender discrimination in federally funded education programs, including athletics. This led to a surge in female participation in a wide range of sports, promoting physical fitness and team skills among girls as well as boys.

Yet, despite great strides toward greater gender equality, gender stereotypes do continue to influence girls' and boys' upbringing. Many parents regard their daughters as more fragile and vulnerable than their sons. In general, girls are still expected to take on more household chores and caregiving responsibilities, but in single-parent and same-sex families, parents are especially likely to reduce gender-based chore distinctions. Color coding, pink for infant girls, blue for infant boys, endures. Girls' and boys' rooms are decorated differently. Boys are still encouraged to play with trucks or construction toys and participate in sports, while girls are more likely to be given dolls or playhouses, encouraging nurturing, cooperation, and role-play. The early twenty-first-century popularity of "gender-reveal" parties among some affluent parents prior to a child's birth suggests the ongoing importance of gender, along with consumerist display.

At the same time, naming patterns that have changed significantly in recent years reveal marked shifts in attitudes toward gender. Unisex and gender-neutral names, like Riley, Alex, Charlie, and Jordan, have become much more common, reflecting a societal movement toward greater gender equality and fluidity. There has also been an upsurge in the number of unique or uncommon names that underscore a child's individuality. Vintage names, including names from defunct occupations, like Mason and Cooper; Old Testament names; and old-fashioned names, like Eleanor, Hazel and Oliver, have made a comeback. There has also been an increase in ethnic names that pay homage to a family's cultural or religious traditions, as well as a surge in nature-inspired names, like Luna, River, and Willow.

While it is still the case that boys are more encouraged to be stoic and girls are typically allowed and even encouraged to express a wider range of emotions, there is certainly more pressure on boys to become more emotionally expressive. And even though boys are still given more freedom to engage in risky play and explore their environment, while girls are more often cautioned about dangers and risks, safetyism has influenced boys' behavior, with significantly fewer boys breaking arms or legs.

Gender-based concerns persist nevertheless, both old and new. These include worries about juvenile delinquency, illicit drug use, and binge drinking, which are much more common among male adolescents, yet they represent only the tip of the iceberg. Another source of concern is that many boys, including many from middle-class homes, appear to be uninterested in education, even though schooling is increasingly viewed as the only reliable route to a secure middle-class life. Scary statistics reinforce this sense of concern. Boys in elementary and middle school are roughly 50 percent more likely to repeat a grade, twice as likely to receive an out-of-school suspension, and nearly three times as likely to be expelled. Boy are also nearly 40 percent more likely to drop out of high school. In addition, boys tend to be less realistic about the requirements for success in today's service-oriented and information-intensive economy and remain reluctant to consider future careers in high-demand fields that involve caregiving like teaching, social work, or nursing.

Not only are young men significantly less likely to enroll in college immediately after high school, they're also about 20 percent more likely to drop out of college. Once in college, male students perform more poorly than their female counterparts, recording lower GPAs and earning fewer credit hours. This is partly due to lower levels of college readiness (evident in lower high school GPAs) and partly to differences in course and major selection. The result is stark: since 1982, women have earned 13 million more bachelor's, master's, doctorate, and professional degrees than men. A likely consequence is a dwindling pool of marriageable men and mounting anger and alienation among the growing number of young men who feel cut off from the opportunities to achieve a middle-class standard of living.

The stark gender gap in illegal, anti-social, and counter-productive behavior has been explained in many conflicting ways, including the notorious and grossly exaggerated claim that that anti-male prejudice has contributed to a "war against boys." Nor is there much evidence to support the claim that video games, hip hop, a "school-ain't-cool" ethic within boy culture, or female-dominated schools, explain these gender differences. Recently, a great deal of emphasis has been placed on the role of "hegemonic" or "toxic" masculinity—the dictate that manliness requires a boy or man to suppress emotions, mask distress, refuse to admit vulnerability or neediness, and be physically strong, competitive, and aggressive. But such a constricted conception of masculinity does little by itself to help us understand academic underperformance and what to do to combat it.

What do we actually know about why young men—except at the most elite colleges and universities—are underrepresented in higher education? Several factors stand out, beginning with academic under-preparation. On average, cognitive development and development of self-regulatory behaviors occur at differing rates among boys and girls. Grade schools, in recent years, have placed greater demand on reading and writing skills, areas in which many boys' skills lag behind girls', leaving many discouraged and disaffected. Many withdraw and direct their energies elsewhere. There is also reason to believe that schools are insufficiently attentive to the needs of active, inquisitive students who are unable to sit still and control their emotions, whether these are girls or boys.

Then, there is young men's declining academic aspirations. Beginning in the early 1990s, young men's educational aspirations began to fall, with significantly more women than men planning to attend and graduate from college or go on to further education in areas like medicine and law. Girls' aspirations rose, boys' fell. Nor is the gap in academic aspirations confined to low-income students. Even among middle-income students, men were less likely to aspire to pursue a college education.

We might add schools' unresponsiveness to the differing needs of girls and boys. In certain respects, K-12 classrooms tend to focus more on boys than girls. Teachers, according to some older studies, are more likely even today to call on boys, attribute ideas advanced in class to boys, ask boys more abstract questions, and elaborate on points made by male students. Boys are also more likely to blurt out answers without raising their hands, speak out more frequently and for longer in class discussions, and adopt a verbal style that is more argumentative, assertive, and self-confident—all ways to establish status, dominance, and hierarchy. Yet despite this bias, a subset of boys is much more likely to act out in class, become distracted, and not take their classes seriously.

The challenge for teachers is to develop the abilities of all students as fully as possible. This requires attentiveness to classroom dynamics, including gender dynamics; responsiveness to students' needs; and the ability to differentiate instruction. The concept of learning styles has been subject to withering criticism, but the fact remains that students differ in their interests, prior knowledge, ability, motivation, attitude toward schoolwork, detail orientation, time-management skills, and degree of extroversion or introversion. The most effective teachers tailor learning experiences and activities as much as possible to students' diverse needs. They also give students multiple ways to demonstrate their learning, which can include verbalizing, visualizing, writing, performing, presenting, debating, and creating.

So, what is to be done? Schools and parents need to help young men better understand the skills needed to prosper in today's knowledge and service economy and then help them develop the communication, critical thinking, collaboration, and quantitative and statistical skills essential to success. Support services need to be highly attentive to the challenges that boys and young men face.

Of course, saying that educational institutions are not doing a good job of serving many boys does not imply that we should redirect our efforts in serving girls and young women. Women remain grossly underrepresented in two of the highest-demand, highest-paying fields of study, computer science and engineering, and underrepresented in mathematics, statistics, and the physical sciences. At the same time, young women now report higher levels of disorders such as anxiety and depression, if only because these have become more obvious given new levels of education and aspiration. These, too, warrant attention. Gender gaps, in short, matter regardless of sex. Here, clearly, is a category where diversity has greatly changed but where it still counts thanks to a combination of continuities from the past and confusing new distinctions.

Race

To grow up Black, irrespective of socioeconomic class or gender or immigrant status, differs profoundly from growing up white. For one thing, it typically involves early awareness of the importance of race in American society, whether from direct experience with racism, discrimination, or prejudice or from discussions about race within one's family or community. Black children also learn from an early age the history and legacy of racial discrimination, from slavery to Jim Crow to the systemic and structural disadvantages and inequalities that continue to exist today. Many realize from an early age that a far larger share of the Black population lives in poverty than among whites and suffers from disparities in housing, health care, and education, and that even many middle-class Black Americans are unwelcome in many neighborhoods and businesses. Also, Black achievements and contributions to America are often underplayed in school classrooms.

Black children, especially sons, are given "the talk," a frank conversation about how to interact safely with the police in order to avoid a potentially violent confrontation. Black children also encounter various stereotypes that denigrate their abilities, intelligence, or behavior and that might influence the way they are treated by teachers, salespersons, and others. Yet Black children often grow up with a strong sense of community and cultural pride rooted in family traditions, music, religion, and other cultural practices. These practices play an essential role in fostering identity and belonging.

The past half century has brought far-reaching changes to Black childhood. The Black community has grown much more diverse. Today, about a fifth of Black children are the product of the recent Black diaspora from Africa, the Caribbean, or other regions. Even as the Black middle class has expanded, high rates of poverty and gross disparities in wealth persist, and rates of downward economic mobility are much higher than among whites. About a quarter of Black babies and toddlers in rental households face the threat of eviction in a typical year.[17]

Forms of Black cultural expression have become more central to American music and other modes of popular entertainment. Meanwhile, awareness of systemic and structural racism—evident in entrenched and persistent inequalities in criminal justice, education, health care, housing, jobs, and the distribution of wealth—has also increased. These developments carry profound but contradictory consequences for Black childhood. Despite the legal end of segregation, disparities in education persist due to factors like the concentration of many Black students in high-poverty schools that offer fewer advanced classes, clubs, and other extracurricular activities. Racial biases in discipline practices and the resegregation of American schools through housing patterns and districting also contribute to educational achievement gaps. Gaps in income and wealth between Black families and their white counterparts remain substantial, a product of historical injustices like redlining and ongoing discrimination in employment and housing. These economic disparities impact the resources available for Black children, affecting their living conditions, access to health care, and extracurricular opportunities.

Black communities continue to navigate complex relationships with law enforcement and the criminal justice system. Racial profiling, disparities in sentencing, and other forms of systemic bias contribute to a climate where Black children may grow up with heightened awareness of and concerns about racial injustice.

Certainly, the affirmation of Black culture, history, and identity has grown, fostering a sense of pride among Black children in their racial and cultural identity. But alongside increased racial pride, there is a growing awareness and, in many cases, anger over the persistence of racial bias and inequality. Social media and widespread coverage of incidents of racial injustice have heightened this awareness among Black youth, leading to a renewed focus on advocacy and activism. Advocacy has taken many forms, contributing to demands for more inclusive, culturally responsive school curricula and more concerted efforts to advance academic equity, by addressing disparities in enforcement of school discipline policies and expanded access to advanced and specialized courses and schools. The result is a generation that is increasingly empowered to celebrate their identity and advocate for change, while also facing the task of confronting and overcoming systemic barriers that persist from the past into the present.

Hispanic Children

The experience of growing up Hispanic varies widely, since the very word encompasses a wide range of ethnic backgrounds, including individuals with origins in Mexico, Puerto Rico, Cuba, Central and South America, and other Spanish-speaking cultures. The product of a unique melding of cultures and of a distinctive history, Hispanics include descendants of Spanish, Indigenous peoples, and Africans and may come from families that have resided in the United States for generations or from recent immigrants. This diversity means there is no single narrative that can capture the experience of growing up Hispanic in the United States; rather, it's a mosaic of stories influenced by factors such as immigration status, socioeconomic status, geography, and generational differences.

Hispanics are among the youngest and fastest-growing American ethnic groups, but they are also among the oldest, predating the arrival of the English colonists by a century. As recently as the 1960s, the Hispanic population was highly concentrated in the Southwest and New York City, and its history was largely invisible to most white Americans. Few white Americans knew anything about the large-scale migration to the United States from Puerto Rico, Mexico, or other parts of Latin America or about the recurrent efforts in the 1930s, 1940s, and 1950s to "repatriate" Mexican Americans. Discussions of industrialization focused on the great factories of the Northeast, overlooking the growth of large-scale mining or commercial agriculture in the Southwest. Nor were many aware that there were civil rights movements among Puerto Ricans and Chicanos that paralleled the Black struggles for equality. The result was to render invisible a whole group of Americans.

During the twentieth century, a prevailing American attitude toward the absorption of immigrants was assimilation, the essential abandonment of immigrant ways for the customs of the established majority. In reality, assimilation did not mean the disappearance of European, African, or Asian heritages. Ethnic groups practiced an assertive multiculturalism, maintaining distinctive religious traditions, foodways, and cultural practices and using politics to defend their groups' interests. The result was the creation of a hybrid culture, a culture shaped by blending, borrowing, and the mutual influence of cultural groups. Languages were blended into an apparently uni-ethnic English. American music, diet, fashion, and sports all reflect a process of borrowing and intermixture.

Hispanics, even in the 1950s and 1960s, did not experience multiculturalism or assimilation; instead, they suffered outright exclusion and discrimination alternating with studied neglect. Across the Southwest, Mexican American children were segregated in separate schools. Not until 1968, when the Bilingual Education Act was enacted, did the federal government begin to encourage instruction in Spanish as well as English. Meanwhile, even after World War II, many available jobs in the Southwest, which were heavily concentrated in agriculture, mining, or railroads, forced Hispanic families to frequently move.

However, Hispanic children now, as in the past, tend to grow up in environments where cultural traditions, language, and heritage are central to their family and community life. Celebrations, cuisine, music, and other cultural expressions play significant roles in shaping their identity and sense of belonging. Bilingualism is also a common aspect of the Hispanic experience, with Spanish often spoken at home.

The experiences of Hispanic children in the United States varies widely based on cultural background, geographical location, immigration and generational status, socioeconomic class, and race. Hispanic children growing up in areas with large, long-established Hispanic communities, such as parts of the Southwest, Florida, Chicago, or New York City, have very different experiences from those in areas where Hispanics are a smaller minority. The local community can influence the availability of cultural resources, the prevalence of bilingual education, and the level of societal acceptance or discrimination they face.

Children of recent immigrants face different challenges and opportunities compared to those whose families have been in the United States for generations. Issues such as legal status, acculturation stress, and family separation can impact the experiences of first-generation children, while second- or third-generation Hispanic children may navigate the complexities of retaining cultural heritage while assimilating into broader American society.

Economic disparities affect the quality of education, housing, health care, and extracurricular opportunities available to Hispanic children, with those from lower-income families facing significant barriers to success and well-being. Since Hispanics can identify with a range of racial backgrounds, affecting their experiences of identity and potential encounters with racism and discrimination. The intersection of Hispanic ethnicity with Black, white, Indigenous, or other racial identities adds layers to the complexity of growing up Hispanic.

Whether they are immigrants themselves or the children or descendants of immigrants or come from families that have lived in the United States for many generations, many Hispanic children have migration narratives as part of their family histories. These stories of sacrifice, suffering, perseverance, and dreams of better opportunities play an important role in shaping children's identities.

Like their Black counterparts, many Hispanic children grow up with a distinctive double consciousness, as participants in mainstream American culture but also as the possessors of distinct cultural and religious traditions. How individual children define their identity varies widely. Also, like Black children, many Hispanics grow up in communities with strong extended family and communal bonds. Religion, especially Catholicism in many Hispanic families, can play a crucial role in daily life and traditions.

Today, Hispanic peoples are changing American life irreversibly. More than any other ethnic group, they have transformed a biracial society into a truly multiracial society and a monolingual society into a multilingual society. At a time when many Americans feel a void in the culture, regarding it as bland, denatured, and overcommercialized, Hispanic culture seems richer and more varied and dynamic, and it is regenerating American food, dress, music, and artistic, literary, and cultural expression.

Immigrant Childhoods

Among the most striking recent developments in childhood is the rapid increase in the number of children of immigrants. These children inevitably straddle two worlds, one rooted in their family's cultural and religious traditions and another that grows out of the American context. This dual identity can be a rich source of pride and understanding, but it can also lead to feelings of being "in between" or not fully belonging to either culture.

The sharp increase in immigration since 1965, when restrictive national quotas were abolished, has had profound consequences for children. We've seen a sharp increase in the diversity of the youngest Americans. Currently, over 18 million children—one in four—are immigrants themselves or the children of immigrants. Slightly more than half are of Hispanic origin, 17 percent are of Asian descent, and 9 percent are non-Hispanic Black, usually from Africa or the Caribbean.

About half of all children of immigrants live in low-income households, about a third more than those with two US-born parents. Nearly two in five have parents with low English proficiency, which makes it difficult for those parents to navigate the educational system or to access many public services. About one in six children of immigrants has limited English proficiency. However, most second- and third-generation immigrant children experience substantial upward mobility by the time they reach adulthood. In fact, children of immigrants achieve more upward mobility than do children of US-born fathers. This is the case, in part, because immigrant parents are more likely to move to high-opportunity areas than their native-born counterparts.[18]

Many children of immigrants face intense pressure, either overt or subtle, to assimilate. In the United States, there is a great deal of emphasis on fitting in and shedding "foreign" customs. They may feel compelled to adopt American dress and behaviors, even at the expense of their cultural identity. It is also likely that they'll encounter prejudice, discrimination, and racism, along with stereotypes associated with their ethnic or cultural background.

Family tensions can be another result of living within two cultures. Immigrant parents and relatives may have cultural expectations about behavior, gender roles, academic achievement, and career aspirations that differ from prevailing American values. This can lead to generational clashes as well as internal conflicts for the child. Growing up in a culture different from that of their parents can foster adaptability and resilience, but it can also stir tensions involving family loyalties and obligations.

Immigrant families often rely heavily on each other, especially if they have limited incomes and weak support systems. This dynamic can create strong family bonds but also added responsibilities for children, like caring for younger siblings or translating for parents. Immigrant families tend to attach a great deal of value to family connections and obligations. Many children of immigrants feel pressure to succeed academically and professionally to honor their parents' sacrifices. But this stress on family responsibilities can clash with the dominant society's emphasis on individualism and social mobility.

What about the approximately 1.5 million children without documentation or the 5.5 million children who live with at least one undocumented parent? Thanks to the 1982 US Supreme Court ruling in *Plyler v. Doe*, undocumented children have a right to a free public K-12 education, but they face many barriers to success; many are unable to work legally, obtain a driver's license, or attend college.

There is reason to think that many first- and second-generation immigrant children grow up with different expectations than those of native-born children. Among many immigrant families, there appears to be a greater emphasis on family interdependence than is found in the stereotypical non-Hispanic, white, upper-middle-class nuclear family. There is a heightened stress on reciprocal family obligations and greater respect for the elderly, growing out of a strong awareness of the sacrifices made by the older generations. In addition, children and adolescents are often given more family responsibilities, including caring for siblings and family members, cleaning the home, cooking meals, and sometimes assisting in a family business.

Many immigrant families attach a high value to family harmony and children's academic achievement, yet immigrant parents express these values differently. They are apparently less likely to cheerlead for their children than native-born, upper-middle-class, non-Hispanic, white parents who exist within a culture that tends to expect mothers to boost their child's self-esteem, entertain their children, ensure that they are happy and never bored, express love frequently—physically and verbally—intervene and advocate aggressively on their behalf, and seek to insulate them from risks to their physical and emotional well-being.

On average, Asian American children, even those from lower-income backgrounds, tend to perform better academically than any other group, earn higher grades, score better on standardized tests, and are more likely to attend highly selective colleges than other groups. Not only are Asian Americans the only group that has met the Obama administration's attainment goals—of 60 percent receiving a college degree—they are the only group whose standardized scores have consistently risen over the past two decades.[19]

These students' outsized level of academic success has given rise to facile and disingenuous cultural explanations, like those advanced by Amy Chua and Jed Rubenfeld, who link the high achievement of Chinese, East Indian,

Iranian, Jewish, Mormon, and Nigerian Americans to a "triple package" that consists of a sense of cultural superiority, feelings of insecurity, and high levels of impulse control. Other supposed explanations emphasize strict parenting, a unique receptiveness to learning and a drive to excel academically, an unusually strong work ethic, stable marriages combined with intense multigenerational family bonds, and a value system emphasizing filial respect and family obligations.[20]

This level of academic success is not because their parents have higher levels of education than the average American.[21] In part, it reflects the fact that Asian American students study for twice as many hours as other ethnic and racial groups. Whereas the average white child dedicates about five and a half hours a week to studying and homework, with Hispanic and Black students allocating less time, the average Asian American student devotes 13 hours weekly.[22]

Asian American students are not only more likely to attribute academic achievement to greater effort, rather than innate ability, than other groups but also to possess unusually high expectations for their own school performance. Equally important is a zealous focus on education as the key to upward mobility—an attitude reinforced by the belief that education offers the surest form of protection against discrimination within and outside the job market.[23]

Lower-income Asian American parents tend to place a premium on getting their children admitted to highly competitive high schools. Even lower-income Asian American students are more likely than Black and Latinx students to attend schools with higher-achieving non-Asian American classmates.

Among the strategies that these families use include leveraging community connections and extended family ties to move to neighborhoods with especially strong schools and emphasizing the importance of competitive testing by disproportionately enrolling their children in after-school, Saturday academies and test preparation programs. In New York, 43 percent of the low-income students enrolled in the city's free test prep courses are Asian.

For households of comparable wealth, Chinese Americans invest more heavily in education because of the discrimination they anticipate their children will face.[24] Cross-class social networks have contributed to the development of a robust array of ethnic community institutions that add significantly to the success of many low-income recent immigrants.

These include weekend schools, after-school programs, ethnic churches, temples, and mosques.

Disproportionate academic success has fed into a cultural stereotype that is superficially positive: the notion that Asian Americans are especially intelligent and industrious.[25] But even seemingly positive stereotypes can be dangerous. High and sometimes unrealistic expectations for academic achievement and intense internalized pressures to succeed can harm students' mental health while narrowing their sense of career possibilities. The view of Asian Americans as particularly smart, hardworking, and successful coexists with other gross generalizations, such as an excessive focus on academics or an absence of interpersonal skills. Such caricatures result in many poisonous consequences. There's a tendency to pigeonhole individuals into narrow categories and to ignore or stigmatize those who don't fit the mold.

Asian American children are not a monolith. The Asian American/Pacific Islander umbrella is a political construct that's just forty years old and combines people from forty-eight national, ethnic, and religious backgrounds: Bangladeshi, Burmese, Cambodian, Chinese, Filipino, Guamanian or Chamorro, Native Hawaiian, Hmong, Indian, Indonesian, Japanese, Korean, Laotian, Nepalese, Pakistani, Samoan, Thai, and Vietnamese, among others. A highly heterogenous composite, this category fails to take account of the peoples with very different histories, languages, religions, and social statuses.

Lumping Asian Americans and Pacific Islanders together can easily blind us to those with low rates of college enrollment and degree attainment. Southeast Asians and Pacific Islanders are much more likely to drop out of high school or college than East and South Asians. Also, gross generalizations about outsized Asian American academic success obscure a more complex reality. Over 40 percent of Asian American undergrads attend community colleges not elite, highly selective four-year institutions. In addition, Asian Americans are the most economically stratified racial or ethnic group in the United States, and some of the generalizations about Asian American economic success are deceptive because these households are more especially likely to contain multiple wage earners.

The fact is that many Asian American college students face invidious stereotyping, receive less academic support or counseling than other students, have less access to culturally relevant programming, and are underserved in terms of student life initiatives. The most obvious example involves the gross underrepresentation of Asian American undergraduates in college athletics.[26]

Gender and Sexual Identities

At a time when thousands of young people openly identify as a gender different from the one assigned at birth, and well over 100,000 under the age of eighteen have received "gender affirming care," it is striking that only in 1973 did the American Psychiatric Association (APA) remove the diagnosis of "homosexuality" from the second edition of its *Diagnostic and Statistical Manual* (*DSM*). The growth of the numbers of children who are transgender or gay is one of the most striking new features of diversity in contemporary American childhood.

Although today's adolescents tend to initiate sexual activity later than their late twentieth-century counterparts, young people have become far more knowledgeable about and accepting of diverse gender identities, including transgender, non-binary, and gender-queer identities. Increased media representation and activism by the LGBTQ+ movement have contributed to a growing acceptance of diverse sexual orientations. In addition, the young are less likely to hold traditional gender norms that prescribe specific roles and behaviors for men and women and place less emphasis on marriage and parenthood as essential to adulthood happiness. Today, more than one in five young adults (that is, 21.8 percent of those born between 1997 and 2003) identify as LGBTQ+, with young women three times more like to identify as LGBTQ+ than men. Among Generation Z respondents to a recent Gallup poll, 15 percent self-identified as bisexual, 2.5 percent as gay, 2 percent as lesbian, and 2.1 percent as transgender. Among Baby Boomers, in contrast, just 2.6 percent identify as LGBTQ+.[27]

Growing up as a gay or lesbian child has changed considerably over the last half century, but that has not necessarily made this process easier. Growing up as a gay or lesbian child in the United States today varies widely depending on such factors as family acceptance, religious background, and geographical location. But it is difficult regardless of circumstances.

Compared to past decades, there is a growing acceptance and visibility of the LGBTQ+ community in the United States today, and many young people find crucial support and validation among their peers. LGBTQ+ youth groups and gay-straight alliances can provide essential resources, mentorship, and a sense of community. There are more positive representations of gay and lesbian individuals in media and popular culture now than ever before, which can offer validation and role models for young people coming to terms with their sexuality.

Yet despite progress, gay and lesbian youth face unique challenges and stressors, including stigma, bullying, and discrimination based on their sexual orientation. A failure to encounter positive or relatable role models can leave many feeling isolated. Worse yet, in a society that still defines heterosexuality as the dominant and assumed norm, it is easy for gay and lesbian youth to worry that they are abnormal or deviant and to suffer from intense feelings of guilt or shame—and in some cases, parental hostility. Even under the most supportive circumstances, understanding one's sexuality and navigating relationships and intimacy in a heteronormative society can leave many gay and lesbian youths suffering from depression, anxiety, and high rates of suicidal ideation. Some gay and lesbian individuals struggle to reconcile their sexuality with their religious beliefs, especially if they belong to faiths that historically opposed homosexuality.

The process of coming out and disclosing one's sexual orientation to others is often extremely stressful. Many, for good reason, fear rejection by family and friends, especially in certain religious or culturally conservative communities. Without access to a supportive network and caring professionals, the stress can seem overwhelming. Current culture war debates contribute further to the complexities faced by this category of American children.

The Importance of Identity

Today's children struggle with identity issues from a much earlier age than in the recent past. No longer do children wait until adolescence to define, express, assert, and celebrate their gender, racial, ethnic, or religious identity through their dress, demeanor, hairstyles, presentation of self, the music that they embrace, and the peer groups they form.

More children than in the past are willing to speak out when they feel that their ethnic or racial identity is marginalized and is not treated with the respect it deserves. There is now a greater expectation that girlhood will be regarded as a source of pride and empowerment. Others at a young age may openly explore their gender identity and grapple with societal expectations, pronoun usage, and how to express their identity.

No longer are identities, whether racial, ethnic, gendered, political, or sexual, taken for granted or treated as a given. In today's society, identities have become politicized and problematized in ways that were much less true half a century ago. From a wide range of sources, including the

Internet, movies, social media, and, of course, peers, children become aware of the many forms that identities can take. As they grow up in an extraordinarily multicultural society that emphasizes diversity and mainstreaming, and that is highly attuned to issues involving bias, discrimination, exclusion, stereotyping, and stigma, it is not surprising that many are eager to explore and affirm their distinctive identity.

It is far too simplistic to attribute the politicization of schoolchildren's identities to assertive parents or activist groups or to blame this on cultural confusion. The fact is that today's children are navigating and expressing their identity from an early age. They are asking what it means to be male or female, or to be Black or Latino/a or Asian American, or to be gay or lesbian or straight. Even surprisingly young children may demand that their identities and their unique life experiences and perspectives be recognized and respected.

Much more than in the past, childhood cannot be insulated from the issues that stir the adult world. As adult society debates issues involving gender, gender norms, gender identity, sexual orientation, disability, racial and ethnic representation, equity, and inclusion, children have grown more aware of these issues. The increased representation of diverse identities in children's media, literature, and toys allows children to see themselves in ways that were difficult in the past and helps them validate their feelings and emerging self-image. The rise of digital technology and social media has transformed how children explore and express their identities. Online platforms offer spaces for connection, self-expression, and exploration of diverse identities, even if these platforms also make children vulnerable to cyberbullying.

Children's increased awareness of diversity has many sources. In their classrooms and in media they see a more diverse array of identities and encounter a wider range of perspectives on history and politics. They are encouraged to treat diverse classmates with respect. Exposure to diversity can be empowering to those who earlier in time would have felt unseen or marginalized. But the increased attention to diversity has also led to backlash and polarization, and children may encounter tensions over diversity even within their own families. School bullying also can still target diversity, particularly concerning sexual identity, but race and ethnicity can factor in as well, particularly in predominantly white settings. As norms shift and as language and labels are redefined, the young may feel freer to explore non-traditional identities more openly than in the past. But they may also experience confusion and uncertainty and encounter peer pressure and harassment. It is not easy to grow up in a culture in which issues of identity are highly charged, polarized, and evolving.

Conclusion

Diversity and inequality combine in ways that differ profoundly from those that existed half a century ago. Inequality has intensified, while diversity defined in terms of ethnicity, gender, immigration status, race, religion, sexuality, and other sociological factors has deepened. Sexual identity plays a more explicit role than ever before, and gender distinctions have undergone significant shifts. Not only has increasing inequality and diversity exerted a powerful impact on the experience of contemporary children, but these developments carry profound political implications as well.

Increasing diversity and inequality do not mean that overarching generalizations about contemporary childhood are not possible. The lives of all of today's children are, to some degree or other, colored by certain broad developments, including the proliferation of new kinds of families; the psychologizing of childish behavior; the intensification of schooling; the declining birth rate; reductions in access to free, unstructured outdoor play; and, of course, nearly universal access to the Internet and social media. At the same time, each of these developments is mediated by the kinds of inequality and diversity that have emerged since the 1950s. As we will also see when we turn to new kinds of childhood disabilities and disorders, these too are heavily influenced by inequality and diversity.

The rise of new forms of diversity and inequality among children has also had a powerful effect on American politics, as Democratic- and Republican-dominated states respond in very different ways to issues involving children, from juvenile crime to immigration, gender identity, labor law, and care for transgender minors. A central issue is whether American society will think about children and childhood in a unitary way or whether, instead, it will differentiate kids on the basis of their skin color, class, nationality, and sexual identity.

The American Child: The Transformation of Childhood Since World War II. Steven Mintz and Peter N. Stearns, Oxford University Press. © Oxford University Press 2025. DOI: 10.1093/9780197797112.003.0004

5

More Schooling. Less Joy?

Children have been complaining about school since it was invented. Contemporary American children, however, are adding some twists to the theme in ways that reflect changes in education and the ways it impacts the childhood experience. Comments by high schoolers, recorded on the Quora response website around 2016, provide some sense of the issues. Thus Taya May, after slamming the dress codes that limit freedom just so "the boys" don't get distracted, launches into her main complaint: "School is definitely stressful, we take multiple tests a year leading up to even bigger tests so a lot of people would rather stay at home and miss all the tests, preparation and yelling." Martha Ruth is a bit more nuanced. Clearly being steered toward college, she is placed, as a freshman, in a sophomore biology class, and she doesn't always understand what is going on. "I have an A in this class. It was probably the right decision. But I didn't have a choice. I have to work a lot for this grade....We only get 43 minutes a day for lunch...it's not even technically lunch, it's 'independent learning time' and we're supposed to be going somewhere to study....I love learning and I have good grades. So maybe we don't think school is awful. It's more about how much better the absence of school is."[1]

* * *

The realization that more formal education was essential—or unavoidable—plus a decline in the enjoyment of schooling created a vital tension in the emergence of contemporary American childhood from the late 1950s onward. The tension was not entirely new, nor was it uniform: many kids still (mostly) liked school at all levels, while an important though shrinking minority simply left as soon as was legally possible. But for many young people a growing sense of constraint was a reality, beginning with the sheer increase in the portion of life that would be spent in a classroom. It showed up at many levels, but quite dramatically in the disparity between rapid expansion of college enrollments and significant indications that expectations of enjoying college were declining at the same time.

College attendance began to soar in the United States from the 1950s onward. Growth was 49 percent during the initial decade, then rose to 120 percent in the decade following. The surge slowed slightly after this point, though absolute numbers would begin to mount again when the Baby Boomers hit college age in the late 1960s and 1970s. But overall expansion remained impressive, and it affected many segments of the population. The attendance gap between Blacks and whites persisted but narrowed, and women, about a third of the college population in the 1950s, overcompensated with a vengeance, reaching parity by 1980 and then beginning to gain preponderance; even in 1980 they were outnumbering men in two-year institutions. The recalibration of the balance between male and female aspirations was clearly underway: by the 1980s as high a proportion of women as men, for example, hoped to go into medicine or law.[2] For virtually every category of American children, however, the rise in educational levels, and also often aspirations, constituted one of the fundamental components of the new, contemporary framework for childhood.

At the same time, polls of first-year college students indicated a fairly steady, if less dramatic, decline in anticipatory excitement. In the 1960s, 60 percent of the incoming class were looking forward to a positive educational experience, but this had dropped to 48 percent by 2001 (though they expected to do well personally). Correspondingly, prediction of boredom in class went up—to 41 percent of the total by 2000, along with heightened anticipation of periodically missing class or arriving late—plans that were fairly easy to carry out. Indeed, the percentage of students who had been bored in class, missed class, or overslept during high school rose by 25 percent in the 1990s alone. Here was one area where children, at least after grade school, were becoming less obedient.[3]

The college attendance figures correctly suggest that schooling became more important for American teenagers in the later twentieth century, going well beyond the basic levels that had been well established earlier—and the implications would spread into earlier childhood as well. Here is the clearest indication of how the structures of the new economy impinged on children. If the modern period in American childhood history had introduced the obligation of children to receive some schooling, the contemporary period upped the ante considerably. More aspects of childhood and youth now centered in and around schools than ever before. But even granting the possibility that American kids, now raised on television, were more easily bored by the century's end, the simultaneous growth in lukewarm projections about the college experience suggested an interesting, if moderate, disjuncture. Though hard to measure, the evaluation of education by children and teenagers may have shifted downward at least slightly—arguably another important feature of the postmodern experience.

This is at best a complicated claim. Many kids had disliked school earlier: the most obvious change during the later twentieth century was the declining opportunity to end the ordeal relatively quickly. At the same time, many students would revel in the extension of schooling or at least grant it had some merit; there was no single reaction. But the overall tension between educational expansion, which can be clearly measured, and the more elusive topic of student enjoyment may have applied to a significant range of students, with gender distinctions increasingly playing in as well. It is no surprise, in this context, that reports of student anxiety began to swell from the late 1950s onward.

It is also true that professional historians, writing about education, must admit to their own peculiarities. They are likely to have enjoyed schooling and done well at it so that discussing even a mild mismatch between studentship and satisfaction imposes its own burdens. But the probability that new educational trends introduced important complications into American childhood—even before the more widely publicized problems such as massive college debt, which came into play only in the twenty-first century—deserves serious consideration.

Causes of Change and the American Context

Two or three basic factors pushed for reconsideration of established educational patterns during the second half of the twentieth century and continuing into the twenty-first: the combination was one of the fundamental differentiators between contemporary childhood and its earlier counterpart. Most obviously, growing global economic and political competition prompted periodic official attention to the educational state of play, with general pleas and concrete measures aimed at making American schooling a more serious business. Soviet success in launching Sputnik, the first manned spacecraft, in 1957, introduced new doubts about the adequacy of American education, particularly in its capacity to produce the expertise needed in the contemporary world. This was a theme that would persist through the remainder of the century, highlighted for example by dire reports such as *A Nation at Risk* (1983),[4] warning that "the educational foundations of our society are being eroded by a rising tide of mediocrity that threatens our very future as a Nation and a People." It is worth noting that this impetus, which guided a number of crucial changes in policy, had nothing to do with children as children.[5]

It was also true, however, that new educational and psychological research increased awareness of learning capacities in children, even among the very young. This was an optimistic finding in many ways, inviting new appreciation of the ways even babies make inferences and inductions and test hypotheses, even countering some of the other concerns about children's competence. However, in connection with the new policy priorities, the same findings invited more attention to testing educational achievement even in fairly young children, as educability and schooling seemed more connected than ever before.

More important still, but moving in the same direction, was the shift in the economy and job market toward greater emphasis on managerial and professional skills and opportunities, less reliance on blue-collar and agricultural options. More and more parents or young people, or both—and more and more high school counselors, themselves a growing breed—began to emphasize the importance of education for successful job entry. This, in turn, meant more schooling, and arguably more serious schooling, not only toward expansion of college ranks but toward growing insistence on completion of high school—something that only half the population had been achieving in the early 1950s. It might also reflect growing concerns, particularly among parents, about assuring that their children would be able to match or exceed their own achievements in a rapidly changing environment.

Pressures of this sort were not unique to the United States, even in countries less directly involved in Cold War competition. Expansion of both personal and national educational goals was a common experience, toward generating new levels of expertise and more extensive educational credentialing in increasingly knowledge-based economies.

In this general process, however, the United States faced a few particular challenges that would complicate, though not prevent, successful response. Most obviously, the overall educational system was notoriously decentralized, making national and sometimes even state-wide policies more difficult and encouraging awkward compensatory efforts, like the No Child Left Behind testing movement. It was telling that the increasingly important task of sorting students for more advanced educational opportunities, in most countries already the province of government-sponsored tests, was left in the United States to private agencies, like the College Board, amid a more haphazard and confusing set of overall standards.

Furthermore, the crowning achievement of the American educational tradition to that point—the high school—was arguably harder to adapt to the changing educational environment than the more differentiated secondary systems characteristic of Europe or Japan. Of course, high schools had never been as democratic as some claimed. Based on residential boundaries, they had always been differentiated by race and ethnicity, with variable resources depending on local tax base. In principle, however, and within individual communities in fact, the high school system gave American students a longer period of grace before the toughest kinds of educational decisions had to be made, than was true of counterparts in other countries where significant examinations already regulated the nature of entry into secondary schools.[6]

Building a more intensive educational experience, in other words, may have been somewhat more difficult in the United States than elsewhere, with results that could both burden and confuse some of the young people involved in the process. Clumsier methods—like the multiplicity of government-imposed tests that became part of the student experience—and more damaging processes—like the distorted competitions among college admissions programs that began to emerge in the later twentieth century—would complicate the educational adjustment process.

Additionally, though this must be a particularly tentative claim, the United States came into the period of educational intensification with a more ambivalent attitude toward education than was characteristic of some other countries. The nation had embraced the idea of schooling fairly readily in the nineteenth century, at least outside the South. But there was simultaneous concern about surrendering too much authority over children to teachers—and the teaching profession that developed from the nineteenth century onward never gained the prestige that it would acquire in Europe. As many experts and parents alike worried that intensive schooling or burdensome homework might damage young people, yet another constraint emerged. In other words, aspects of American culture may have complicated the new efforts to extend schooling—not preventing them but surrounding them with some misgivings on the part of some parents and students alike. Never a hotbed of enthusiasm for intellectualism or intellectuals, the United States now had to figure out what to make of the growing insistence on more education.[7]

Growing concerns about children's competence factored in as well, at least on the part of educational policymakers and quite possibly among adults more generally. For US students experienced not only an expansion in the number of years they were in school but also a particularly marked growth in the time they spent in classrooms—suggesting a clear belief that children could be counted on to learn only when under the direct supervision of adults. Many other affluent countries, witnessing similar trends, for example, in expanding university enrollments, placed far less emphasis on classroom confinement.

Finally, the surge of interest in extending education, beginning as it did in the 1950s, occurred amid two other, if ultimately temporary, challenges. In the first place the American Baby Boom, more pronounced than its European echo, made for painfully crowded schools and classrooms through the 1960s. Many school districts had to adopt a two-shift system during the school day simply to deal with the numbers involved. Crowded classrooms, in turn, could send confusing signals about what kind of student responses were possible or necessary in dealing with new educational expectations. For some male students, the school environment was also shaped by the relationship between school results and eligibility for the military draft (until its termination in 1973). Good grades and even more specific achievements such as class rank, in high school and college, could take on particular importance.

School Diversity and Inequality

Any assessment of patterns in American schools must emphasize the extraordinary diversity involved, the twin of decentralization, even as the policy role of states and the federal government has increased. Differences among urban and suburban schools remained massive. To be sure, outright funding disparities declined in some cases, at least within individual states—and New York City even exceeded the state average on a per-student basis. But the continued dependence of most schools on a local funding base, and the vast economic differences between one locality and the next, created an ongoing problem. As crusaders like Jonathan Kozol have pointed out for decades, many children from poor families (disproportionately

African American, Native American, or Hispanic) continued to attend schools with burst pipes, mold, and other blights.

Even where funding was not such an explicit issue, teacher quality as well as school facilities still diverged massively—teachers in the districts with a higher percentage of children from poor families were far more likely to quit, sometimes creating outright teacher shortages and certainly reducing experience levels—quite apart from the huge differences in needs between children from low- versus high-income backgrounds. Structural inequalities, in other words, compounded the social class differences in approaches to education. Indeed, income gaps may have been the most decisive determinant of different levels of educational achievement, and some studies suggest that the effects actually became more severe from the 1960s onward—part of the new contours of inequality in contemporary childhood. Certainly, educational inequality counted for more than in the past simply because education itself, including college entry, was becoming more important. Access to Advanced Placement courses and other educational and extracurricular activities varied sharply—again, precisely in the decades when these opportunities were becoming more significant.[8] Language differences added in. While suburban schools have seen growing immigrant populations since the early twenty-first century, their experience has contrasted markedly with schools in which second-language learners, many of them recent arrivals, were a vast majority—and where attrition among teachers reached twice the levels of the national average. These distinctions were often compounded by regional divides, increasing in many ways as a result of red-state/blue-state polarization. Larger trends can be identified and, with 40 percent of students overall, suburban schools embrace the largest group. For many students, however, the differences in resources and offerings overwhelm any simple generalizations about change.

Furthermore, structural differences are only part of the issue. Racial and socioeconomic divergences among students add to the complexity of any effort at generalization. In California, for example, less than 40 percent of Black and Hispanic high school graduates have completed a college prep curriculum, rendering them ineligible for admission into the state college and university system and contrasting massively with the experiences of white and Asian American students. The growing gender distinctions in educational achievement and aspiration add further complexity.

Inequality was also reflected in varying rates of school attendance even before the optional years of later high school and then college. Though absenteeism gained national attention only in the 2020s, in the wake of the pandemic, American rates had long been comparatively high—predictably increasing with the age of the student involved. But absenteeism varied considerably by race and family income, reflecting the distinctive school experiences and expectations of Native Americans, African Americans, and some immigrant children, but also comparatively high levels of poverty, including homelessness. Absenteeism often responded to family needs, including keeping a child at home to care for younger siblings or simply to work, but it also reflected wider recalcitrance among a minority of children and their parents and the fact that the nature of school itself varied so widely. The expansion of schooling was a general phenomenon, cutting across many divisions among children, but it did not erase the diversities of childhood.

Basic Changes: More Years

Extending the amount of time children and teenagers spent in school was hardly a new phenomenon. High school attendance, for example, still fairly rare in the late nineteenth century, had been expanding steadily in the first half of the twentieth century. However, the acceleration from the 1950s onward, affecting virtually all levels of education, significantly altered the balance between formal education and other activities for children.

The high school focus was dramatic. It was during the 1950s and 1960s that a relatively new term, "dropout," began to gain attention; only after 1965 did the commentary begin to trail off, quite simply because the message had been received. Arguments for high school completion centered on job market implications, but they could also pick up other concerns—for example, about juvenile delinquency—and the Cold War needs for expanded training loomed large as well. As one writer put it, urging the imperative of high school completion: "if we would train everyone in the limit of his capabilities, we must adopt a policy of attracting and holding every student in school for as long as he has the ability to achieve and the willingness to co-operate." This kind of rhetoric easily became self-fulfilling: the number of jobs requiring a high school diploma steadily expanded, making the dropout option, which was still common in the 1950s, increasingly self-defeating and extending the centrality of the high school experience in American adolescence.[9]

Thus, after hovering in the 50 percent range through the 1940s and early 1950s, graduation rates began to move up briskly. By the mid-1960s, 78 percent of the relevant age group was graduating, and by the twenty-first century the figure had advanced to roughly 84 percent. However reluctantly and unevenly, more and more families were recognizing that investing at least twelve years in education—at least two years more than legal requirements—had become a necessity.[10] The minority that still dropped out must be noted, including the fact that it is disproportionately Black and especially Hispanic, but partly because they now contrasted so vividly with the standard experience.

For the then-large middle classes, a similar recognition increasingly applied to college—at least to the point of initial enrollment: further commitment seemed essential. Here too national policy was involved: the National Defense Education Act of 1958, the response to Sputnik, raised the profile of college attendance and provided relevant financial aid, particularly in science and mathematics fields. But the real driver centered on decisions being made by young people and their parents, about what kind of preparation would generate entry into appropriate sectors of the job market and, more diffusely, offer the kinds of social experiences that seemed to be an increasingly normal part of middle-class life. By 1970 a full 40 percent of all Americans of the relevant age group were at least entering college. Whereas in 1950 only 13 percent of all Americans over twenty-five had attended some college (6 percent for four or more years), by 2000 the figure was 51 percent (25.4 percent for four years or more). And though it pushes beyond the experience of any reasonably defined childhood, growth in master's degree recipients was similarly steep.[11]

With shifts in high school completion and college entry combined, the experience of older teenagers was significantly transformed. In 1950 only 30 percent of people in this category were still in school, but by 1991 the level was 60 percent and rising. Correspondingly, the average American, who in 1950 could expect to spend about ten to eleven years in school, by the early twenty-first century could anticipate at least fourteen.[12]

These changes were striking, reflecting for many people an expansion of a period of at least partial economic dependency, certainly increasing the extent to which the full range of childhood and adolescence would revolve around school.

At the other end of childhood, more and more children began to be enrolled in kindergarten programs, again from the late 1950s onward.

The kindergarten experience was not new, but into the 1950s it had not yet become standard. Only twenty-six states were providing any funding for these programs, and many schools had no kindergarten at all. This now changed dramatically as all but two states signed on and as more parents agreed to the need for an earlier start to formal education (and, given the increasing involvement of mothers in the workplace, welcomed a place to park young kids). Kindergarten enrollment soared in the early 1960s, increasing by 30 percent in just two years, and became a standard experience for most five-year-olds. By the later twentieth century nineteen states plus the District of Columbia were in fact requiring kindergarten attendance. To be sure, the kindergarten year included a lot of play time (though with adult supervision—it still entered into the growing institutionalization of childhood), but emphasis on academic content increased steadily. Whatever the content, the growth of kindergartens meant that, at both ends of childhood, the years spent in school were expanding.

The Changing Structure of the School Day

Another kind of expansion, at least as dramatic though of a different sort, began to affect the experience of grade- and middle-schoolers, and it may have had more impact on children's perception of schooling than the years spent. This surge started in the 1980s in response to the growing sense of educational crisis and reflecting the realization that adequate preparation for later stages of education required an earlier start. Here is where the new expectations or requirements began to transform childhood more widely.

The focus, interestingly, was not the school year itself, despite recurrent discussion: at an average of about 180 days, approached earlier in the twentieth century, the American figure was actually rather low on an international scale. It was true that reduced absenteeism moved actual attendance up, to a 160-day level by the 1980s, after which it remained fairly stable; this arguably mattered more than official levels and confirmed the trend of spending more time in school. Furthermore, in the early twenty-first century, a few states incentivized districts to up the ante to 200, and a number of charter schools extended the year as well. Overall, however, despite some pressure, the 180-day average held fairly firm.[13]

What did change more substantially was the structure of the school day and the extent to which classroom attendance commanded an ever-larger portion of the child's time. On the days when Americans did send children off to school (unusually early in the morning by most international standards), they committed them into a surprisingly full day—about seven and a half hours. And while this too did not expand greatly despite the new pressure for educational achievement, the amount of time spent in the classroom began to soar.

The targets were recess and mealtime. Before the intensity push from the 1980s onward, many American children had enjoyed at least an hour of recess during the school day—twenty minutes in the morning, twenty during a forty-minute lunch period, and then a final twenty during the afternoon. Alternatively, some schools granted a full sixty-minute lunch break, during which some children simply went home to eat, along with at least one recess. By 2000 these niceties were largely a thing of the past. Little recess if any now combined with a lunch period squeezed into thirty minutes or less. One 2016 report claimed that the average student now had twenty-six minutes for lunch and recess combined. Increasing numbers of kids had no recess at all: 7 percent of first and second graders, but 11 percent of sixth graders according to one study, while recess was often entirely eliminated in middle school. Along with this, physical education classes were also curtailed or abandoned.[14]

These changes generated debate, of course: advocates for the importance of flexibility and play made a valiant pitch. But they fought a rearguard action at best. Arguments against recess—though counter-indicated by virtually all relevant studies of learning—focused primarily on a need for more academic focus, with an intuitive argument that "if you give more time to do something, they'll do better in school." Basic concerns about children's competence to learn without adult direction may have entered in here. But worries about safety, bullying, and overexcitement also contributed to the new pressures to keep kids in classrooms, and there were even intriguing claims that contemporary children, conditioned by solitary hours in front of television, no longer wanted or knew how to play. Whatever the pitch, the trend was clear well through the first decade of the twenty-first century. By 2016 only sixteen American states required any recess at all.[15]

The result, by the twenty-first century, was a school classroom career, grades 1 through 8, that was about 1,300 hours longer than the 8,894 average of the thirty-eight nations in the Organization for Economic Co-operation and Development (OECD). Most of these additional hours, in turn, had been applied to the school day over the previous quarter century, in what was a rapidly changing educational experience.

The overall point is clear: when Americans responded to the changing needs for education after the mid-twentieth century, the emphasis rested on time literally in school, often directly in classrooms—affecting students of all types, regardless of the many other inequalities in experience. Many of the resultant trends resembled patterns in other developed countries, particularly the pressure to complete secondary school and, increasingly, to enter college (though it is worth noting that, at four to six years, the American college experience itself was longer than that of many European countries). However, the patterns for younger American children suggested a commitment to an unusually intense allocation of time, and one in which children themselves had no real voice and where parents themselves, though sometimes concerned, were largely silent or ineffective. (Interestingly, in the context of standard American eating patterns, the increasing abbreviation of lunch periods drew little comment at all. Good Americans should know how to eat fast.)

These developments, particularly at the primary and secondary levels, occurred in a school environment that had changed in one other respect: schools, on average, had become a great deal larger and correspondingly more distant from home. Between 1930 and 1970 the average American school burgeoned from eighty-seven students to 440, as deliberate consolidation paired with the ultimate expansion of the school population. The process was not uncontested, for it significantly altered the balance between school administrators and parents: but there was no question about the trend. The result was that, just as time spent in class began to increase, students were also exposed to a more impersonal environment: a variety of studies showed that the result, particularly for groups such as African American students, increased a sense of estrangement and could even measurably worsen educational outcomes. Interestingly, the parallel growth of some huge universities, while significant—Ohio State's size, for example, would more than triple between the 1950s and 2000—was arguably less burdensome, for there were a larger number of smaller, less impersonal options.[16]

For younger children, school growth also increased the time spent on school buses. The experience applied to about half the student population by the early twenty-first century. Here too a variety of factors contributed:

school consolidation heightened distance from home, particularly in rural and suburban areas. Worries about safety and more dangerous traffic reduced interest in letting students walk or bike, even when this was potentially feasible. Suburbs themselves began to extend fences or other barriers that reduced opportunities for shortcuts. In 1970, 42 percent of students were still getting to school on their own, but by 1995 the figure had dropped to 29 percent and to 13 percent by 2001 (the figures do not count high school students who drove themselves). And while the average bus ride might seem fairly modest—at twenty-six minutes—there were many longer jaunts, with African American as well as rural students particularly burdened. Furthermore, even the standard duration added to the daily time that children were spending passively cooped up. It contributed as well, from another angle, to the elimination of any possibility of going home in the middle of the school day, as had been common for many grade-schoolers into the 1960s.[17]

One final change, this one from the 1970s and 1980s onward, involved time spent in a slightly different sense: a growing movement saw many parents (or teachers or both) working to delay the onset of grade school by a year, keeping children in nursery school and kindergarten for a longer period. The practice, dubbed "redshirting" because of its resemblance to a comparable practice in college sports, was designed to improve chances of school success by capitalizing on slightly greater maturity, and it seemed particularly attractive to anxious middle- and upper-middle-class parents who could afford an extra year of childcare. By 2003 the proportion of six-year-olds who were enrolled in first grade or above had dropped to 84 percent, in contrast to 96 percent in 1968. While part of this change resulted from shifts in law, the bulk reflected adult efforts to manipulate the system to advantage their offspring, another sign of the growing importance of educational achievement, but also its growing challenge. The result added to the overall time spent in school for some students.[18]

Some of these developments, admittedly, had compensatory bright sides. Delayed grade school did indeed improve results for some students in the early years—though not, interestingly, over a larger school career. More clearly in the plus column: consolidated schools could afford much more elaborate equipment and a wider range of activities, which could appeal to many students. While there was fluctuation and state-by-state variety, class sizes did not systematically increase and indeed dropped on average from the heights of the Baby Boom. From thirty-five in the 1950s, average public school classes were in the mid-twenties by the early twenty-first century. While this was larger than the norm in many other advanced industrial countries, particularly in Europe, the change might have alleviated some of the drawbacks of consolidated schools. And whatever the overall balance of factors, many children continued to thrive in and through their educational careers.[19]

It was also true, given the transitory nature of the school experience, that few children themselves were directly conscious of change. They had no remembered baseline by which to assess developments such as the elimination of recess or even the increasing compulsion to finish high school. At most, middle-schoolers could recognize that they had less free time than they remembered from grade school, a frequent source of complaint, but there was little opportunity to articulate any larger concern about trends.

Still, it is impossible not to wonder if, for many students, the measurable increases in the hours and years spent in school affected the way education itself was experienced and evaluated—even if the children involved had no direct recollection of a more relaxed past. As student comments suggested, the sense of rigidity and imposition was striking. By 2000 an impressive number of children had a daily schedule surprisingly similar to that of adults: about the same commuting time or slightly more and about the same obligatory hours (in a shorter daily frame but with a restricted lunch break). If many adults came to chafe at this schedule, the possibility of childish discomfort for an activity that did not always carry direct rewards may have been greater still. And the possibility was only enhanced by a second development: the growing importance of tests and grades.

Homework

Overall, in keeping with the growing intensity of in-school focus, the level of homework increased from the 1950s onward. Many areas had in fact outlawed homework before the response to the Soviet threat—California was a case in point. But now it seemed essential to add to what could be covered during the school day. However, the results were complicated, and it was not clear how much homework actually altered the school experience for many students.

In the first place, patterns fluctuated. Burdens tended to ease again by the 1970s, only to go up in response to the *Nation at Risk* anxiety. The twenty-first century, shaped by No Child Left Behind, saw another surge compared to the 1990s, with some claims that burdens actually doubled, particularly as students were urged to prepare for tests. A 2015 report suggested that even some kindergarteners were spending twenty-five minutes a night on homework.

However, in the second place, what was assigned and what was done were often two different matters, qualifying any sense of a major intensification. One study thus suggested that between 1981 and 2000 actual average daily homework had risen—but from sixteen daily minutes to nineteen. Furthermore, polls of college freshmen suggested that the amount of time actually devoted to homework declined in the final decades of the twentieth century: the number who had spent at least six hours a week on homework during their high school senior year dropped by 25 percent, to an all-time low of 35 percent using the 1960s as a baseline. Eager to see their offspring do well in the college admissions stakes, more parents were now worrying about too little homework than too much, though there were partisans in the latter camp as well.[20]

Overall conclusions are difficult. Homework almost certainly went up for conscientious grade-schoolers, who were, however, less vocal in their response than some of their high school counterparts. But after that experience varied, and a 2004 report noted that "claims about large increases in the homework load carried by most students are seriously overstated."[21] Many high school students managed to get a lot done in study halls. Many, clearly, did receive more burdensome assignments but did not actually invest much time in completing them (or got their parents to help, another interesting option). Amid constant debate, changes in homework took a distant second place to the outright extension of time in class in affecting children's experience.

Another development might be added, not insignificant to children's daily life: at all grade levels, but particularly for people in middle school and high school, the size and weight of textbooks went up fairly steadily from the 1960s onward. As textbooks became heavier, a growing number of parents and physicians expressed concern that the books' weight might contribute to back and posture problems. One obvious side effect: backpacks increasingly replaced school bags. Here too the experience of getting to and from school became less pleasant.

Testing

The idea of testing and grading students was not new: both features had advanced earlier in the twentieth century. They became increasingly prominent features of the school experience from the 1950s onward. Here too change emerged first at the high-school level, reaching the primary level more clearly from the 1980s onward.

As early as the 1950s, with a few forerunners in the previous decade, an interest in studying test anxiety among students, at various levels but particularly high school and college, gained ground steadily among academic psychologists. Researchers routinely found that a quarter to a third of the students examined had significant issues with testing, which in many cases severely hampered their academic performance. The research was not directly predicated on changes in the level of testing, but it was at least suggestive. There is no question that, for students intimidated by exams, problems were beginning to multiply.[22]

By international standards, American students had actually been undertested prior to the 1950s. They did not face the make-or-break exams characteristic of European countries and Japan (and newly installed in Britain after World War II). To be sure, the College Board SAT exam had been devised earlier in the twentieth century to help elite colleges sort applicants, but by the 1950s only a relative handful of colleges actually required it, and few college seekers actually took the test (1 percent, as late as 1940). It did not loom large. In fact, for most of the relatively small number of students aiming for college, the whole process was rather unintimidating: most applied to only one school, usually local, and in most cases admission rates were very high.

This began to change with a vengeance amid the flood of new college applicants. More and more universities shifted toward exam requirements (furthered as well by a 1951 government decision to factor SAT scores into military draft decisions, where the scores were available). While in 1955 fewer than two hundred colleges and universities sought test scores, by 1965 the number had quintupled, including massive state systems such as California (in 1958). By 1990, after doubling yet again, 1,839 colleges were on the list, which now included an ACT option (introduced in 1959, reflecting the new pressures) along with the SAT. In 1955 only 23 percent of all college applicants had taken a test, but by the mid-1960s the number soared to 80 percent. The changes went beyond percentages. Before the mid-1950s students who did take the exam normally gave it one shot, usually in April of their senior year. In the new environment, multiple efforts became common, stretching into the earlier high school years or even middle school. The National Merit Qualifying exam, introduced in 1956, morphed into the PSATS in 1971, creating in some students as early as their sophomore year of high school a sense, as one put it, that "time was running out" for their best chance to qualify for a good college.[23]

It is important not to exaggerate. The group of students most susceptible to the most extreme new exam pressures was a minority—perhaps 5 percent of the total. Many students were still not aiming for college at all; many others retained more modest ambitions that were not dependent on tests or at least not on top results. Still, the signs of higher stakes were clear. New training courses, like the Princeton Review, launched in 1981, reflected greater pressures. The College Board itself began to up the ante: it had begun reporting scores to high schools only in 1937, leaving it to them to decide whether to inform students directly. By the 1970s, however, the Board started providing information about average test scores by college while directly contacting students as well.[24] Many students, and their parents, were on increasingly high alert.

Furthermore, school systems themselves began to encourage students to participate and do well, whatever their college plans. This additional facet would morph, early in the twenty-first century, into actual requirements that students take the SAT or ACT as part of their high school graduation requirements: twenty-six states were in this category by 2020.

To some extent, the spread of secondary-school testing requirements over the past half century or more simply placed American students in the same pattern as their peers in other advanced industrial countries. But the SAT/ACT complex was a different animal from counterparts like the French baccalaureate or German Abitur, for it was in principle an aptitude test, not based on any particular pattern of subject matter study. As such, it seemed more democratic, more open to talent, in keeping with American educational tradition. However, as relevant psychologists were now routinely concluding in their exam anxiety studies, this was exactly the kind of test that created the greatest nervous stress, precisely because students had less sense of what to expect or how to prepare.[25]

It also became clear that preparation did matter. The College Board, though still clinging to the aptitude claim, began releasing sample tests and providing study advice in the 1970s. This provided interested students (and their parents) with some welcome guidelines, though it could also encourage more frenzied concern about preparation in advance of the exam and the growing commitment to multiple test efforts by individual teenagers.

While the shift toward greater emphasis on test results for college entrance (and later for high school graduation in many cases) was the most obvious change in the secondary-school examination pattern, the later twentieth century also saw growing reliance on final examinations (most commonly at the end of each quarter) in standard high school classes as well—usually to the tune of 20 percent of the overall final grade. Periodic pressure points increased as part of the normal school experience. Further, as state testing programs expanded, standardized test requirements for high school graduation also multiplied. In some Texas programs, for example, students had to master a test battery in English every year, again as a condition of graduation. As one child noted, in 2018: "Well, nowadays students aren't taught to be taught. We're taught to pass the test.... These test scores don't reflect us or how smart we are."[26]

Some of the same pressure began to move to the grade-school and middle-school levels from the 1980s onward, again impinging on childhood regardless of aspirational levels. Both state and federal education officials responded to growing concerns about lagging educational quality by imposing a new battery of tests designed to measure student progress but even more to provide the basis for assessing school and teacher performance. Thus in 1995 Virginia introduced its Standards of Learning program, aimed at testing third and eighth grade students as well as secondary school students in four core subject areas, concentrated heavily on English and math. This was followed in 2001 by the federal No Child Left Behind program that effectively imposed a similar testing pattern across the nation. While the goal was improved student performance, the basic philosophy involved—that "only what's tested gets taught"—had wider implications for the student experience.[27]

In the first place, children who struggled with testing now had an additional batch of obligations that were particularly novel at the grade-school level. The sense that education involved mainly a series of nervous hurdles could easily increase, particularly for the "low-performing" students who were the particular target of the legislation. The gender component often factored in here: boys typically picked up on schooling more slowly than girls in the early grades, and now it was increasingly easy to feel discouraged. Second language learners also faced particularly intimidating test batteries. For other children more skilled at test-taking, the new requirements had less significance, though the periodic exercises hardly spurred enthusiasm for the educational process and could measurably increase the boredom component. Furthermore, for all levels and for all types of students, the sheer amount of time devoted to examinations, sometimes involving weeks of straight testing, became an increasingly intrusive feature of life at school.

More important, and increasingly recognized, was the larger impact on classroom experience. Quite simply, mindful of severe consequences to individual teachers and schools for bad test results, grade- and middle-school teachers began teaching more to the test, eliminating arguably more imaginative and interesting exercises. Drilling and repetition increased, and somewhat ironically—given the stated concern about reading—the likelihood of assigning whole books declined from the early grades onward in favor of other kinds of reading promotion (a change further encouraged by the advent of electronic media). Even at the high-school level, English classes often filled with reading texts crammed with excerpts and quotes, along with the inevitable drills to test comprehension. The new test pressures contributed directly as well to the growing erosion of recess periods and physical education. School, for many children, became a more limited and limiting experience, often including the inescapable sense that the purpose of learning centered on the ability to take and pass examinations.[28]

The new pressures also increased the instability of the teaching corps: during the initial decades of the twenty-first century annual attrition reached 8 percent, over twice the level of countries like Finland that generated better overall educational results; and in schools dominated by poorer students, the level was double the overall average. For students, teacher volatility could add further difficulties to the school experience.[29]

Finally, the new testing focus impacted subject matter emphasis as well. Growing attention to English and math increasingly eclipsed attention to civics, history, and other subjects that at least for some students might have heightened a connection between schooling and understanding the world around them. Only science courses were spared. Further, when standardized tests did embrace a larger subject range, as with the Virginia Standards, they emphasized drill and memorization over any wider learning goals. Writing assignments, when they existed, also became shorter and more structured. There was of course room for debate about the impact of the shift in content emphasis, and students were variously affected depending on their interests and aptitudes. For some, however, particularly before high school, schooling became a narrower and more pressured experience.

Grades and Performance

In the 1950s Harvard University instituted a new national recruitment program, providing scholarships to two able students in each state every year (Mississippi and Alabama were combined), with the deliberate goal of escaping the school's disproportionately regional base. The program was successful in many ways, but it yielded an unexpected result. The students involved, even when they adapted to the university's disproportionately prep school population, remained inordinately concerned about their grades, uncomfortable with anything short of an A. University officials, accustomed to a more relaxed atmosphere, and some of them visibly skeptical about a potential flood of high school graduates, urged them to ease up, but to no avail. After all, high evaluations (including SAT results) had won them entry in the first place, and they were not about to relax.[30]

Not surprisingly, given the growing emphasis on examinations, grade results and attendant class rank became more important in students' experience and self-perception, at least from high school onward. The result proved to be a basic feature of the newly competitive educational environment—beyond any objective necessity. Older ideals of a "gentleman's C," based on deliberately modest educational striving combined with an array of leisure activities, clearly declined. Derisive use of words like "grind" to describe students who simply worked too hard did not end but measurably dropped at least from the 1950s to the end of the century, and most contemporary students have never heard the term.[31]

This aspect of school intensification did not clearly reach into the primary schools. Grades at this level were not taken particularly seriously—as opposed to test scores—except perhaps by concerned parents who might transpose their own remembered worries about grades onto their offspring. But for other student sectors, from high school onward, the emotional investment in grades could be considerable.

The most obvious spur was college admission itself. As more and more students began to apply to multiple institutions—not just the local option that seemed standard for many in the early 1950s—their sense of the importance of competitive qualifications rose in tandem. Ambitious students now realized that they might be competing against a national pool. By 1967 only 43 percent of college freshmen had applied to only a single institution, and by 2006 this was down to 18 percent. Correspondingly, multiple applications soared: already in 1967, 26 percent were venturing four or more, and by 2006 this figure was 57 percent. Along with good SAT or ACT scores, good grades now seemed increasingly vital to parents and students alike, and—as the Harvard experience suggested—the linkage easily carried into college years as well. Here again the contrast with patterns in other nations, where college entry depended on standardized test performance far more than school record, was vivid.[32]

Grades and class rank carried other benefits as well. For men, it could be a crucial determinant for position in the draft; indeed, draft board requirements helped promote calculation of class rank in the first place. Beyond this, periodically through the late twentieth century, individual states rewarded class rank directly. Texas, for example, in 1997 granted students graduating in the top 10 percent of their high school class automatic entry to a state university, and similar patterns prevailed elsewhere, though with varying percentages. Not surprisingly, periodic lawsuits over calculating and publicizing class rank highlighted the importance attached.[33]

Attention to grades—and, again, tests—was also promoted by the growing interest in College Board Advanced Placement (AP) courses in high schools, which launched in 1955 and steadily expanded. Doing well on the AP exam might provide college credits (while also counting toward the high school grade) but even more obviously served as an additional selling point in college admissions. AP courses were attracting only a minority of high school students, but it was a steadily growing minority and added to the intensity of the school experience. By 2022, 1.2 million high school students were taking 4.4 million AP exams in the year (up from 75,000 test takers in the mid-1970s), hopefully focused on substantive learning but eagerly awaiting the grade as well.[34]

This was the climate, from the 1960s onward, when grade inflation added to the complexity of the school experience—or at least to the complexity of evaluating the school experience. In the early 1970s, as the inflationary pattern was just setting in, the average college freshman brought in a C average from high school. By contrast, in 2000 a clear majority had A's. Something of the same pattern took shape in college, though at a slightly more modest pace. As grades began to matter more, student results seemed to improve.

The phenomenon has been interpreted, and often decried, from several angles. The Vietnam War may have had a role in launching the process: more and more high school and college instructors were loath to condemn students to the mercies of the draft boards by maintaining traditional grading standards. Some instructors may simply have sought greater popularity, though when grade inflation first launched student evaluations of faculty were not yet common. Yet grade inflation reflected new pressures from students and their parents as well, precisely because awareness of graded results was mounting: the causes of the new patterns were complicated. The result was a rising set of expectations. Students and parents alike easily adapted their standards to the new normal. It was not clear that the changes cut into the heightened levels of emotional investment—indeed, the reverse may have applied. It was revealing that no equivalent sense of the adequacy of a "gentleman's B" emerged in the new climate so much as a frequent belief that the grade was slightly inadequate or unfair. "Can't you at least give me an A-?"[35] From an objective vantage point, grade inflation arguably reduced the meaningfulness of the grading process, but from the standpoint of students and their parents, the process reflected and may have encouraged new intensities. It was and remains a complex phenomenon.

For even as getting good grades became easier, the challenge seemed more urgent than ever, which is where a changing student culture entered in along with objective factors like more tests, more pressure to go to college, and, often, ambitious parental expectations. By 2017, 47 percent of American high school seniors were earning an A average, the clear fruit of grade inflation (up from 38 percent two decades before) and a development that might have reduced anxiety levels at least for a large minority. But to many high school students, the pressure had only increased, both because of fears of falling into the below-A group and because of the growing compulsion to share grades with peers—and to measure oneself by the results. Ironically, new federal laws had prohibited older practices like posting grades in public (in 1974)—but student culture moved in the opposite direction. Any dissemination of grades brought an immediate flurry of conversations and text messages that would reveal the student's place in the competitive pecking order. Adults had created the range of new educational hurdles, but children themselves often made it worse.

A New Student Outlook?

Many changes in the school experience are easily documented: the longer days, the extended years, the heightened testing and test-based instruction, even the new pressures on grades. Figuring out what this all meant to children and teenagers themselves is more challenging, quite apart from the obvious point that reactions doubtless varied widely. Yet there are data to suggest, at least from the high-school level onward, that outlook toward education was shifting in several respects. The purpose of the whole process was significantly reconsidered between the late 1950s and 2000; expectations became more ambitious—the clearest link to grade inflation—and, most notably, the competitive environment became more intense.[36]

Among college freshmen, polls suggested a steady movement toward a more utilitarian evaluation of schooling during the second half of the twentieth century. Responses in the late 1950s saw a majority noting that improving personal understanding and philosophy ("achieving a meaningful philosophy of life") was a top goal in going beyond high school; by 2000 this had faded dramatically, replaced by a desire to earn more money (priority number six in the 1960s). Spectacular growth in new fields, like business, accompanied this transition. The change may simply have reflected the surge in numbers, with people who had always seen education through a pragmatic lens now translating their goals into the college level, but it was an interesting shift, potentially related to other changes like the greater anticipation of boredom. The change also corresponded to the major alterations in subject matter focus imposed on the primary and middle-school grades by No Child Left Behind.[37] To be sure, attitudes shifted somewhat after 2000, with more reports of interest in socially relevant jobs, but selection of college majors continued to move to toward the apparently utilitarian, so the extent of change was not easy to assess.

The heightened expectations were at least as interesting and persistent, born of grade inflation but extending into sometimes unrealistic hopes. Quite simply, more college freshmen expected top marks than would achieve them. In the 1960s, 27 percent of entering freshmen expected a B average or better, but by 2000 the figure was 57 percent (about 10 percent higher than probable results at that point). A corresponding increase applied to anticipations of gaining entry to an honors society: at 19 percent in 2000, this was at least twice the level that would actually qualify. Despite grade inflation at the college level, it became at least slightly easier to be disappointed.[38]

The big shift, however, centered on the increasingly competitive atmosphere in schooling for many young people. The pressure was not entirely new: already in the 1920s high schools had transformed the selection of a valedictorian from a student who could give a good speech in Latin to the student with the highest grades. But the "gentleman's C" ethic and the fact that only a minority of students were educational strivers limited the competitive sense: it was uncouth to try too hard.

Now, however, new competitive pressures came from a variety of directions, though of course students varied in their susceptibility. By the 1970s colleges were developing elaborate and intrusive marketing programs aimed at enticing student ambitions, with mailed solicitations pressing into sophomore and junior years of high school. The contrast with the 1950s, when most colleges had no professional admissions operation or brochures at all was striking. Part of the new boasting process involved explicit advertisements of the average grades, class rank, and SAT scores of applicants. It was in 1983 that *US News and World Report* introduced its college rating system, which emphasized not only average applicant scores but also the number of students each admissions office turned down. In response, many high-prestige institutions (while officially lamenting *US News* but gamely participating) began to encourage multiple applications, well beyond any reasonable expectation of success. Finally, though more gradually, high schools themselves began to produce data about student results in the college application game. It was hard for many students and their parents not to feel enmeshed in a competitive struggle.[39]

The new level of concern was in one sense somewhat misplaced. Student crowding and the surge of college applications in the 1960s created some genuine tensions, and this may have been the source of anxieties that long outlasted necessity. Over time, the number of college slots easily expanded to accommodate new numbers: thanks in part to the rise of new colleges, seats for first-year students rose by 297 percent between 1959 and 2010, while the ranks of high school graduates expanded by 131 percent. During the later twentieth century only about 10 percent of American colleges actually tightened their admissions standards.[40]

However, the sense of challenge amid the college feeding frenzy remained high. While only about 5 percent of all high school students fully entered the fray—sending off applications to fifteen to twenty-five colleges on average by the early twenty-first century—many more participated in part. The temptation to try at least one high-profile college, even if a student admitted this was really a "vanity" effort, was considerable—at the very least, students wanted a shot at the choice public institution in their state, even if there was a declining chance of getting in. Never before had so many students faced such a wide range of choices and setbacks (for tens of thousands would now be getting one or more rejection letters). Small wonder that growing numbers referred to the admissions process as "judgment day" or "moment of truth"—and small wonder that many parents deeply invested in their offspring's success, defined through college prestige, became wrapped up in the process as well.[41]

Other changes both reflected and furthered the competitive atmosphere. Calculation of grade averages became ever more complicated as high schools began to factor in different levels of difficulty. The student who took several AP courses and did well overall easily built a grade point average significantly above the maximal 4.0. Seeking to respond to pressures, many schools began to select multiple valedictorians—sixteen or more, in some cases. While this presumably eased envy among the top group, it only confirmed the larger competitive process.[42]

Perhaps most important, students themselves began to turn the college admissions process into an open exercise—much like they were doing with grades, eagerly seeking to determine their standing among their peers. News of college admissions results, trickling out during the final semester of the high school senior year, gained wide purchase, facilitated ultimately by social media. The whole admissions process, as one counselor noted, turned into a public sport, at least by the early twentieth century. Here too, high schools themselves contributed—often skirting the 1974 law that banned public disclosure of student performance—by listing successful students by name in publications, plaques, and display cases in the corridors.[43]

While the sense of school as competition developed most vividly at the high-school level, it had its quieter grade-school counterpart, with evidence accumulating in this case as well from the 1960s onward. Here, the crucial mechanism centered on teacher preferences, which often established distinctions among categories of students quite early on. Thus, Ray Rist's study of a public school kindergarten in the 1960s found that by the eighth day of a new school year, the children in one classroom had been divided into three tables, each table grouping students by their differential likelihood of success. Other practices extended the sorting process. Many schools, for example, began awarding children green, orange, or red badges, designating behavior and daily achievement in descending orders of magnitude, the results publicly visible to students and parents alike. While explicit shaming of individual students had eased—dunce caps were a thing of the remote past—a more general sense of competitive pressure clearly mounted. In the process some children doubtlessly gave up, accepting a designation as school losers and reacting accordingly. Others, however, would continue to play the game, trying to measure themselves by their position in relation to their colleagues.[44]

The importance of academic sorting among students was a common challenge in advanced industrial societies by the later twentieth century. What was arguably unusual about its American version was twofold: first, a well-established national emphasis on the importance of individual competitive achievement in general, but second, an unusual reliance on school performance—grades and other ratings—rather than more impersonal national examinations as the basis for advancement. The system placed a premium on the competitive atmosphere in the schools themselves.

This spilled over, finally, into one other feature of the American educational environment during the past half century: the unusual (and, again, highly competitive) emphasis on extracurricular activity. Here too there were precedents. American schools had long since developed a larger array of sports, clubs, and artistic activities than their counterparts in most other countries. Now, however, amid real or imagined college admissions pressures, many students began to multiply their efforts, guided by colleges that insisted that grades and even SAT scores would not be the only criterion for success, that a robust activity profile was vital as well. To a much greater extent than their counterparts in other countries, many high school and even middle school students pushed themselves into a dizzying array of after-school and community service activities—often, in families that could afford it, following a grade-school experience filled with organized sports and lessons as well. The results could be rewarding in many ways, but they also could contribute to a sense of competitive tension throughout the years of schooling, and they certainly contributed to a sense of busy pressures.[45]

Security

While the increasing focus on academic instruction and drilling dominated the school experience for many students, other changes are worth noting. On balance, their overall impact on the children involved is hard to assess—some developments impacted particular groups rather than students in general, but there is room for further assessment.

At two crucial points since the 1950s unusual concerns about safety significantly distorted student life, in each case with some measurable psychological consequences. Nuclear war fears drove many schools to introduce "duck and cover" bomb drills from 1950 onward. Los Angeles students were told that an atom bomb "is a bomb that blows up houses and makes the earth wiggle. Children have to be ready when it drops." From 1951 onward many students were also issued dog tags, designed to facilitate identification after incineration. While teachers were told to reassure students, a number of studies suggested that some children became seriously concerned—losing sleep and expressing fatalistic thoughts—in a pattern that would extend, particularly for urban children, into the early 1970s.[46]

The second episode, still ongoing, followed from the Columbine school shooting of 1999 and the seemingly endless array of similar episodes thereafter, at schools and colleges alike. Responses varied, but overall the number of schools with full- or part-time security staff increased notably—to about 65 percent by 2015. The use of metal detectors, though much discussed, was far more limited, applying to only 14 percent of all high schools by 2020 and far fewer lower schools. Efforts to reduce school entry points further isolated schools from communities. Students themselves often found it more difficult to move freely in and out of school, a shift in the high school experience. Lockdown drills constituted the most widespread new burden, ultimately affecting about 98 percent of all students. The exercises frightened many students, raising serious questions about whether they were worth the distress. And the number of children directly involved in a shooting incident, though a small portion of the total, was not negligible: over 43,000 in 2022 alone.[47]

As with the nuclear fears, but with greater immediacy, school shooter concerns and responses measurably added a further source of tension for many students, without clear precedent in the earlier history of education.

Discipline

Changes in discipline may have made school more palatable for some children, running counter to the increased academic pressure. However, evaluation is complicated, and there were some significant countercurrents.

The big news was a decline in corporal punishment, particularly from about 1980 onward; California, for example, abolished spanking in public schools in 1983. In 1977, when the Supreme Court ruled that the practice was legal in schools, only a handful of states had moved against it, headed by New Jersey, which had acted in 1869. By 2023 physical discipline in public schools remained legal in only seventeen states and was extensively used only in the South—with Mississippi heading the list in the infliction of paddling. However, private institutions and home-schooling parents could and often did maintain corporal measures more widely.

The problem in assessing the significance of the change is the scattered evidence about frequency of past practice. Some recollections suggested common use of rulers over knuckles in the 1950s, or in a few cases more severe paddlings administered by physical education teachers. But many schools seem to have avoided the practice altogether. Geography was undoubtedly a factor, with the South unusually severe; and private Christian schools were more severe than the publics. For many children, however, changes in the law simply systematized what their own fairly benign experience had been.[48]

Further, as corporal options declined, a new move against disciplinary infractions took shape in the 1980s and 1990s, extending into the early twenty-first century: under the new label of "zero tolerance," the practice of suspending offending students, particularly but not exclusively at the high-school level, took off as never before. Whereas in 1973 only 4 percent of all students experienced a suspension in a given year, by 2010 the figure had almost doubled to 7 percent—after which it did begin to drop back slightly. The practice extended into early grades and even preschool; one report suggested that as many as 250 preschoolers were suspended every day. (Another practice also applied to younger students: isolation in an enclosed space, which shared many features and results with suspension.) Many students were suspended or secluded for relatively trivial offenses. Students of color and those with learning disabilities were disproportionately affected, and the impact on their further schooling could be substantial. Defenders of the policy argued that removal of disruption benefited students more generally; however, the overall impact on school experience was hard to assess.[49]

For college students, disciplinary trends moved resolutely toward a reduction in regulation, particularly as institutions stepped back from efforts to prevent sexual activity. The classic "parietal rules" of the 1950s, designed to limit heterosexual contacts in dorm rooms, faded to the extent that the term became entirely unfamiliar. Even this trend, however, raised difficult questions. Students now faced new choices about their own sexual behavior, and the decline of regulation unquestionably exacerbated issues such as date rape or simply unwanted pressure, in what became a newly complicated aspect of the student experience. By the twenty-first century, declining drinking and sexual activity among older teenagers suggested new responses in these domains.[50]

Distractions

American schools had long offered various kinds of entertainment as complements to academic activity, and many of these persisted from the later twentieth century onward. Sports events, particularly Friday night football, continued to entice many students, along with the wider local communities—though amid new concerns about injury there was a measurable decline in the football option after about 2010 outside the South. Musical events were significant as well, though there was great variety depending on the relative affluence of the school district; and amid challenges to school finances, there was some tendency to cut back after about 1997.

Field trips took a measurable hit, again from the late 1990s onward. Budget concerns combined with worries about student safety and, above all, the growing pressure to focus on academic basics. Between 2010 and 2015 school administrators reported a 30 percent decline, after which the pressure eased somewhat.[51]

The role of schools in providing food for students from poor families, on the other hand, steadily increased. The national school lunch program was launched in 1946, and amid some fluctuations it tended to expand, in some cases extending to the provision of breakfast as well. By the twenty-first century, some schools provided the service to students more generally. Results suggested definite though modest improvements in test scores for the students involved, plus reduced absenteeism. From the 1960s onward the addition of vending machines in many schools was another significant innovation, offering quick, though usually unhealthy, pick-me-ups.[52]

The advent of computers and cell phones, particularly after 2000, provided another set of potential distractions for students during the school day, depending on the vagaries of school policy. Many students managed to use the devices for games and social contacts, though both schools and parents tried to set boundaries.

From the standpoint of formal policy, school became a somewhat narrower experience for many students, as certain kinds of amenities were reduced in favor of the focus on academic drilling. The pattern paralleled the decline of recess. However, new opportunities for individual entertainment, and for some the growing availability of food, may have improved the livability of the school years—particularly after grade school, though in some tension with the goals of academic authorities.

For students going on to college, the theme of compensatory entertainment was far more explicit, even apart from the ultimate availability of social media. Expanding student services units devoted extensive resources to a wider array of club activities and intramural sports programs. First-year orientations became steadily more elaborate from the 1970s onward, with days of games and free food, and sometimes camping excursions, along with academic advising sessions. Investments in exercise facilities expanded massively, in some cases including amenities like climbing walls or even artificial waterways. For students with funds, and particularly the minority of residential students, opportunities to combine education with consumerism clearly blossomed, in some contrast to the more complicated patterns at the primary and secondary levels.

Twenty-First-Century Adjustments

A variety of concerns, including growing awareness of student mental health issues, led to interesting if modest efforts toward reconsidering some of the innovations of the previous decades, particularly after the first decade of the twenty-first century. A growing number of colleges dropped the requirement of SAT or ACT scores; this would turn into a flood, at least temporarily, under the impact of the Covid pandemic. In several parts of the country, school districts decided to abolish identification of valedictorians, an interesting shift designed to reduce competitiveness and envy. Several regions moved to restore a bit of recess: Florida, for example, now required thirty minutes a day. Concerns about homework levels and disciplinary suspensions ratcheted up. A few experiments delayed the start of the school day for high school students, an effort to reflect adolescent sleep patterns.

By the 2020s a tentative move also suggested growing interest in reducing the pressure to attend college by opening more jobs—for example, in state bureaucracies—to high school graduates and expanding technical training as an alternative route to college, and state officials from both political parties joined in. Whether this would have much impact on overall expectations and pressures was not yet clear. Another interesting trend involved the installation of "dual-enrollment" lower-level college courses in the high schools, designed certainly to save states money but arguably also to ease transitions in the later secondary years—though the educational results were dubious at best. Even more significant was a striking decline in enthusiasm for college attendance after about 2010. Partisan tensions contributed here, but the big villain was growing college debt. By 2023 only 41 percent of all parents said they wanted their children to attend a four-year college, and actual matriculation rates did drop. The shift contrasted with patterns in almost every other country and obviously raised questions not only about tertiary education but also about the larger intensification of educational ambition that had so deeply affected American education for over half a century. The main driver of reduced college enrollment numbers was the numerical decline of the relevant age group, but it was clear that, beyond this, some students were opting out.[53]

The pandemic introduced another set of variables: the disruptions prompted growing levels of absenteeism at most school levels, along with a new surge of disciplinary problems in many schools, plus wider reluctance to turn assignments in on time, if at all, even in college. Explicit absenteeism—the percentage of students missing ten days or more of school without authorization—soared from 15 percent in 2019 to 26 percent by 2023. Similar trends occurred in other countries but, with the partial exception of the United Kingdom and Canada, at lower levels and from a much lower base (1.5 percent in Japan, for example, or about 4 percent in Germany). In the United States the increase affected all racial and economic groups to some extent, but it was most pronounced among lower-income families and racial minorities—except for families of Asian origin. Explanations varied, apart from the vital fact that the pandemic had disrupted routines and shaken confidence in the schools. Parents in more precarious economic circumstances sometimes faced increased need for children to work (even before the legal age) or care for younger siblings. Even some wealthier families seemed more cavalier about pulling kids out of school for an extended family skiing trip. Growing concern about children's mental health made some parents more tolerant of the kid who simply said they could not stand to go to school several times a year. And, of course, some children cut out without their parents' knowledge or consent. School districts employed a variety of tactics to address the issue, but it yielded slowly at best. At the same time, growing tolerance for some absences or tardiness with assignments—as officials and teachers tried to take student distress into account through greater leniency—may have compounded the problem.[54]

Evaluation is complicated. It is too soon to say if these developments—declining college interest as well as school truancy—reflected durable readjustments for some young people, or if they were simply pandemic aftershock. It is vital to remember as well that American absentee rates had been comparatively high even before the pandemic. A minority of students (and their families) had never bought into the expansion of schooling, and this group was growing. It is not fanciful to suggest that, whether consciously or not, an important subset of students was seeking to rebel against contemporary school pressure by literally voting with their feet.

The rise of homeschooling was another new variable, prompted by concerns about school violence and pandemic restrictions. By 2022, 5 percent of relevant-aged children were being homeschooled. The results were varied, but they could involve less subjection to frequent testing; less pressure to join in extracurricular activities, though this was not uniformly the case; harsher physical punishments; and greater curricular diversity. The system was surprisingly unregulated and unquestionably added to the complexity of schooling trends.

On another front: some school districts began to recognize the lack of student voice in most aspects of education. By 2022 Baltimore, for example, began to urge teachers to give students some choice in lessons and activities, building this into the process of teacher assessment—though it remained unclear whether students experienced much change.

Most of these innovations were tentative, as well as varied. Testing did not drop overall, despite the discrediting of No Child Left Behind policies. Many states actually added requirements for high school graduation, for example in including SAT or ACT results. By 2024 a few colleges actually reintroduced testing mandates for applicants. With educational officials concerned about learning loss during the pandemic, reliance on standardized testing actually increased in many cases: in 2023 almost half of all teachers reported growing pressures to "teach to the test" even though in their view the assessment results were inferior to other options.[55] Other continuities were clear as well. Application rates for the "top" colleges and enrollment in AP classes remained robust. At the same time, the drumbeat of school shootings and lockdown drills continued unabated. If this was a new transition period, in other words, its dimensions were not yet clear.

Certainly, there was no wholesale review of the schooling experience that had become so central to contemporary childhood, nor were the economic pressures toward higher levels of educational achievement really reversed. Most recent policy changes—a bit of recess, a half-hour shift in school starting times, less mandatory testing for college—tinkered with prevailing patterns without altering them fundamentally. Newer developments, like more absenteeism and homeschooling, were hard to assess and still involved only a minority of children. It was hard to shake the national notion that contemporary education depended on time in class followed by a test. Even advocates for disadvantaged children often bristled against the idea that schooling should open up to a greater sense of play and flexibility, arguing that while wealthy white kids might survive this, thanks to family environment, poor children needed as much drilling in basic subjects as possible if they had any hope of staying afloat.

Conclusion

The idea of a decline in student joy seems accurate enough, but it should not be pressed too far, quite apart from the obvious fact that many students a half century ago were not exactly joyous. The variety of changes in children's educational experience since the 1950s do not yield easy judgments about impact. Yet it seems highly probable that, on average, the new trends in schooling worsened the quality of childhood, at least modestly, for many young people, as the role of the school and tensions associated with school expanded from the 1950s onward. And while ongoing (possibly worsening) educational inequality remains a vital issue, it is more than likely that a sense of pressure and dissatisfaction—if for somewhat different reasons—cut across many categories of childhood. At an extreme, this contributed to the growing number of students who sought to regain some control through irregular attendance without dropping out entirely given the drawbacks this now involved.

Teachers certainly felt increasingly pressed to try to make school fun—in spite of the system in which they were enmeshed. As one teacher put it, "the assumption seems to be that school sucks, kids hate it, and the curriculum and resources we are given are lackluster. And therefore, part of our job is to make it as sparkly and captivating as possible."[56]

Data from students themselves are certainly stark. A 2019 survey (pre-pandemic) found 75 percent of all high school students reporting a negative experience overall. Their dominant mood during the school day combined fatigue, stress, and boredom. Almost 80 percent of all students reported stress, and 70 percent reported boredom. By contrast, 24 percent reported feeling happy and 5 percent excited. Student complaints centered on school environment, including fears for safety, apparent classroom goals—"mostly the focus is just on the statewide tests"—and the huge tensions and uncertainties of the college admissions process.[57] The Yale researchers responsible for the study were taken aback by the extent of malaise and discontent.

Unfortunately no comparable 1950s survey can be unearthed for comparison. But—and changing college freshman polls do provide some confirmation—it seems likely that the results would have been less severe, and only in part because some of the most disgruntled would have left school altogether.

Results for grade school students may be less dire. Some twenty-first-century polls suggested majority satisfaction up to about the third grade. But as early as middle school, evaluations had turned downward for a majority. School had become more difficult at these levels as well, probably academically and almost certainly emotionally, and a number of the very specific changes—in time spent, intensity, and evaluation—contributed strongly.

The changes involved invite evaluation from a variety of standpoints—the intentions of policymakers; the frequent gap between goals and results; and the complicated roles of parents in the whole process, at once protective of their kids but often heavily invested in academic success. Despite intense awareness of international competition, the reluctance to learn from more successful foreign examples is also intriguing. A number of scholars also argue, plausibly, that the increasingly rigid association of education with professional preparation and productivity enhancement has driven happiness out of the equation, in the United States and elsewhere, reducing earlier interests in using schooling for exploration, including emotional exploration, and preparation for participation in a wider public good.[58]

The impact on childhood itself warrants serious attention, and here an additional measure, more vivid in the United States than elsewhere, comes into play. As children's school experience changed, a variety of new ailments, many of them virtually unknown before the 1950s, surfaced as well. Consistent with the negative polling results, a growing minority of children began to be identified with school-based disabilities that had either not existed or had not mattered so seriously before this point. It had become harder—at least, a bit harder—to succeed at this aspect of being a child, yet it had clearly become more important to do so.

The American Child: The Transformation of Childhood Since World War II. Steven Mintz and Peter N. Stearns, Oxford University Press. © Oxford University Press 2025. DOI: 10.1093/9780197797112.003.0005

6
Children in a Changing Family

By the twenty-first century the American family was a considerably different entity from its counterpart a half century before. It was less stable and far more varied, and both features inevitably impacted children. It also depended a great deal more, in dealing with young children, on some structures outside the family proper.[1]

The idea of family breakdown has been a common theme for several decades in the United States, beginning with growing awareness of the sharp rise in divorce rates during the 1960s and 1970s. (Indeed, middle-class observers were pointing to family decline in other social groups even earlier.) We have seen references to family decline, or at least to major changes, enter into discussions of new levels of childhood diversity. The theme risks oversimplification, given the growing variety of family forms and successful adaptations by many family members—including children. Some of the worst fears have not come to pass. Certainly, determining the relative importance of changes in the family in shaping a distinctive contemporary childhood is far more difficult than charting the growing significance of schooling. It remains true that families have changed in many ways since the 1950s, placing new burdens on many parents and forcing a number of adjustments on children.

There is some danger in taking the 1950s as a point of departure, for this proved to be an unusual decade in American family history. Never before had such a high percentage of the population married, and at such a young average age. Many young Americans reacted to the combination of the Depression followed by world war and then growing prosperity with a deep enthusiasm for family formation. Even the divorce rate dipped a bit. The concurrent increase of the birth rate—the famous Baby Boom—was an expression of the same enthusiasm, with most of the families involved assuming that mothers would stay home to take care of the brood. At the same time, popular culture bathed the family in a warm glow that concealed a variety of common problems, a point to which we will return. Certainly, the 1950s family, and its celebration in the movies and TV shows of the decade, was a historical anomaly sharply out of line with long-term trends—and, not surprisingly, it did not last.[2]

What happened in the ensuing decades, however, went beyond undoing the special features of the 1950s. By choice or circumstance, growing numbers of Americans moved away from conventional family structures, either through rising divorce rates or by deciding not to form marital units in the first place. Growing individualism and an increasing desire for self-fulfillment pushed against the constraints of family life. New economic opportunities and aspirations for women, though still impacted by gender inequality, contributed strongly, affecting decisions by both men and women.[3]

The Rise of Family Variety and New Debates over the Importance of Children

Innovations combined with growing variety, making generalizations about family patterns increasingly difficult. The rise of gay marriage at the end of the century and then its legalization (after 2004 in some states, after 2015 nationally) was a case in point. At a time when the conventional marital unit was challenged overall, a significant group adopted it as a more explicit goal, creating an important new family subgroup and, often, a new source of parenting as well. There was even a modest "lesbian baby boom" as early as the 1980s, when a growing number of lesbian couples decided it was possible and desirable to have kids, and the result actually contributed to the increased acceptance of the idea of gay marriage.[4] On another front: the most striking symbol of the changing family from the 1960s to the early 1980s—the rapidly rising divorce rate—unexpectedly stabilized, and by the early twenty-first century a couple's marriage was considerably more likely to survive than had been the case two decades before. On the other hand, the number of Americans who decided against conventional family formation, either by avoiding families altogether or by other forms of cohabitation, increased steadily.[5]

Variety directly impinged on parenting. While the decline of the birth rate was a fairly general trend—families with more than two or three children became increasingly rare—interest in having children ranged from none to intense. By the twenty-first century the number of couples (officially married or not) who claimed disinterest in having children rose steadily. A 2021 poll found 56 percent of all nonparents under fifty saying they were in this category, citing costs, nuisance, medical concerns, and other factors. A large minority of adults, including about a third of all women, no longer believed that having children was essential to a fulfilling life.[6] Even earlier a family type emerged—captured in a famous British study called *The Symmetrical Family* (1973)—that saw family life as a source of sexual pleasure, a base from which both adults involved could work, and a consumer unit in which a couple could share leisure interests, including elaborate vacations, and other related expenses. In the United States many so-called Yuppies, or Young Urban Professionals, fell into this category by the end of the twentieth century. Family for this group was a real entity, again with or without formal marriage—it just did not include kids.[7]

New terms highlighted this rising family culture. As early as the 1970s, the word DINKS (Double Income, No Kids; or Dual Income, No Kids) touted childless marriage as a delightful option, creating a new set of cultural disputes that would simmer into the 2020s. The term "childless," long associated with some kind of failure or disappointment, was replaced for this group by the label "child-free." By the twenty-first century a variety of newspaper accounts highlighted increasingly negative portrayals of having children: the costs, certainly, but also the health risks to mothers as well as the loss of freedom. The same could apply to word of mouth: one young mother noted how many of her peers, learning she was pregnant, rushed "to tell me all the terrible things about motherhood, and how it only got worse over time"—a marked shift from the idealization of the past and probably, in some cases, a reflection of the older age of the average first parent.[8]

Decisions on having, or not having, children were facilitated after 1960 by further improvements in the effectiveness and availability of birth control devices, beginning with the pill. The legalization of abortion after 1973 was another factor—though after an initial flurry abortion rates did not actually rise, the procedures simply became safer and easier to arrange. Couples that did not want kids, or wanted to limit how many they had and regulate their timing, had more opportunities than ever before. The separation of sexual activity from procreation widened. (Even so, a surprising 5 percent of all pregnancies in the early twenty-first century were unplanned—a figure higher in the United States than in other developed countries. Still, even 5 percent was far lower than had been the case in earlier periods of American history.) Certainly, most Americans now experienced a period of sexual activity before there was any interest in having children or, often, any thought of marriage—part of the heralded "sexual revolution" of the 1960s that highlighted lower ages and increased frequency of premarital sex. A focus on children increasingly competed with other interests, and the reduction both in the numbers of children and the percentage of families with children was a key result. The rise of "only" children was another crucial outcome of shifting family goals and methods of birth control: where 11 percent of all children grew up without biological siblings in 1976, the figure had doubled to 22 percent by 2020.[9]

On the other hand, cutting against the trend toward a declining birth rate, a growing number of married and unmarried couples who found it difficult to have children began to pour significant money and deep emotion into the expanding range of options available from the 1960s onward for alternative forms of conception. An initial experimental sperm bank was established in the United States in 1964, aimed at addressing infertility problems in existing families. In 1978 the first successful in vitro fertilization occurred, enabling many men with low sperm production or women with other barriers to pregnancy to have children. By the 1980s it became possible for women to freeze their eggs, creating other opportunities to time pregnancies into the future. By 2006 over 54,000 children a year in the United States were being born thanks to in vitro procedures, over 1 percent of total births in that year; by 2024 the figure had risen to 2 percent. Sperm banks were even more widely used, though estimates varied: by the 1990s possibly as many as 170,000 children a year resulted from women's use of sperm banks via donor insemination. In a small but interesting number of cases, surrogate mothers could also be used, an option variously legal in all but three American states and also sometimes involving women in other countries. Wanting kids could be a deep passion, triumphing over a variety of impediments that previously would have precluded biological parenting.[10]

The results both confirmed and challenged conventional family structures. Many couples eager for children but faced with fertility challenges could realize their parental hopes. But single people, particularly women, could now achieve parenthood as well. American sperm banks were disproportionately patronized by relatively affluent, college-educated women, many of them single but eager to form a family without a man directly involved. Lesbian couples were also using this option in some cases. The numbers involved were not huge—at most 4 percent of the total babies born in the 1990s—but they represented a new family option and tended to increase over time.[11]

American families had always varied, depending on economic circumstances, community standards, and personal decisions. After the 1950s, however, as economic constraints eased to some extent and community tolerance for family variety visibly increased (amid no small amount of backlash), individual choice loomed large—and family structure became less predictable, and certainly less uniform, in the process.

In this new setting, children—having them or placing their interests first—began on average to decline as a primary concern in favor of consumer goals, work interests, or other individual aspirations. Again, the picture was (and still is) uneven, as the rise of new parenting options or the intense commitment to compensating for fertility problems attest. For some individuals—particularly women—having a child actually became more important than forming any other type of family: hence the growing rate of intentional single parenting.[12] Other, more traditional families continued to assume that having children was part of God's purpose or at least a standard function of normal adulthood.

But the overall statement stands: amid rapid family change, children were more likely to be downplayed than prioritized, resulting in one of the major and most troubling shifts in the overall context for American childhood in recent decades. Even adults who did finally have children—like a happily working mom—often expressed a certain amount of guilt that the kids were not as high on their priority list as the parents themselves still thought they should be. Kids could react to the major changes in a variety of ways, often demonstrating impressive resiliency—further complicating generalizations about the outcomes involved. The decline in the centrality of childbearing and child-rearing for many adults was not matched by lessened needs on the part of children themselves, and in response a number of different patterns resulted.

The Big Changes

Between 1960 and 1980 the divorce rate in the United States surged from 20 percent to slightly over 50 percent of all marriages, a startling 156 percent increase. The earlier marriage age that had followed World War II was partly responsible: young couples were particularly likely to decide that they had made a mistake. Community opprobrium for divorce steadily declined, though stigma remained high in some sectors, particularly when traditional religious views persisted. Legal changes also facilitated the process. Beginning with California in 1969, "no-fault" divorce opportunities spread, while waiting periods declined, a pattern that ultimately reached most American states.[13]

During the 1960s and early 1970s, rising divorce rates were also promoted by a widespread belief that divorce was better for children than the continuation of a conflict-riven marriage. This provided a comforting sense that divorce did not necessarily contradict a high valuation of child welfare, and research showed that in some particularly bitter relationships the belief was probably accurate. By the 1970s, however, relevant family scholarship became more nuanced, with increasing attention to the damage divorce did to many children—but this did not initially dent the trend. Many people who divorced thought or hoped that the kids would be okay, but this was not their primary concern.[14]

Rising divorce rates combined with frequent remarriage. Of divorced men in the 1960s, 75 percent would remarry; the same applied to two-thirds of all women. Not all the people involved had children, but the rates of remarriage—an ironic tribute to the continued popularity of the institution—signaled a rapid increase of "blended" families. On television the popular show *The Brady Bunch*, launched in 1969, offered a sunnily optimistic take on the results of this growing phenomenon.[15]

These same decades saw far-reaching changes in family patterns in inner cities, particularly among African Americans. In 1959 only 10 percent of low-income Black Americans lived in a single-parent household, but by 1980 the figure had climbed to 44 percent. Two-parent Black families, 72 percent of the total in 1967, fell to 63 percent in 1973, and would continue to decline. Divorce was a factor here, but the simple increase in out-of-wedlock births was the bigger trend. At the same time, improved welfare provisions enabled more single Black mothers to move away from their parents, amplifying the incidence of female-headed households. Explanations for these trends were hotly debated. Conservatives blamed the welfare programs of the Great Society era; others cast back to the family instability caused by earlier enslavement. Welfare rules particularly affected marriage: a man marrying a single mother was required by law to support her children, which did not prevent cohabitation but certainly discouraged marriage.

Further, in many states unemployed fathers were ineligible for assistance, which prompted some to desert their families, at least officially, so that wives or partners and children could obtain benefits. At the same time continued poverty and frequent unemployment or underemployment, along with high rates of incarceration, most obviously contributed to family instability.[16]

From the 1990s onward, official divorce rates actually declined among American families overall, and while this did not boost the overall incidence of two-parent households, the shift is worth noting, particularly given the popular assumption that family instability of all types continued to mount. Whereas the divorce/marriage ratio was 50 percent in 1990, it had already dropped to 44 percent in the 1990s, and then to 30 percent by the second decade of the twenty-first century. The increase in the average age of first marriage was probably primarily responsible, leading to greater maturity and, usually, increased prosperity among initial marital partners. Of course, at 30 percent, divorce rates remained higher than they had been in the 1950s and earlier in American family history.[17]

Remarriage among divorced individuals remained fairly common but noticeably dropped. It was only 63 percent for men and 55 percent for women by 1980, an indication of faltering faith in marriage as an institution. Interestingly, new divisions opened up between people under fifty—increasingly unlikely to divorce—and those a bit older who took part in "gray" divorces, suggesting some new interest in protecting young children against the stress of divorce but moving toward the split when the children were mostly grown.

From the standpoint of childhood—and too often ignored amid the understandable concern about overall family instability—the most important divorce development by the later twentieth century was the substantial increase in shared custody arrangements as opposed to the earlier pattern of maternal privilege. In 1985 only 13 percent of all divorced couples with children agreed upon shared custody, but by 2013–14 this had risen to 34 percent. Shared custody was particularly common among more affluent families, disproportionately but not exclusively white. While it could harbor its own tensions, shared custody arguably constituted a buffer for many children against the worst stresses of divorce and particularly the possibility of disappearance or exclusion for the father. It also signaled a continued or renewed commitment to children even amid the decline of traditional marriage.[18]

Against this trend, however, the big news of the turn-of-the-century decades, and on into the 2020s, was the sheer decline of the marriage rate and the increase both of cohabitation without marriage and of single-adult households (including, of course, a growing number of people who had divorced and dropped out of the marriage game). The pattern continued to spread in the inner cities, but now it affected other sectors of society as well. In the 1960s fewer than half a million Americans lived together as unmarried couples, but by 2012 this figure had increased by 900 percent, with 7.8 million couples involved. In 1960, 72 percent of all adults over eighteen were married, but by 2019 this had dropped to 51 percent. For children, the chance of having one or more unmarried parent rose steadily with every passing decade.[19]

Three other, related structural variables should be noted: the percentage of children in foster care, the number of children adopted each year, and the dramatic changes in the treatment of severely disabled children. Those in foster care, at about 0.5 percent of the total population of American children, remained roughly stable from the 1960s into the twenty-first century, though the percentage fluctuated year to year depending on varying adoption rates. Orphanages, important during the Depression, literally ceased to exist by the end of the 1950s, so foster care was the only real option for children without an identifiable or willing family. And the system was consistently overburdened, partly because the number of available foster care facilities declined in the turn-of-the-century decades. The category is small in terms of percentage but important to keep in mind, though its stability suggests that the worst kind of family collapse for children was not increasing.[20]

Adoption rates were also fairly stable during the turn-of-the-century decades, though they did drop a bit. In the early 1980s about 2.2 percent of all children under eighteen were adopted, compared to 2 percent in the early twenty-first century. Of babies, 0.5 percent were adopted each year. On the other hand, 8–10 percent of American adults claim to have been adopted, suggesting higher rates in the past when the issue of orphans loomed much larger than it does today. International adoptions drew much attention, but the sources dried up after the 1980s, yielding only a total of 2,900 placements in 2011. Among domestic adoptions, children under eleven, whites, and females were preferred. By the twenty-first century many adoptions were by stepparents after a new marriage, not a classic case of rescuing a young person from uncertainty. As with foster care, adoption trends remind us that the most severe instabilities for children did not seem to be mounting—though some of the children involved often faced serious challenges.[21]

Sharp shifts in the treatment of severely disabled children occurred during the 1960s and 1970s, and the changes were quite dramatic. A variety of exposés in the 1960s revealed hideous conditions in many of the state institutions that housed children with mental or other disabilities, creating growing pressure to dismantle these options in favor of family care. The 1975 federal law that required that disabled children be given a public education capped the new trend, resulting in far more parental responsibility—another complication in the overall family trends, in this case pointing to heightened commitment. Many parents with a disabled child began to invest unprecedented amounts of attention, with results that impinged on any relevant siblings as well.

The Ramifications for Childhood

The implications for children of the seismic shifts in American families varied widely. In the first place, growing numbers of American adults were not intensely involved with children at any stage in their lives when the rates of (often deliberately) childless marriages are combined with the massive increase in unmarried and unpartnered individuals who also did not have children. It is worth considering how much this might affect the larger environment for American childhood, including the policy environment.

More obviously important was the increase in blended families, in which children were living with one stepparent, most commonly a father, and often with at least one stepsibling. By the twenty-first century, 16 percent of all children—one in six—lived in a blended family—and this does not count the units where cohabitation was not accompanied by marriage. (A still higher proportion—21 percent, more than one in five—lived with a stepparent or partner who had children by more than one partner.) By 2010, 30 percent of all Americans had at least one stepsibling, and 13 percent had at least one stepchild. Not surprisingly a majority of those involved with step relationships, 56 percent, said that their families had not turned out the way they had expected (compared to only 41 percent of those who were step-less). Problems of preferential treatment for biological kin undoubtedly existed, particularly for children dealing with a stepparent.

On the other hand, a majority of those involved with step relationships professed themselves satisfied with their family lives. Once again, the impact of new family patterns on children was complex. Adults could prove to be deeply devoted, children impressively resilient.[22]

But the headline news was clear: children growing up in a traditional two-parent household became a minority by the twenty-first century—a privileged minority in many cases, because their families were also disproportionately white and enjoyed a higher-than-average living standard. In the 1960s, 87 percent of all children could expect to reach eighteen with still-married parents; by 2018 that had dropped to 46 percent—far from negligible, but obviously no longer the norm.[23]

By contrast, the percentage of children born to a single parent mounted steadily. In 1980 this category had constituted 21 percent of the total (already rising from 5 percent in 1960 and 11 percent in 1970), but by 2013 it had mounted to over 40 percent. Obviously, this figure concealed a host of variables. Single parents were primarily mothers (80 percent)—but not always. They were, on average, concentrated among lower-income groups, where poverty added to the strains of single parenthood. But this also was not invariably the case, as an increasing number of single female professionals deliberately decided on parenthood.[24]

Of the growing number of children born to an unmarried parent, about half became part of a cohabiting household, and about half were in the care of a single parent alone. A full 23 percent of all children lived in a household with only one adult (mostly mothers, but in a significant minority of cases, fathers)—the highest percentage in the world. But children living with unmarried couples faced their own challenges. As critical authorities were quick to note, cohabiting households often fluctuated—the term merry-go-round was frequently employed—as partners shifted or departed. The boundary line between single and cohabiting parenthood was often porous. Further, both single parents and unmarried couples faced economic constraints or other pressures more often than two-parent households (including those involving stepchildren).[25]

The twin themes for children among all these developments were variety and instability. The variety was obvious. The possible settings for childhood had never before ranged so widely, from what one author would call the "Two-Parent Privilege" to the single mother whose children had been abandoned by their biological father. But instability was inescapable as well. Many children continued to experience their parents' divorce. Some dealt not only with stepparents and stepsiblings, but a fluctuating cast over time. Children of single parents often grew up in considerable poverty, frequently changing residence.[26] And even kids who benefited from more stable circumstances, aware of the variety of family dynamics around them, often among their own school classmates, might wonder about the predictability of the future.[27] One of the reasons children's knowledge of the adult world has increased since the 1960s is the direct exposure to varied family patterns and their possible application to their own lives.

Not surprisingly, the Covid pandemic added to instabilities for a noticeable group of children: about 200,000 lost a parent or caregiver to the disease, interrupting a trend in which the outright death of a parent was becoming less common.[28]

Yet statistical change, no matter how dramatic, does not tell the whole story. The devotion and care of some single parents might easily compensate for what on paper seemed a precarious pattern. Indeed, some single parents so concentrated their emotions and expectations on their child that the problem was less instability than overprotection and overinvestment. As already suggested, step relationships could prove to be quite positive. (Amusingly, the first episodes of *The Brady Bunch* were predicated on conflict between the two sets of stepchildren, but soon, based on audience demand, they turned warm and fuzzy.) Divorce, like the frequent death of a parent in more traditional societies, devastated some children but found many, usually after a brief adjustment, quite able to cope. Further, other family patterns, relationships, and non-family structures must be taken into account as well.

Day Care

By the second decade of the twenty-first century, 58 percent of all American children aged four and five were in some form of day care, and the same applied to 38 percent of all three-year-olds. Without question, given changes in family structure and the increased involvement of mothers in the labor force, day care (and, for five-year-olds, the rapid expansion of kindergartens) served as a vital supplement to family supervision in the lives of young children. Yet day care has experienced a particularly fraught history in the United States, yielding a far less comprehensive system than its counterparts in many other developed countries.[29]

Charitable efforts to offer some day care help to poor mothers began in the nineteenth century, but the first network to provide any systematic option arose with federal government support during World War II as a means of freeing mothers for vital factory work. This system collapsed after the war, however, and during the 1950s no comprehensive options were available beyond the family. Some nursery schools offered programs, but usually for short periods each week rather than providing more comprehensive care.

The situation began to change, haphazardly, in the 1960s. YMCA youth workers, for example, realized that a growing number of teenagers were providing childcare, and in response started opening day care options from 1968 onward. Aware that more and more mothers were working outside the home, the federal government developed some interest. The establishment of the Head Start program in 1965, focused on children from families or (ultimately) single parents below the poverty line, was a major step forward, quickly enrolling 560,000 children in new centers. The program offered a variety of services, including preschool activities, primarily for children aged three to six. However, despite some subsequent expansions, Head Start never handled more than a minority of eligible children—a million out of three million from families whose incomes qualified by the twenty-first century, leaving many parents, including those barely above the poverty line, casting about for other options.[30]

And here the federal government remained singularly hesitant. Eager not to challenge the primacy of parents, and with some conservatives hopeful that many women could be induced to stay or return home, the most general moves involved offering tax rebates for childcare expenses, rather than actual facilities. This approach helps explain the patchwork system that in many ways persists to this day—in contrast to the better-funded and -regulated institutions that have emerged in Western Europe and elsewhere. A major opportunity for a more comprehensive response was rejected by the Nixon administration in 1972, on the grounds that it might weaken the family. Subsequent federal action was limited. Tax cuts during the Reagan administration in the 1980s, favoring the wealthy, encouraged the formation of new for-profit day care centers. Some new subsidies were voted on in the twenty-first century, including as part of the Covid response, but they were modest and often short-lived. The early months of the second Trump presidency saw serious discussion over whether support for Head Start itself should end.[31]

The checkered history of American day care policy must not distract from the fact that, amid changing family patterns, a growing number of parents absolutely depended on some kind of option beyond the family itself. The 1970s saw the most sweeping transformation. At the beginning of the decade, about 4.2 million children aged three to five were enrolled in some kind of day care, but by 1980 that number had more than doubled, reaching a figure that has essentially remained steady, with only a few brief fluctuations. The majority of American children now had some kind of day care experience, in some cases from infancy onward, but otherwise usually by age three.[32]

And this meant that the same majority of young children were exposed to a clearly inadequate patchwork. By the twenty-first century, 51 percent of all Americans lived in "childcare deserts" where there were not enough slots to go around. Even in better-served areas, the strain of finding available and acceptable options was a real burden on parents—and, by extension, on many young children. In some cases, transfers from one center to another because of financial issues, the volatility of many centers themselves, or other factors might add additional stress for the children involved.[33]

Variety and class stratification were the other major features. While fortunate low-income families had some subsidized options, many parents were left casting about. A substantial industry grew up around home-based day care, handling six to twelve children (state rules varied here) in a domestic setting, operating without detailed regulation or supervision—though in some cases a limited amount of staff training was required. At least 20 percent of all children in day care clustered in facilities of this sort, where fees were not negligible but were definitely lower than the options that featured more elaborate equipment and staffing. For white-collar and professional families, employers frequently provided day care, though usually for a fee and typically with limited spaces. Other operations expanded rapidly, like the highly touted Montessori schools, which featured 2,000 centers by the twenty-first century at an average annual cost of $10,000–15,000 (though about 500 were publicly supported).

Evaluations of the American day care system, or lack of system, typically focus on the stress and cost imposed on parents, quite properly noting that the challenge helps explain why some families shy away from having children in the first place. For children themselves, assessments usually center on the extent of academic preparation. Head Start offerings, particularly, are often judged by later results in formal schooling, with widely disputed findings that usually suggest some limited and often short-lived benefits.[34]

But there are other angles as well, beyond the obvious fact that American day cares clearly further deep social and often racial divides among children. Opportunities for play and social development are limited for many young children (another area where Head Start is frequently found wanting). Stress on parents can be transmitted to kids as well, particularly when it combines with some of the other instabilities of American family life.

Finally, the inadequacies of American childcare put some of the other changes in American family structure in sharper relief. High costs have certainly contributed to the falling birth rate, though other factors are also involved. Difficulty accessing childcare helps explain recent compensatory developments, like the rise of joint custody, which can buffer some of the vagaries of the institutional system. But there can be no doubt that the inadequacies of childcare options impinge particularly intensely on single and unmarried parents and their offspring.

Other Relationships

While the growing instability and variety of family structures, combined with the challenges of the day care system, most obviously altered the framework for childhood in the decades after the 1950s, other changes and continuities in family patterns warrant attention as well.

The increase in the average age of first-time parenting deserves special emphasis and applies not only to married couples but to cohabiting and single parents as well. Teenage parenting declined, though it did not disappear. Somewhat older first parents, even if unmarried, might provide a degree of greater maturity that could promote some compensatory stability, at least in some cases. On the other hand, older parents may be more anxious on average, which has its own impact.

Other family links could prove vital in a child's life, though they are harder to track than the overall contours of the nuclear family or its absence. A major theme in modern family history, and certainly in American family history, is the decline of the extended family, thanks to geographical mobility and changing patterns of residence. In this vein, some authorities in the 1980s claimed that only 5 percent of all children had any regular contact with a grandparent. And it was true that co-residence with a grandparent became much less common in the United States from the 1920s through the 1950s, while rapid suburbanization disrupted ties as well. Interestingly, the

Leave It to Beaver TV show, often held as emblematic of the 1950s family, never surfaced a grandparent, though a (decidedly unpleasant) great-aunt appeared in one story line. Divorce might also disrupt contacts with grandparents or other relatives, and this factor would merely intensify in ensuring decades. However, extended family patterns were not as constrained as some of the generalizations suggested, and they might continue to play a significant role in children's lives.[35]

Indeed, there is significant evidence that the extended family rebounded in some respects after the 1950s. Causes varied and included simple adjustments to new residential patterns, such as suburban living, plus growing opportunities to take advantage of new technologies, like cheaper long-distance telephone rates or, later, Zoom calls to keep in touch. They reflected rising longevity rates for older Americans. On the darker side, they also included reactions to the newer issues of family disruption.

In the first place, relatives, most commonly grandmothers and/or aunts, often stepped into the childcare void, taking care of young kids at least part of the time, sometimes alternating with a day or two of some kind of preschool, sometimes shouldering the whole burden when a parent was at work or incapacitated. For young Americans overall, 20 percent were involved in this pattern at least some of the time. African American and Hispanic children were particularly likely to be cared for by relatives; over 45 percent of preschoolers in both groups regularly interacted with relatives, again sometimes in combination with a bit of day care. The option was less common for whites and Asian Americans, but it was not unknown.[36]

This option harbored some predictable tensions. On the one hand it could be a huge financial relief, compared to complete reliance on institutional day care. And it might offer greater reliability and familiarity for parent and child alike. On the other hand, it could bring some unwelcome criticisms of parental inadequacy, particularly when single mothers were exposed to the strictures of their own mothers. While this was mainly an issue for adults, children could be caught in the crosshairs.[37]

At least as significant was the increase in three-generational households from the 1980s onward, where one or more grandparent was directly co-resident with grandchildren. At only 3 percent in 1970, the percentage of children living in a grandparent's household surged to 7 percent by 2010. These extended families in turn were of two types: some with parents present as well, where the combined household might better cope with income and childcare issues, And others where the parents were simply absent and grandparents were entirely responsible for childcare. The latter type, particularly important in inner cities, expanded in response to particular adult crises, like the results of drug use and higher rates of imprisonment in the late 1980s and 1990s or the unemployment surge following the Great Recession of 2008. Results for children varied: when grandparental care began only in the teenage years, tensions often ran high. But results for younger children could be more favorable, particularly when compared to the alternatives. Whatever the outcome, the partial revival of extended families provided yet another strand in the growing variety of family forms.[38]

Beyond childcare, however, interactions with a wider range of relatives could offer some additional family structure for children in ways that might at least slightly modify some of the other instabilities or, in other cases, bolster the advantages of a two-parent household. Here is another area where assumptions about the decline of the extended family partially break down.

Maintaining extended family ties could unquestionably be complicated given a number of postwar trends. Many American families are notoriously geographically mobile, putting distance among family members—though by the later twentieth century this type of mobility declined markedly. Divorce remained frequently disruptive of ties between children and grandparents or cousins. Single parenthood might limit options as well, though it could also promote ties with other relatives, including grandparents. And certainly a strong impulse for contact has remained. Over 30 percent of all Americans report attending a family reunion at least every three years, and the occasions can provide unexpected opportunities for children to bond with cousins as well as gain a larger sense of family identity. Holiday travel often aims at family links as well. Use of social media can work to the same end, though Zoom options are more attractive for adults than children when it comes to extended family ties.[39]

Cousins continued to provide vital social contacts for many children, particularly of course when they lived nearby but even when they were simply regular visitors. They were often a child's first friend. The combination of friendship and relatedness might create durable bonds. Family magazines recurrently touted the joys of cousin contacts into the twenty-first century, though unfortunately there is no indication of the frequency of significant cousin interaction. Emotional bonds with loving aunts also came in for warm comment (with benefits on both sides of the relationship), again, however, without assessments of frequency. For some deliberately childless adults, more energy was available to put into contacts with nieces and nephews.[40]

Grandparents earned a more consistent press, even apart from those directly providing childcare. References to an "intensification" of grandparenting gained ground, and while the most obvious target involved actual caregiving, a wider range of relationships drew comment as well. For one thing, medical improvements meant that grandparents were more likely to be healthy and active than ever before—and while their interests varied, many rated grandchildren as a major focus in life. Regular visits or other contacts with grandparents provided many children with a further source of treats—which some grandparents could overdo—but also a wider sense of family identity and support. And the interactions were frequent. A full 43 percent of children saw one or more grandparents at least once a week—obviously going well beyond the important caretaker group. Despite some continued geographical mobility, 55 percent of all American families lived within an hour's drive of one or more grandparents, and most took advantage of the fact. Diversity was important as well, but in this case the patterns ran counter to other indicators of family instability: contacts were least frequent (for geographic reasons primarily) in the upper middle class, and most important in rural and inner-city families and among many immigrant groups.[41]

By the twenty-first century, only 1 percent of all American families with children reported no kind of extended family contact. For many, a combination of persistence and new needs and opportunities generated a significant feature of children's family life in the decades after the 1950s. The result added to the complexities of assessing the family environment, mostly in a positive way. Evaluating the emotional impact of extended family ties on children is not an easy task—they may not have recovered earlier intensities as fully as the greater frequency of contacts suggested. But they could be meaningful.

Inside the Family: Changes and Continuities

Charting the structural shifts in family life as they bore on children builds on considerable available data. The variety admittedly complicates generalization. It would also be good to know more about extended family links, including relationships among cousins. And evaluating how the major shifts actually affected children is a major challenge. But a general framework can be sketched.

Dealing with more subjective changes *within* the family is another matter, and in some cases they might be more important than structure. A few points can be suggested, though, as with structure, they point in several different directions. Patterns of punishment within the home were more stable than one might expect—more than in Western Europe, though there were a few developments. Americans continued widely to approve of corporal punishment, and again in contrast to Europe there were no efforts at government regulation beyond strictures against outright child abuse.

Still, measurable shifts did occur. About 84 percent of American adults approved of spanking in the 1970s, but that had dropped to 71 percent by the early twenty-first century. About 5 percent of parents reported spanking babies as early as three months of age, but most waited until the toddler stage. There was wide disapproval of using instruments other than hands. Patterns were class-specific: the upper-middle class used almost no corporal punishment, the urban and rural lower classes relied fairly heavily, and the middle class waffled. A number of evangelical Christian families were particularly severe. Overall, children became somewhat less likely to experience physical chastisement after the 1950s, but many American parents continued to ignore systematic expert advice against the practice.[42]

Shaming punishments are harder to trace. The relaxation of toilet training suggested a growing desire to avoid shaming, and polls found that American parents were widely opposed to deliberate shaming—as well as being very sensitive to school practices that suggested blatant shaming. Here too children on average enjoyed somewhat greater leniency in the turn-of-the-century decades than their predecessors had, but amid considerable variety.[43]

Informality also predominated in American family life, though this was less novel. Parents, eager to seem friendly, accepted casual labels. Except in some immigrant families, grandparents also required no special honorifics. Children were exposed to few occasions demanding elaborate etiquette. Indeed, by the twenty-first century some business schools began to hold formal dinners for college students to show them what structured manners involved, in case this might later be professionally relevant. Before high school, few children had to dress up frequently. Religious services were the most obvious exception, but many families eased off on these occasions by the turn of the century. More than their counterparts in some other societies, American parents did try to inculcate "thank-yous," but otherwise the approach to instilling manners was rather relaxed.

Some key patterns of contact with parents shifted more decisively. On the one hand, the family dinner steadily declined (another prompt toward greater informality). With more women working and greater reliance on take-out or prepared meals, more vagaries in adult schedules, plus extracurricular activities for the young, plus in some cases a child's preference to huddle in their own room, this classic family gathering faded. A survey early in the twenty-first century suggested that 40 percent of modern families dine together only three times a week or less.[44]

On the other hand, the time parents spent directly with children probably increased—at least in the more intact families. By the 1990s many parents were deliberately attempting to compensate for hours spent at work, while at the same time many children, faced with an absence of playmates in their neighborhood and restrictions about going outside unattended, were more available for parental contact. Thus, fathers reported a massive increase in "quality" time spent: from five minutes a day in 1974 to thirty-five by the early twenty-first century. For mothers, the average fifteen minutes in 1974 rose to a full hour. Findings here, though possibly surprising, have been pretty consistent in recent decades, running counter—for the family units involved—to the theme of family collapse, at least in terms of parental intent. Many children, though probably particularly in the middle and upper classes, were encouraged to see parents to some extent as pals, sharing games, shopping excursions, and other pleasures. Indeed, the growing role of parents as entertainers-in-chief, in a variety of family structures, has become steadily more prominent in the contemporary era.[45]

Evaluation of these trends can be tricky. Increased time with fathers was an important development—but only if a father was around, which was becoming less common. Shared tasks with parents—for example, boys and their fathers tinkering with a car—may have declined even where entertainment contacts increased. It may well be that father-child interactions were most intense during early childhood, rather than during adolescence, reversing earlier patterns. Trends in the parent-child contact category were not entirely bleak, but they must be assessed with the increasing variety of family settings in mind.

The growing use of cell phones in the twenty-first century could enhance parent-child connections from another angle, though it could also create resentment about parental interference. Many children called parents quite regularly. College advisors who addressed freshmen, in the past eager to urge calls or letters to parents, now actually reversed course to argue for less frequent contact, given how many adolescents seemed to depend on excessive parental guidance. On a related front: about 30–40 percent of all parents reported using cell phones to keep track of where their kids were—which admittedly went beyond social contact. Of course, it was also interesting to note that a majority of parents, for whatever reason, did not do this and had less detailed notion of what their older children were up to.[46]

Turn-of-the-twenty-first-century American parents eagerly wanted their children to be happy. A 2015 international poll showed this as the top goal for 73 percent of American parents—not the highest figure in the world, but well above levels in non-Western nations, where achievement or other goals took pride of place.[47] A child-rearing expert, Robin Berman, echoes the point: "When I give parenting lectures around the country, I always ask.... 'What do you want most for your children?' The near-universal response it, 'I just want my children to be happy.'"[48] This rhetorical commitment was not brand new in the postwar years; it had been building since the nineteenth century, but it now became commonplace, at least on paper.

The commitment raises a variety of interpretive issues. First, did American parents really mean what they said? Growing concerns about children's school success and pressure to do well in sports and other extracurricular ventures might raise real questions about whether happiness was a genuine goal—no matter what parents thought they believed. Correspondingly, the parental commitment contrasted with growing evidence that kids in fact were becoming more troubled. The theme was double-edged, as Berman herself noted. It might be sincere, but it also made parents impatient with signs of sadness—eager, possibly, to seek therapeutic help to restore the image of the gratefully smiling child. It could, in sum, be counterproductive, putting unexpected pressure on children.[49]

The most obvious example of a heightened commitment to children's happiness and to spending a bit more time with the kids showed up in growing levels of consumerism and the more elaborate celebrations of children's birthdays and other family holidays. Family vacations, particularly car trips, loomed large as well, with at least 35 percent of American families attempting this on a regular basis. A host of new facilities sprang up to accommodate this interest from the later 1950s onward, with the Disney parks and amusement park chains like Six Flags only the most renowned. Focused efforts to make children happy, and a deep desire to believe that they were, formed vital components of American family life in the turn-of-the-century decades. It carried the potential for real enjoyment, for parents and children alike, but it might also cause disappointments on both sides as well.[50]

Amid the various trends in family life, both structural and qualitative, overall assessments of changes in parenting styles are difficult. The rise of the helicopter parent, intensifying from the 1960s onward, was the clearest trend, probably affecting about 40 percent of American parents at least to some measurable degree. This pattern was most readily achieved in middle-class settings and particularly with two parents involved, though it could develop in other situations as well. Other parents, probably a bit more traditional though not necessarily hidebound, did not fit this category, and economic pressures on parents might profoundly affect the time and attention available for children. In many cases, a stricter approach to discipline in the child's early years yielded to considerable loss of control over teenagers. Even for older children, however, immigrant groups often maintained tighter family environments than the contemporary norm. Considerable variety predominated in this, as it did in many other categories of the child's family environment.[51]

Finally, and not surprisingly, the environment continued to shift. The Covid pandemic of the early 2020s, so disruptive in many ways, found a growing number of middle-class parents able to take advantage of working from home, and the trend caught on. Many professional and white-collar workers found they greatly preferred this arrangement and resisted returning to 9–5 office schedules. Avoiding the commute was one key advantage. So, in many cases, was the opportunity to move out of center cities, to more spacious but cheaper housing. But high on the list was the greater flexibility the arrangements created in caring for and maintaining contact with children. Female employees were particularly adamant. To be sure, many employers pushed back as the pandemic eased, and it was not clear how widely online work would survive. But it seemed probable that some change would prove durable, creating another, and probably more favorable, domestic environment for parent-child relations. Yet, as in so many other cases, the gains were class specific. Blue-collar and lower-class families did not have the online option; for most of them, Covid simply strained an already challenging family setting.[52]

The Family and Religion

The turn-of-the-century decades saw a dramatic reduction of Americans' commitment to organized religion, and the results inevitably spilled over into childhood. In the 1950s family involvement in religious life had clearly embraced children, providing another dimension of parent-child relationships and also a weekly environment for children apart from formal school settings.

This did not change entirely. Polls in the early twenty-first century saw a majority of children sharing religious life with their parents—a pattern particularly marked in evangelical Protestant families but not confined to this category. However, a third of all American children were now growing up without any formal religious experience. Only 46 percent of all teenagers attended a religious service at least once or twice a month. And even where families remained more religious, some gap opened between children (or at least teenagers) and their parents. In a 2020 study 32 percent of all teens professed religious unbelief, compared to 24 percent of their adult counterparts.[53]

Here was another evolving pattern that highlighted stark diversities in American family life. Overall, however, trends suggested yet another category in which shared experiences between parents and children were declining at least to some extent, with implications that invited continued scrutiny in the future.

The Dysfunctional Family

Pulling together the numerous and significant changes in family life over the past half century plus, as they bore on children, is no easy task, particularly given variety and some ongoing continuities. There is, however, a compelling overall image, which deserves exploration before turning to a final conclusion.

Large numbers of Americans today—80 percent in some polls—believe that the American family has become dysfunctional, and their views are echoed by many experts. The term itself is new: references to dysfunctional families crept into the lexicon in the 1960s but really took off from the late 1970s onward.[54] And while this is arguably revealing—doesn't the need for a new term reflect growing instabilities?—it also seriously complicates historical judgments.

Here's the picture as it has been developing for the past three decades—ever since a major 1998 study by the CDC and Kaiser Permanente.[55] More than half of all American children experience some form of serious family dysfunction: physical, emotional, or sexual abuse; exposure to domestic violence; parental alcoholism, drug abuse, or mental illness. The 1998 study, focused mainly on the white upper and middle classes, showed that about a quarter of those surveyed, even in this group, had experienced childhood sexual abuse or parental alcoholism or drug addiction. Many subsequent studies, particularly since 2011, with more representative samples reveal even higher levels of dysfunction. In one study 64 percent of those surveyed reported at least one adverse event during childhood, and 17 percent reported four or more.[56]

The findings are deeply troubling. Without question, they highlight many childhood problems that will later show up in higher rates of disease, mental illness, alcoholism, and other issues among adults. While they also reveal diversity—inner-city and Indigenous families and those whose parents have less than a high school education display considerably higher rates of dysfunction than others—they also show that problems extend to many families more broadly, including even a minority of white, two-parent, upper-middle-class households.

But a rush to conclude that a characteristically dysfunctional childhood is the clear result of the various, often complex family changes of the past seventy years is challenged by at least two factors—despite the ominous figures revealed by all the studies of the past quarter-century. First, dysfunction remains very hard to define, and both the studies and the popular impressions cover a range of experiences, from mildly challenging to clearly ominous. Levels of dysfunction range from childhoods where parents sometimes shout angrily or criticize frequently, to outright and frequent physical violence, parental rape, or severe deprivation. Growing sensitivity to family imperfections is itself a fascinating development—another result, possibly a good one, of the psychological turn—but involves important imprecisions.

And the sensitivity is at least to some degree ahistorical. Eagerness to identify family dysfunction has undoubtedly increased faster than the phenomenon itself. Many families in the cherished 1950s harbored problems just as great as those today (including greater likelihood that a parent would die), but they were far less commonly identified—which makes evaluation of the level of change, the extent that dysfunctionality is somehow newly baked into contemporary childhood, problematic at best.[57]

Two examples highlight the challenge. In 1960 a poll suggested that 12 percent of Americans blamed alcohol for family troubles; in 2015 the comparable figure was 30 percent. But rates of heavy drinking had actually declined in the interval. This does not mean that the 30 percent figure was wrong, but it may suggest that the change reflected greater awareness of a problem more than, or at least along with, an increase in the problem itself.[58] The same applies to some aspects of the discussions of sexual abuse. Here too Americans have become far more sensitive, desirably so. The Kinsey reports on American sexuality in the late 1940s and early 1950s suggested that 25 percent of all children (mainly girls) experienced sexual overtures short of intercourse, often involving genital exposure, typically from older male relatives; but the finding drew no particular comment at the time, as opposed to concerns about adultery and premarital sex. Without much question, many of the same behaviors today end up on the dysfunction list, but that does not mean that they are more common.[59]

The clear point is this: in a more psychological age, many Americans expect more from the family than they did before, even as changes in the family may make success more elusive. Some problems have measurably increased: drug taking and mental illness among parents and, in some cases, rates of imprisonment of a parent. Others, like violent discipline or sexual abuse, may have changed less while at the same time not keeping pace with new standards. Some of the rising family forms, like single parenthood, may also make dysfunction more likely, particularly when combined with poverty; the rise of stepparenting might increase possibilities for sexual abuse, though this is not certain. *Somewhat* greater dysfunction overall is probably accurate in summing up the various impacts of family change over the past seventy years, and there is no question that both the forms and the levels of dysfunction warrant serious attention. However, there is risk of oversimplification.

Conclusion

By the second decade of the twenty-first century, social science researchers interested in comparative issues were startled to discover that couples without children were happier in many countries than those involved in parenting. And the gap was by far the widest in the United States—20 percent higher than in Ireland, the next on the list, and massively below countries like Portugal and Sweden where parents were actually happier than their childless counterparts. The parent-nonparent contrast was greatest when parents had children still at home, but it persisted even after children had left.[60]

Unfortunately, no comparable international poll exists for the 1950s and 1960s. Possibly, the strains of the Baby Boom would have produced similar results back then, but far more likely American parents were still geared to emphasize the positive rewards of having children around. Other polls suggest that the pleasure of parenthood was beginning to decline among Americans, from the 1960s to the 1980s.[61]

At the least, then, analysts are faced with a comparative issue: are American parents really distinctively dissatisfied, and if so, why? And they almost certainly face yet another historical question as well: why has dissatisfaction overcome the far more positive vibes associated with the baby boom and even its immediate aftermath? Does this touch base with the possibility of increasing dysfunction?

Explanations for both the comparative and the historical questions have involved three primary targets, related but in descending order of reliability: national policy differences, the structural changes that had buffeted the American family, and the more qualitative issue of parenting styles.

The many deficiencies of American family policy unquestionably top the list: the absence of systematic paid parental leave, the lack of comprehensive and affordable day care, and the unusual dearth of support for children in low-income families.[62] But structural change enters in as well. Not surprisingly, one-parent households report the lowest average satisfaction with parenthood. But divorce and other instabilities have complicated parental satisfaction as well. Beyond this, the extent to which so many parents feel special burdens because of their fears or competitive aspirations may contribute to making American parenthood seem particularly fraught. Being a helicopter parent, to take the most obvious case, is an onerous task.

How much does all of this redound on children themselves? Charting the impact of structural changes and other shifts and continuities in family habits on American young people is at best a speculative venture. It seems safe to argue that family conditions have contributed to making the experience of childhood by the twenty-first century more difficult than it was a half century before. Having parents who, comparatively, feel unusually hard-pressed, unsupported, or put upon is surely not a great formula. But—except for at least occasional stress reactions or some of the most grievous forms of dysfunction—children may be largely unaware of their parents' angst. Indeed, the happiness imperative, though it can place its own burdens on children, encourages some camouflage on the part of the parents involved.

The big analytical challenges center on the growing variety of family situations, the accommodations that have been made in some cases, and the unpredictable adaptability of children themselves. Children of divorce have been widely studied, and while the optimism of the 1960s has vanished, most analysts conclude that, particularly if treated sensitively, many children bounce back from the disruption of divorce fairly successfully—but an important and unpredictable minority do not. Other shifts—the decline of the divorce rate but also the rise of joint custody—have probably contributed to easing the burdens over time, but they have not eliminated them. Children of divorced parents—particularly those whose parents divorce before their teen years—are more likely on average to have behavioral difficulties and other problems, though they also can develop a useful degree of resilience and empathy.[63]

The same verdicts—disproportionate problems but also important possibilities of adjustment—apply to the still larger number of children who grow up without regular contact with fathers not only due to divorce but to other disruptions or to single motherhood. Problems are compounded when, as is common, greater poverty is involved.[64]

By the same token, the measurable changes in family life since the 1950s have widened the social and economic gaps among children, with the minority of children in two-parent households clearly advantaged, on average, over their counterparts involved in other situations. The variety of family structures combines with growing inequalities in defining key aspects of contemporary American childhood.[65]

Overall evaluations are also complicated by some of the other factors involved. The decline of physical punishments, though not as systematic as many experts would like, has eased burdens for some children. The same applies to the increased time available for interaction with a parent or parents—though this can also lead to the counterproductive extremes of helicoptering. The decline of teen parenting is probably a boon for many young children, even apart from its impact on the divorce rate. Contacts with extended family members are more significant for many children than is sometimes acknowledged, another factor to keep in mind. The possibility of greater flexibility in work arrangements for some adults may prove to be a significant shift. For severely disabled children, the increase in family responsibility, over-institutionalization, often involves significant gains.

Changes in the American family, developing now for over half a century, have made childhood less predictable in a number of ways—for scholars trying to understand the experience, for a wider American public, but above all for children themselves. The results interact with other changes in the framework for childhood, including the nature of schooling. They certainly correspond to measurable symptoms of growing malaise. Yet they are, on balance, less systematically severe than images of family collapse sometimes suggest. Clearly important, they may combine with the other new factors affecting children's lives in complicated ways.

In 2019 a restaurant chain commissioned a poll on children's attitudes toward their family. About 90 percent of the children tallied said they felt close to their family, and 56 percent felt very close. A minority felt their parents did not understand the current generation, and 73 percent wished they had more family time (compared to 70 percent of the parents involved). Shared entertainment activities topped the list of children's family delights (a tribute to this growing parental priority). A more systematic 2023 poll, surveying 9,000 children, generated similar though slightly less optimistic results, with 67 percent of children reporting good relationships with parents (with preteens featuring a measurably higher percentage) and 83 percent noting they had fun with their parents. Only 3 percent of younger children, 6 percent of those aged twelve to fourteen, reported bad relations.

Poll results can always be debated, of course, but these remind us not to overdo the understandably pessimistic assessments about contemporary family life, though the evidence about the adverse effects of the newer forms of family instability must be credited as well. Many children seem to make do with the family they have—and for better or worse, they are not in a position to assess historical trends. Their reactions surely deserve some attention, along with the more obvious challenges of variety and extensive dysfunction.[66]

One final point: any evaluation of the major changes and diversities in contemporary family life, and their potential impact on children, inevitably invites hopes to put the genie of change back in the bottle, to return to the family patterns of seventy years before. The temptation is real, but almost certainly misleading, even in certain forms of dysfunction. Older patterns were not as uniformly benign as is often imagined: there have been some positive gains. Most important is the probability that most of the new forms of parenting, including single parenting and reasonably high divorce rates, are here to stay, at least for the foreseeable future. The challenge, for American society, is to devise more effective means of support and adaptation.

The American Child: The Transformation of Childhood Since World War II. Steven Mintz and Peter N. Stearns, Oxford University Press. © Oxford University Press 2025. DOI: 10.1093/9780197797112.003.0006

7

The Decline of Children's Play—and the New Alternatives

American children do not play tag nearly much as they once did. This game, with its many variants, dates back almost 3,000 years—records exist from Greece in the fourth century BCE, from India and other places not long thereafter—and quite probably its real origins stretch much earlier. It is a game that requires no equipment, combines physical activity with a bit of excitement and uncertainty, and traditionally could also include children of various ages. It also was normally played without adults. Tag remained popular with American children into the later twentieth century, for example in schoolyards or simply around neighborhoods. But while it has not disappeared, it has measurably declined, and a growing number of children do not play it at all.

The clearest retardant involves changes in school policy, which began to surface by the 1990s. Individual schools or school districts in states as diverse as Wyoming, Kansas, Washington, and South Carolina instituted bans, or in other cases imposed severe restrictions that required extensive teacher supervision. The motives were revealing. Atop the list was a concern about physical harm. As one approving teacher put it, "What typically happens is, rather than touching someone to tag him…someone ends up getting hurt." The tags were too forceful, and occasionally other dangers were cited: apparently in one case early in the twenty-first century a boy playing tag collided with a metal pole and ultimately died. Opportunities to act on the safetyist impulse were steadily mounting.[1]

But physical issues were combined with concerns about psychological harm. Tag might be an occasion for bullying. A child singled out to be "It" could feel put upon, unfairly treated. Tag games that involved children of varying ages—not uncommon during school recess, for example—seemed particularly problematic. Much of the new protective apparatus being developed around children was now applied to this play tradition.

There was debate, with some adults vigorously defending the merits of tag as a source of exercise (particularly amid rising rates of obesity) and informal lessons in conflict resolution and fair play. And the bans on tag were not universal. But even many tag defenders hedged their bets: "much like any other activity, teachers must modify rules...and ensure people are safe." Children, in other words, should no longer fully control an aspect of their play that had long been in their domain.[2]

While new school policies were the clearest source of limitations on tag, other factors may have been even more significant and probably began to kick in a bit earlier. There was, of course, the sheer reduction in recess time. More important still was the increasing difficulty of assembling neighborhood groups of children to play games like tag apart from the school setting.

Here, a number of barriers combined, from at least the 1970s onward. Increasing age-grading limited the willingness of children to play with counterparts of different ages. Neighborhood fences and other barriers reduced the capacity to roam around. Growing parental fears about traffic hazards and "stranger danger" kept many children inside for longer periods of time. Brian Sutton-Smith, an expert on children's play, has noted that the classic maternal gambit—"don't bother me, go play outside"—virtually disappeared in this new context.[3] For children themselves, the impulse to stay indoors might well be furthered by the new charms of air conditioning and television. Most notably, there were simply fewer neighborhood kids to play with—because there were fewer children. Many suburban tracts, as the Baby Boom ended, saw similar-aged children separated from potential contact by a block or two, though of course there were exceptions.

In this setting, tag was not the only traditional game to experience decline. Hide-and-seek also faded somewhat. Data here are less clear, partly because it was less common as a schoolyard game and thus drew less attention from authorities. And the game was featured on popular television shows such as *Sesame Street*. But some familiar objections did surface. What if a child was not found for a while—would this produce a sense of abandonment, a feeling that no one cared? But the greatest barrier, again, was the neighborhood situation and the difficulty of finding peers close by: by the late twentieth century hide-and-seek was most commonly a game for very young children, within the home, played by parents and the child alike, possibly with a sibling joining in when one was available. The traditional group game, for kids themselves out of doors, faded dramatically.

Some versions of hide-and-seek, such as "sardines," where children crowded together with a "found" playmate, now died out altogether.

Kick the can was another victim. The game had been immensely popular during the Depression, because it could be played in any outdoor space and required only a garbage item for equipment. It maintained some interest into the 1960s, where it figured in several television shows, but by the end of the century it had largely died out, another casualty in what a number of experts describe as the larger decline of outdoor and unstructured play.[4]

A Pattern of Change

Indeed, of all the categories of children's activities, including family and school, the transformation—and, many would argue, the tragic decline—of established patterns of children's play was by far the most dramatic, and at least to a considerable extent it affected children across economic and other divides. The change went beyond reversing systems of the previous few decades or even the earlier century. Many games that had been around for millennia, like tag, now virtually disappeared. Most of them had featured interactions among a number of children, with little or no equipment, with scant adult involvement, and, arguably, a considerable opportunity to learn how to deal with a variety of peers as well as the occasion for a good bit of physical activity. Whether or not this was the most important of the many adjustments in contemporary childhood, it was unquestionably the most revolutionary. Teasing out both causes and consequences is a vital part of assessing the lives of children in the past half century.

Certainly, the transformation of play was one of the most striking features of the larger shift in American culture, where child-centeredness clearly declined and commercial concerns, enhanced by new technologies, took a growing role. Though not a widely familiar topic outside the ranks of scholarly experts, the transformation is easy enough to chart: the challenge is to figure out the impact on children themselves.

Other Victims

The list of traditional losses must clearly include the virtual disappearance of marbles and jacks. Marbles may have been the first children's toy ever, crafted from balls of clay in the heyday of hunting and gathering. Jacks, largely for girls, was a more recent entrant but had similar characteristics of simple equipment, dexterity, and usually amicable competitions. American kids, and particularly boys, played marbles extensively in the 1920s and 1930s: a national tournament for seven- to fourteen-year-olds was launched in 1922. Marble games were cheap, usually spontaneous, and filled with specialized vocabulary that provided connections even among kids who did not know each other very well. By the 1970s, however, the game had virtually disappeared, another striking change. Familiar factors were at work: competition from commercial games, including electronic offerings, and greater attention to adult-organized sports activities. Safetyist impulses entered in as well: by the 1990s several school authorities openly worried about the dangers of glass or clay fragments from broken marbles, though there was no actual evidence of harm. But even more important were the decline of recess and walking to school and the disappearance of extensive patches of unregulated neighborhood dirt on which the game could be played.[5]

A few traditional games persisted slightly more strongly, like jump rope and hopscotch (which was, after all, an activity for pavements). Simon says still featured at parties for fairly young children; here there were no physical safety concerns, though at least one twenty-first-century study worried that the confusion that was fundamental to the game might damage children cognitively. (Psychology could provide its own forms of safetyism.) Games of this sort did decline, however, reflecting the same new combination of constraints and alternatives.

Evidence accumulated about the decline of other children's outdoor activities. Bike riding largely succumbed to traffic safety concerns; helmet requirements, spreading from 1987 onward, also complicated matters for some children, a really interesting new constraint that was pushed particularly aggressively in the safety-conscious United States. Hiking with friends seems to have suffered. By the twenty-first century one CDC estimate suggested that only 6 percent of all children aged nine to thirteen were playing outside at all—spontaneously or not. A few politicians sought to respond: a Healthy Kids Outdoor Act was proposed to Congress in 2015, but it was referred to a committee.[6]

On another front: reading for pleasure declined, particularly among boys. A substantial proportion of the activities that had sustained children in the 1950s were being rethought, consciously or not.

The evisceration of Halloween was yet another, though in this case annual, example of change. Well past the mid-twentieth century Halloween had given many American kids one night to kick up a bit of independent mischief—harking back to a much more elaborate tradition of allowing children a few opportunities, given their normally dependent state, to do some minor damage on their own as a form of release. By mid-century community concerns about vandalism had already introduced some constraints, confining typical "tricks" to throwing corn on porches, soaping screen windows, or bedecking trees with toilet paper. But it was the odd and largely inaccurate poisoned candy scare that more fully turned the tide. By the 1980s Halloween had transformed almost entirely into an adult-controlled activity, with supervised treats for little kids—admittedly, along with the pleasure of a costume—and adult-orchestrated (though often very clever) haunted houses for older ones, often in the company of their parents. Plus, there was a growing variety of parties for adults themselves to which children were not invited.[7]

Spaces, as well as activities, were redefined. Many spaces for play shrank or became more structured. Suburban housing booms removed many vacant lots. A few schools began to be built with no playgrounds of any sort. Park playgrounds persisted, but many traditional features were removed because of safety concerns—sometimes even swings and sandboxes, arguably limiting opportunities for exploration and creative construction. Led by McDonald's, many fast-food outlets figured out how to discourage teenagers from hanging out, another constriction of partially independent space. Even in the 1950s, as one observer noted, efforts to get children off the streets and sidewalks were creating a "shortage" of play spaces. And conditions would only get worse, despite a few abortive efforts to revive street games and some dubious commercial ventures designed to lure kids with play space.[8]

Familial Alternatives and Their Limitations

The decline of various activities and places for children did create opportunities for replacements, many of them, like television, increasingly ubiquitous but noteworthy both for their sedentary qualities and for their reduction of meaningful interaction among children themselves. Other innovations, which were somewhat more open-ended, also deserve attention.

The rise of the play date was one. While the term was introduced in American English in the 1920s, its usage and popularity soared from the 1980s onward. The notion, familiar enough today, involves parental arrangements for children to play together in the home of one of the participating families. Interestingly, online advice about the play date by the twenty-first century urged that only two children at a time be involved, otherwise one would be left out—another case of the assumption that children could not manage things well on their own. Whatever the prompt, most play dates did emphasize two at a time. The majority of play dates also occurred largely inside, but under parental supervision activities in a backyard were also possible.

The growing importance of the play date had several sources. The new concern about kidnapping was one. Engagement of many mothers in the workforce was another, requiring special arrangements to make sure an adult was available. The sheer decline of children in a given neighborhood was, again, a vital spur: many children had to be driven to find a similar-age counterpart, which made adult involvement absolutely essential.[9]

Play dates loomed particularly large for the growing number of "only" children after the end of the Baby Boom. Research on the experiences of only children is all over the map, from claims of higher rates of obesity to above-average success in school. But there is considerable agreement that only children indulge in less unstructured play than their sibling-ed counterparts, enhancing the general trend. But kids with siblings needed play dates as well.

By the twenty-first century the importance of the play date even motivated efforts to declare a National Play Date Day (to be held on January 21). Above all, play dates could be immensely significant for children themselves, supplementing preschool and school activities. In contrast to more traditional forms of play, however, the new encounters occurred under closer adult supervision and inevitably suffered in spontaneity. Most importantly, by definition the play date was occasional at best: adults rarely had the time to make it a frequent occurrence.

For slightly older children, the rise of the sleepover from the 1950s onward was another interesting accommodation to suburban sprawl. By the 1980s sleepovers became virtually a requirement for middle-class parents with daughters. More than the play date, they allowed serious tinkering with adult-imposed rules (particularly about when to stop chattering)—but sleepovers too depended on adult initiative.

The common evolution of the American birthday party had a somewhat similar flavor in many respects, though the trends were slightly less decisive. As they evolved from their largely nineteenth-century origins, birthday parties remained largely home-based affairs into the 1960s and 1970s. They were, of course, parentally organized and supervised. They featured a mixture of games, with varying degrees of structure, and largely homemade treats, including the cake. During the final decades of the twentieth century, however, this format increasingly yielded to theme- or destination-based gatherings, usually outside the home, focused more clearly on entertainments organized and provided by a variety of vendors. Chuck E. Cheese became a common destination: the chain began in 1977, highlighting prepared foods—pizza and cake—plus animatronic shows and arcade games. Museums also got into the act, with other organized and arguably more educational options like finding artificial dinosaur bones in a sandbox. The new trends most obviously reduced pressures on now-working mothers, and they certainly still allowed kids to assemble and make a good bit of noise: they were not entirely structured. Arguably, however, the elements of play and spontaneity were reduced, the focus on adult organization and oversight enhanced. The trend was clear. In the process the emphasis on gifts and toys mounted. So did the costs, which could give many parents the sense that they were more than fulfilling their obligations: by the twenty-first century the average birthday party cost $400, and with parental gifts tossed in added up to a $500 outlay, no small investment in terms of average family incomes.[10]

Families also sought to respond to change by providing individual kids with their own space. The middle-class commitment to separate rooms for each child, though launched earlier, picked up steam with the decline of the birth rate after the 1960s. While a majority of families with two or more children still had some room-sharing by the twenty-first century, most middle-class families had long since provided separate quarters, each usually jealously guarded by the child in question. The impact on play was widely debated. Some authorities commended the importance of private time and space, where a child could devise their own activities, particularly as other aspects of life became more structured. In other cases, however, separation, even from a sibling or two, compounded the decline of neighborhood activities and spontaneous interaction. Impact on play was further complicated when the child also had a TV in the room—as was the situation for an estimated 71 percent of all children by the early twenty-first century, in this case often including poorer households.[11]

Changes in patterns of play also highlighted the growing importance of parents not only in providing opportunities but in actively organizing entertainments—one of the new parental functions that kids themselves seemed to recognize quite positively—as in the polls that vaunted this above all other possible parental strengths. For many children, particularly before adolescence, a good bit of daily play typically involved an oscillation between intense engagement with parents and time spent alone, often in one's own room.

Overall, the rise of new contact patterns amid the decline of more traditional play activities, though they provided some new kinds of interaction and opportunities for individual imagination, did not clearly compensate. In some cases they compounded children's encounters with more organized and commercial entertainments, which might soak up attention without the benefit that play could provide.

The Decline of Play?

Howard Chudacoff, the leading historian of American play, argues that the first half of the twentieth century, into the mid-1950s, was the true heyday of children's play in the United States, only to be constricted thereafter. His argument rests on the congruence of two factors: first, the decline of work after 1920 (including, for many, household chores), which was a key distinction from the nineteenth century for many young people, and second, the relatively unsupervised opportunities that existed for group play in parks, school grounds, suburban spaces, and even urban streets. His argument makes the reductions of time and space for play in the past half century all the more vivid. Here was another major change in childhood—according to some authorities, one of the most fundamental shifts not just in the modern era but in the whole of human history, a focus that has been a vital part of children's experience since the species first emerged.[12]

It is important not to overdo this argument. Other historians have pointed to new limits on children's play even from the nineteenth century onward. These included growing adult interest in making sure kids used their free time, or at least some of it, "wisely," often with educational goals in mind. These goals often included urging some regular reading and, by the early twentieth century, enjoyment of toys billed as instructive. Concerns about supervising children's play had increased earlier as well, particularly in the playground movement of the early twentieth century. This movement sponsored spaces that seem amazingly freewheeling by contemporary standards, particularly with climbing structures that would now be seen as dangerous but were nevertheless designed to provide greater structure for the users. Finally, though school took up less of children's time than it does today, its reach was already increasing in the earlier twentieth century, particularly with the expansion of high school attendance and more assiduous efforts to reduce truancy. In other words, constrictions on the time and latitude for free play predate the contemporary decades, though at lower intensity.[13]

The movement to associate play with consumer goods, particularly toys, was also well established by the early twentieth century, though it has reached new dimensions since that point. Many adults sincerely interested in the happiness of the young assumed that giving them things was the best approach, paying less attention to real opportunities for play. The tendency to surround even infants with objects could establish a reliance on things over activities from an early age. Here too some modern limitations on children's play easily predate the contemporary era.[14]

At the same time, there is no need to argue that kids today are joyless. They are not, after all, concerned scholars, nervously charting the decline of play. Many take real pleasure in play dates, in the amount of recess time that is provided, in opportunities in preschool. Many, particularly in the middle classes, gain access to play, including outdoor play and summer camps, though amid adult supervision and some imposed structure. And many may readily agree that a steady supply of new toys, renewed on birthdays and, for many, at Christmas, provide real material for play. Here, another innovation from the 1980s—parental invitations to develop individual "wish lists" in advance of a major holiday—might extend the sense that toys and play intermingled and that there was choice involved. Other compensatory opportunities, such as the proliferation of children's sports groups, clearly work well for many. And while children continue to complain that household obligations cut into their opportunities for play, average chore time spent has dropped considerably, though whether the resultant margin contributes to unstructured activity is hard to determine.[15]

However, a significant reduction of classic play activities and spaces, and with it some potential new problems, is undeniable, and while the most extensive evidence applies from the 1970s onward, there were forerunners in the two prior decades as well. The notion of play, as activities freely chosen and defined at least in part by the participants themselves (and typically without elaborate equipment), did suffer new constraints, and the decline of tag was only one example.[16]

In 1981 and again in 1997, sociologists at the University of Michigan, relying on a large sample of parents, sought to measure how children spent their time. The findings were striking. Among six- to eight-year-olds, researchers found a 25 percent decline in the amount of time spent playing over the two-decade span and a 35 percent decline in the time spent conversing with others in the household. In contrast, time spent in school (18 percent), time spent on schoolwork (145 percent), and, strikingly, time spent shopping with parents (168 percent) all increased, in two cases quite dramatically. The total time spent playing (including indulging in the then-new enthusiasm for computer games) averaged only eleven hours a week. Though it was not precisely measured, the amount of outdoor play declined far more than play in general, a change reported in other studies as well.[17]

A survey of mothers early in the twenty-first century confirmed the reduction of outdoor play: only 31 percent of children were playing outdoors at all, and only 22 percent for periods of several hours. The parents blamed television and computer games but admitted their own rules played a major role as well, spurred by safety concerns including fear of crime and apprehensions about bullying. Yet surveys also insisted that children themselves found outdoor play the most rewarding form by a fair margin, easily outranking television or video games. The decline, in other words, was not of their doing.[18]

Further, while the most precise evidence applies to developments over the past forty years, more impressionistic data suggested a shrinkage in outdoor, neighborhood play as early as the 1960s. Though there is risk of excessive nostalgia, many older adults claim to have noted contrasts between their 1950s childhoods, where a walk through a neighborhood routinely found groups of children playing, and a comparable experience even a decade or two later. On a more scholarly basis, psychiatrist Bruno Bettelheim estimated that free time in the average middle-class childhood dropped from eleven years in the 1950s to between five and eight by the end of the century—thanks mainly to the heightened time at school and with school-based activities.[19]

Studies of children's after-school patterns, though focused on the turn-of-the-century decades, revealed a more specific aspect of the decline of play. Seeking to compensate for concerns about children left on their own by working mothers—the "latch-key kids" problem of the 1980s—more and more parents were arranging for children to stay in school settings after formal instruction had ended, often for up to two hours. A study in 2000 suggested that only 26 percent of all children were spending any time alone after school (for an average of an hour, during which TV watching predominated but some time was devoted to play or study). Social class divisions did apply: wealthier families were more able to afford after-school activities. But the aversion to leaving kids alone was quite widespread, with the result that exposure to adult supervision and more structured activities became increasingly standard.[20]

A gap was clearly emerging, or widening, between what children wanted to do and what they were allowed to do. Specific adult fears played a growing role, as did school burdens and, to an extent, alternatives like television. But it was possible to suggest an even more fundamental clash between the inherent logic of children's play, which involves a certain element of fear and moderate risk-taking, and the growing safetyist approach to childhood on the part of most adults.

And, while children were not necessarily aware of change, some did comment on how adults seemed to misunderstand the purpose of play. One gifted-program grade-schooler noted, "We need to play because play is pretend work.... It helps us to communicate and reduces stress." And another: "Most people think of playing as a waste of time, but it's really not. Grownups don't realize that games like sports, puzzles and also communicating are very important to us. They say that work comes before play, but I think work should involve play."[21]

Replacements

Beyond sponsoring new patterns in and around the home, such as the play date or the provision of separate TV sets for children, parents and other adult authorities moved into what had been extensive play space with a variety of options, seeking to entertain, instruct, or achieve other goals. Motivations varied, but they included a real if implicit understanding that more traditional play options had dwindled (or were parentally discountenanced because of new fears about neighborhood activities) but also an effort to provide something more desirable than a TV (or later, social media) diet alone.

Where funds permitted, for example, and sometimes when they did not, family vacations became more elaborate and, like birthdays, increasingly intertwined with commercial entertainment. This was a category that embraced great variety, but the clearest trend was a growing interest in taking the kids to some kind of amusement park and, at least once, to enter one of Disney's parks. By the twenty-first century, 87 percent of American children had visited an amusement park and 74 percent of them had gone to a Disney. And 18 percent of the parents involved had borrowed money for the trip. Here, clearly, the intention was fun—but not, as purists would insist, real play.[22]

Expanded reliance on summer camps was another important option—though, like vacations, very much a function of family income. Private camps as well as the YMCA, YWCA, and scouting camps had existed before World War II, but they involved a relatively small number of children. Postwar prosperity expanded interest, and so did the growing involvement of many mothers in the labor force. Indeed, for many parents, summer became a rather desperate scramble as they sought to place children in one organized activity after another. Most postwar camps provided a general set of offerings, emphasizing crafts, swimming, folklore, and a variety of outdoor activities, including sports. The camps provided recreation but also fostered independence, teamwork, and leadership skills.

By the later twentieth century, however, the camp experience changed in several ways. It became more expensive, providing yet another social divide in childhood, though most cities tried to offer some opportunities for poorer children. It involved more elaborate adult supervision in the best safetyist fashion. And camps tended to become increasingly specialized, reflecting the growing parental interest in giving children every possible leg up in what they saw as a competitive educational environment. All-purpose camps still existed, and even the specialized camps almost always offered a greater mix of activities than schools did, but increasingly the focus was on music, dance, computers, or particular sports. For the children involved, summer became yet another setting for institutionalized, adult-directed activities, though with somewhat more variety and flexibility than described the standard school year.

Most important, in the quest for alternatives to unstructured outdoor play, was the mounting passion for enrolling children, often quite young, in formal sports activities, even aside from specialized camps. The interest of American children in sports was not at all new. Street baseball or stick ball, for example, had been a vital urban option in the nineteenth and early twentieth centuries. School sports programs were also well established, though interestingly, from a fear of premature competitiveness, few grade schools were involved, which left room for other agencies. Gender segregation had also limited involvement for girls. But for boys, park teams and other informal group activities, often particularly directed at poorer families in hopes of deterring crime, also dated to the earlier twentieth century.

However, what happened from the 1950s onward, though building on precedent, turned out to be a different phenomenon and increasingly involved different kinds of children. Football star Tom Brady, comparing his own childhood to what he was pressed to provide his own children, captured part of the change. His recollection from the 1980s emphasized relatively informal, local team activities, with an interested boy participating in different sports depending on the season (he himself started football only as a high school freshman) and minimal travel times to games. But his children's world, by the second decade of the twenty-first century, was a stark (and in his view, unpleasant) contrast. "It's just hard, because all the parents are doing it...and the competition feels like it starts so early for these kids....I don't know how it's taken that turn, but you know, sometimes it's nice for kids to be kids."[23]

Intensification actually began in the 1950s, though there is no question that further components were added toward the end of the twentieth century. It was in the '50s, for example, that Little League baseball, which had launched as a local effort in Pennsylvania in 1939, began to ratchet up its national competitive activities, increasingly seeking support from the business community in the process. Focused on grade- and middle-schoolers, who largely lacked access to team sports, with a cut-off at age thirteen, Little League gradually began to drain energy away from informal neighborhood sports and even public park groups. The notion of an end-of-the-summer Little League World Series (first ventured in 1947) drew increasing attention as the operation became national. Each state (or in the cases of

California and Texas two regions within the state) began to select regional all-star teams during the summer, with elimination games that would ultimately yield the final cluster that played in Williamsport, Pennsylvania.[24]

A similar though slightly less elaborate pattern applied to children's football. Here too activities began before World War II and also in Pennsylvania, with an initial team formed in 1929 as an antidote to youth vandalism. Efforts extended from 1947 with the formation of the Pop Warner League, and various divisions were established, with age- and weight-level clusters from ages five to sixteen (ultimately another group included three- to four-year-olds). Until concussion concerns began to cut into popularity after 2010, Pop Warner teams regularly included hundreds of thousands of boys.

Ventures of this sort fed into the growing popularity of high school (and in some cases middle school) sports teams. Already well established for boys, team activities expanded only slightly from the later twentieth century onward. For girls, however, there was a genuine explosion from the 1970s onward, encouraged by the federal government's insistence on greater gender parity in sports: the famous Title IX legislation was signed into law in 1972 and prohibited sex-based discrimination in any program in any school that received federal money. In 1971, 360,000 girls were participating in high school sports, but three decades later the number had soared to 2.7 million, not too distant from the boys' figure of 3.4 million. Gender inequalities in sports still existed, particularly in the smaller audiences and television interest in women's competitions, sometimes in inferior facilities, but even here there were signs of change by the twenty-first century.

By 2012, 73 percent of all children aged six to twelve were listed as doing some sports activity, either team or individual, and while only 41 percent actually did team sports with any regularity the percentage was arguably impressive. For children aged thirteen to seventeen, the overall figure was 76 percent, with 42 percent listed on some kind of team. The figures may have been somewhat inflated, with both children and their adult mentors eager to report more activity than actually occurred, but there was no question that organized sports and childhood had become increasingly intertwined.[25]

Within this basic framework, a further intensification began to take shape from the 1980s onward, accelerating after 2000 with the rise of travel teams, ultimately in a whole variety of sports headed by baseball, basketball, and soccer but extending to include cheerleading, swimming, shooting, tennis, golf, and other competitive athletics. The movement actually began in the 1960s—the first North Virginia travel team for women's soccer, for example, dates back at least to 1974, but extensive impact emerged only toward the end of the century.[26] Travel teams were privately sponsored and involved paying memberships. Age-graded, they included activities at the grade-school level into the early high school years. As the name suggested, they emphasized competition over a fairly wide geographic area, heightening the seriousness of the stakes involved. Entry was not easy. Not only did parents have to pay membership fees, but children themselves had to prove their abilities. Entry requirements in turn spawned a growing industry built around lessons—often, expensive lessons—for children aspiring to qualify, extending into the early grade-school years and in some cases even before. In baseball, for example, T-ball lessons and competitions could begin at age four.

By 2020, 20 percent of all school-age children were involved in a travel team of some sort. The focus was actually squeezing some more traditional opportunities, such as Little League. Overall sports participation may actually have declined a bit: one study suggested a 25 percent drop among grade-school children from 1968 to 2016. But for the large minority still involved, or aspiring to be involved, travel teams capped several decades of increasingly serious emphasis on the centrality of sports in American childhood. For the commercial sponsors, the result was a clear bonanza: travel sports constituted a $15 billion industry by 2017.[27]

Sports enthusiasm clearly exemplified the growing eagerness to provide organized activities to replace play or respond to the decline of play. As one psychologist put it, "Our society...is moving rapidly to a complete takeover of (the) traditional franchise of childhood."[28] A variety of motives contributed. Parents became increasingly eager to shield their children from obesity or excessive time with television or social media; sports involvement and helicoptering were natural partners. At least at the grade-school level, given the decline of neighborhood activities, a simple desire to tire kids out might play a role. Competitiveness clearly factored in: parents easily felt negligent if they were not involving their kids in as many activities as other parents sponsored. And at sports events themselves many parents outdid their offspring in their competitive zeal, among other things making the life of volunteer referees increasingly miserable. Like schooling, sports became an arena where childhood was increasingly reorganized to emphasize formal training and competitive success.

Increasingly, and particularly undergirding the rise of travel teams, many parents clearly saw sports achievement as a key to other opportunities for their kids, translating and even magnifying the sense of high-stakes rivalry that developed in education. A few might hope for access to a high-paying career in athletics, as Major League Baseball, for example, became stocked with young (largely white) men of middle-class origin (joining foreign players of much different backgrounds). Far more, however, saw sports success as an entry to successful high school and college teams—hopefully, with scholarships attached. As one father put it, "I don't want my kids to join Major League Soccer, but I do want them to go to Princeton." Sports were meant to shape larger qualities for success, but even more specifically add to college application resumes and possibly—a more and more common goal as college tuitions soared—win scholarships.[29]

The crucial question, of course, is how this evolution affected the experience of childhood itself. Some answers are quite clear, others are more debatable. On the clear side: sports became an increasing differentiator by social class, particularly from the 1980s onward. Except to an extent in football and basketball, successful child athletes normally had parents willing and able to sponsor lessons and team activities that could cost thousands of dollars a year. Older children who had to maintain part-time jobs rarely had a chance even at school teams that held daily multi-hour practice sessions. Whereas sports between the wars had been seen as a device to aid poor children, the effective emphasis steadily shifted, though some charitable organizations continue to try to sponsor inner-city kids. By the twenty-first century children in poor families, and/or with parents who had relatively little education, were only half as likely to be participating in sports as their counterparts from middle-class backgrounds with college-educated parents. The disparities were striking.

Also clear was that the reach of sports steadily extended into early childhood, and obviously to girls as well as boys. Whatever the advantages and demerits of sports, they now applied to childhood rather generally, not just to activities predominantly for teenagers.

It was also striking that the level of organization and adult supervision steadily expanded, highlighting a theme pervasive in contemporary childhood. Informal park activities continued, but they played second fiddle to more structured efforts like Little League, which in turn yielded increasingly to high-stakes training and administration in the travel leagues.

Far less clear, however, was the question of whether the children involved had fun and found in sports some of the qualities their counterparts used to gain in less structured play. Some clearly flourished, including growing numbers of girls who gained new opportunities for physical fitness, team bonding, and individual achievement. They, as well as their parents, talked of the excitement of sport, the benefits to physical health, the friendships formed with teammates, and the lure of competing in different places. Though they might also recognize the rigor involved, it would be hard to convince them that "more genuine" play would have been more useful.

At the same time, some children continued to participate in organized sports without getting drawn into the intensities of travel teams. It was still possible, for example, to play high school baseball without an intense set of prior lessons or participation in teams beyond the park league level. Access to a college team was less likely, but this was not the goal in any event. Or a child might genuinely enjoy playing soccer for a while or getting tennis lessons with no intention of more serious involvement.

But there were downsides for many children as well—even aside from the increasing social inequality. For the apparently successful, the rise of travel teams increasingly encouraged children to concentrate on a single sport from a very young age in order to maximize opportunities for advancement. Experimentation with other sports (or activities) just for fun was discouraged. Boys particularly saw opportunities narrow compared to earlier patterns, sometimes for grade school onward—though for girls increasing opportunity was the more obvious theme. And the burdens of over-organized days were real as well, for both genders, with little free time for any less structured activity, including play. Family life might also suffer. Travel teams took children away from the family as a whole, and while a parent was usually in attendance, relationships with siblings could deteriorate.[30]

Finally, the intensity and competitive demands clearly turned some children off, discouraging them from less formal sports ventures and, possibly, activities of any kind. Though the data are not always clear, peak involvement in sports often centered on grade school years, where parental involvement was most telling. Some children who might have been able to maintain participation had the framework been less intense dropped away. The fact that a full 20 percent of all children were on a travel team or that 42 percent of all high school students played a team sport was genuinely impressive, but the same data showed that a majority of children had turned away or had not been able to try in the first place. The pattern was double-edged.

Other Endeavors

Sports were not the only organized activity aimed at providing some mixture of training and diversion amid the decline of less formal play. Dance activities took on many of the same features as sports for many children, particularly girls. Many were signed up for dance classes as early as three years old, and schools frequently provided dance instruction as well. As with sports, some girls participated without intense involvement, but for the truly dedicated dance could become a consuming involvement, with the usual mix of advantages and drawbacks involved.

Chess clubs and tournaments took on something of the same quality, though a smaller number of (primarily male) children were involved. There were even opportunities to gain special college scholarships, as with sports, that could attract parental interest as well. The US Chess Federation was accused of becoming "child obsessed" in its enthusiasm for recruitment and tournament sponsorship, and the activity also gained in response to the Covid pandemic. As with athletics and dance, however, some children were involved without becoming narrowly specialized.[31]

Widespread interest in music participation shared characteristics with other activities organized for children, though there were also some revealing differences. Many parents, disproportionately middle class, thought music lessons should begin early, in some cases at age two but more commonly a few years later. As with athletics, some children's bands and choruses organized outside the school framework, though there was nothing like the cost or competitive atmosphere of travel teams. Schools themselves varied, most obviously by the wealth of the local school district, though many featured training on an instrument at least by middle school, and many were also eager to tout the cognitive benefits of music participation. A few music educators, though enthusiastic about the rewards of participating in music, also warned that children might be turned off by the amount of time it took to be at all proficient, in contrast to an easier sense of progress in early sports like T-ball.

Indeed, music involvement did turn out to be a bit different, though obviously it featured some of the same kind of adult management that sports or dance did, including the rise of specialized summer camps. Fewer children participated, in the first place. One study suggested that 24 percent of all high school students did at least a year of chorus, orchestra, or band—partly because so many more were drawn away to demanding sports. (Other estimates varied, but they suggested a similar range.) Gender ratios contrasted with sports, with about 20 percent more girls involved by the early twenty-first century. Racial disparities were less marked than with sports overall, though children from wealthier families were somewhat overrepresented; 58 percent of the participants were white. Most importantly, the competitive atmosphere simply did not develop to the same degree, though there was some pressure simply to get into a band and an informal sense of rivalry, particularly among marching bands, from one school to the next in a given region. Parents were less intense. While performance levels mattered—particularly for the handful intending to continue music in college—there was no belief that doing band was going to get you into Princeton. Indeed, even in many universities that had a big marching band program, like Ohio State, targeted scholarships were not offered. Beyond the structured units, some high school students formed their own musical groups, another contrast with sports. Music participation patterns, in other words, offer a reminder that not every organized activity for children was caught up in the same level of frenzy, and there were other pockets, like student theater, that might make the same claim. Sometimes, children still just had fun, enjoying the activity and the chance to socialize with friends, even when some adult structure was involved.[32]

Assessment: Another Crisis?

Changes in children's play since the 1950s raise a host of issues about adult attitudes toward children and about children themselves. There is little question that adults, overall, increasingly soured on spontaneous play for the young, though they may not have been aware that they were doing so. "Safetyist" concerns about risk-taking, anxieties about leaving children unattended, increasing eagerness to see children get ready to qualify for major hurdles like college admission, and the heightened sense of a competitive environment, all combined to produce more effort at supervision and structure. A really interesting issue is whether many adults stopped enjoying the sight of children's play as much as in the past, a point suggested by the larger changes in child-involved culture as well. The increased average age of the new parent might have factored in: older parents, with all the best intentions, might convey a narrower approach to children's play. Practical problems, like the increasing scarcity of children in many neighborhoods, also served to challenge play; here was a huge issue, if not always widely recognized. Yet there was great variety as well, including the special guilty feelings of some single or divorced parents that so often heightened a commitment to providing pleasure but also those parents who, for whatever reason, were unusually sympathetic to childish flights of imagination.

Also impinging from the adult side were the growing number of organizations eager to sell goods and activities to or for children. Here too there was complexity. Howard Chudacoff describes the increasingly careful efforts by toy manufacturers to study cues from children themselves, as they developed the new batch of playthings. Children also played a growing role in shopping. Not everything was imposed from above. Still, children's activities were increasingly surrounded not only by changing parental attitudes but by the ploys of a variety of commercial agents—including the new organizers of the travel team industry or the providers of theme-based birthday parties.[33]

As to children themselves, assessments range from deep pessimism to qualified admiration of the ways many children still manage to retain some autonomy in play. Some play theorists are simply appalled. Convinced of the vital importance of unstructured play, they see the changes of the past half century as responsible for all the ills of contemporary childhood, from rising obesity to the growing reports of mental illness, narcissism, suicides, and breakdowns in emotional control. As Peter Gray, one of many concerned critics, puts it: "Without play, children fail to acquire the social and emotional skills necessary for healthy psychological development." A major 2023 study attributes the rise of new psychological ailments primarily to the decline of play. Some claims go even further, contending that adults themselves now have trouble really having fun—in part because they lacked the experience of play as children.[34]

While no relevant scholar disputes serious downsides to recent trends, some take a slightly more nuanced view, noting among other things the resourcefulness of children and the variety of contemporary situations. Thus, Howard Chudacoff again, in his chapter on the late twentieth century, talks of how children's play goes "underground" but does not disappear. Convinced as well of a substantial and troubling decline of play, he nevertheless notes how children continue to manage using toys for purposes for which they were not intended, to create their own play worlds, or how they manage to defy adult authority directly, gaining time and materials for genuine play.[35]

It is also important to recognize that the many activities that have accumulated to replace play often leave some wiggle room. Team sports, camps, and other ventures are often serious commitments, but intentionally or not they leave space for forming friendships, gaining social skills, and simply goofing off. Younger children can and do take advantage of preschool groups and play dates. Even for older children, some structures are more intense than others. It is also relevant to acknowledge the growing importance of household pets for many children, though this is not an entirely new theme. Data over time are somewhat elusive, but it has been estimated that by the twenty-first century 40 percent of all children were born into a household with a pet and that 90 percent would have some experience with a pet during childhood, and with this there were often some important opportunities for play and emotional development. The decline of play is a real contemporary theme in the history of childhood, but it does not cast a uniform pall.[36]

Along with the general concerns, three issues may warrant particular attention.[37] One, which is not new but has taken on new dimensions, highlights the social inequalities involved in the decline of play and in the rise of substitutes. Children from poorer families may be less afflicted by problems like a dearth of same-age peers in the neighborhood, but they have demonstrably less access to many of the group activities that have gained ground, from well-appointed preschools to travel sports or summer camps. They also are less likely to have pets. They experience at least some of the decline in play, including outdoor play, without as much access to alternatives.

The second issue is the most familiar, aside from the general laments about play, but it is no less important as a result: the extent to which many children, from right before grade school on up, find themselves overorganized, stressed, and fatigued.[38] The grade school girl with a music lesson, dance and soccer practice, along with school, obviously has lost much time for unstructured play, but she may be stretched too thin in other ways as well. The same applies even more clearly to the high school student juggling classes, music, and at least one demanding sport, in a particularly competitive atmosphere, where reports of inadequate sleep time have predictably multiplied. Again, variety must be noted: some children developed admirable time-management skills and seemed unperturbed and others, of course, simply dropped out; but there were potential problems overall.

The third issue is loneliness, perhaps the most troubling but not easy to chart. Often, despite active parenting, many postmodern children were spending more time alone than ever before. One 2017 study suggests that, whereas only about 40 percent of children eighth grade and up spent an hour or more alone each day from the 1960s to 1990, with a dip in the early '90s, rates rose steadily thereafter, reaching about 55 percent right before the pandemic. The same chronological pattern applied to going out with friends: a pronounced dip beginning in about 1984 for eighth and tenth graders, with twelfth graders following suit a few years later.[39] But the sources of the new trends took shape earlier. For some young children, the absence of readily available playmates or siblings, plus the lack of much informal time with peers, might create great difficulties in forming deeper social links later on.[40] There might be less experience choosing and forming close friendships, of the sort many people still registered vividly in recalling their childhoods in the 1950s. Here is where the decline of so many relatively spontaneous, traditional games is most telling. When attention turned to signing slightly older children up for teams or music groups, those involved were often dealing with several different sets of peers rather than interacting more intensely with one set, and there was often little chance for informal follow-ups. Children from low-income families might not face these hurdles, but confinement because of unsafe neighborhoods could impose its own constraints. For all children, school environments provided the most obvious opportunities for contact after the early years, but in structured and supervised settings along with the measurable decline of free play. For many children also the interest in watching television began to cut into opportunities for social interaction, and the same would apply later on to some of the uses of social media after 2006. Here, problems were often particularly severe for children in low-income families that relied on television or cell phones to occupy the kids while adults attended to other responsibilities.

Many children of middle school and early high school age may have faced the greatest challenges. By this point they not only had more separation from hourly parental attention but also usually had more voice over what activities they wanted to participate in, and they might increasingly decide on none. Some might actually have become bored with the force-feeding of their grade-school years, without finding alternatives (other than television or social media, which some of them watch more than they had when they were younger). Or they might be excluded, particularly when sports became more competitive and more dependent on demonstrated skill. Organized leisure for older children had many drawbacks when it came to play, but exclusion from these activities—whether by choice or not—could be even worse. Many children, particularly in the suburbs, found themselves spending hours a day in isolated play with toys, watching their own bedroom television set or using social media in ways that measurably did not substitute for personal contact. For some a new and precarious dependence on the number of "likes" on social media reflected needs that were not being satisfied by more direct interactions with peers. The lack of play experience and play opportunities could be telling. The forced isolation imposed on children by the Covid pandemic made some of these issues more prominent, but they were not new.[41]

For adolescents, the result might spill over into one other measurable and surprising change from the 1990s onward: the measurable decline in sexual activity. Here, the new trend was not attacking centuries of tradition so much as the results of the 1950s and 1960s sexual revolution. And the concept of play may not clearly apply. But the trends were striking, in the United States and several other countries. Teenagers after about 2000 began sexual activities later than their twentieth-century predecessors had, they participated in sex less often even once they did begin, and they had fewer partners. According to one study, the percentage of teenagers reporting no sexual activity at all rose from 29 percent to 42 percent among males between 2009 and 2018, 49 percent to 74 percent among females. Gender distinctions were obviously significant (possibly reflecting differences in candor as well as behavior), but the pattern was general. Explanations ranged widely, but they identified many of the familiar targets. More distraction by more impersonal activities was clearly involved, particularly as social media kicked in. Increasing contestation about consent and gender roles, including greater likelihood of getting into trouble for a wrong move, clearly affected risk-averse young people. An apparent increase in undesired "rough sex" among some young people who did indulge was also cited. The availability of pornography and arguably intimidating portrayals of sexual prowess probably played a role, though masturbation (admittedly hard to measure) apparently declined as well. More broadly, relative lack of social skills, thanks to lessened opportunities for play earlier in childhood might have factored in. Certainly, the decline of sexual activity both reflected and furthered the possibilities for loneliness in later adolescence.[42] The decline of play arguably had a variety of consequences and connections.

A Larger Evaluation

Determining the extent and severity of the decline of play over the past half century is not an easy task. Problems of measurement combine with the obvious role of new opportunities, including the chance to use social media and computer games for new forms of play and social contact. Variety is another vital complication. Divisions by social class and residence loom large, but so do the diverse ways particular children respond to the range of leisure opportunities that are available to them. While it is significant that so many of these opportunities are more structured than before, the extent to which they inhibit playful, imaginative activities and intense social interactions varies greatly depending on the child.

Evaluation is clearly complicated by the fact that young people themselves are largely oblivious to the larger dimensions of change and often deeply committed to a belief that contemporary games and electronic opportunities have actually improved the quality of their leisure. Ask a college class, for example, about the decline of marble playing. The result? First a widespread ignorance of what marbles actually are or were. Second, once this hurdle is crossed, a deep belief that the superiority of electronic games is solely responsible (Apple even introduced an electronic marbles game in 2003, though it was not widely popular). Insistence on the decline of play, among other things, involves adult observers preempting children's own judgments about progress, always at best an awkward process.

Still, two points stand out. The first is simply that major changes have occurred in children's play and social settings, whatever the variety in individual response and whatever children's own beliefs about their new electronic world. Classic games have declined. Available outdoor space has narrowed. Informal time with other children has diminished, and aspects of this run through adolescence. In these important respects, childhood has become different from what it was just a generation or two ago. The contemporary American child is a less playful child.

Second, play theorists and other observers of children have been noting and lamenting these developments for several decades, making the same good, basic arguments about the harm the decline of play does to many children.[43] They have not managed to reverse the tide, though the rise of "free range" parenting picks up their message to a degree. In ending his essay on the decline of play, Peter Gray approvingly cites a statement by Hillary Clinton: "But I'm hopeful that we can regain the joy and experience of free play and neighborhood games that were taken for granted growing up in my generation," concluding that "restoring free play" is the greatest gift we can provide for children today. But he does not say how this can be done.[44] Wise critiques have yet to make a major mark.

How important are the huge changes in children's play compared to the concomitant shifts in family life and school experience (to which they are clearly related) in shaping the contemporary child? For some—given the fact that most people are not play theorists—the temptation to dismiss them as interesting but somehow a bit more trivial may run strong. Yet their magnitude is striking, as are the links to other issues of sociability and mental health. The category looms larger than is sometimes recognized—and, again, it has proved distressingly hard to address.

The American Child: The Transformation of Childhood Since World War II. Steven Mintz and Peter N. Stearns, Oxford University Press. © Oxford University Press 2025. DOI: 10.1093/9780197797112.003.0007

8

The Changing Face of Children's Culture

Since 2000 girls aged eight to twelve have become the fastest-growing market for cosmetics in the United States. Retailers target tween girls not only for basic beauty products like lip gloss, eyeliner, mascara, eyeshadow, nail polish, and blush but also high-end moisturizers, body lotions, eye creams, and perfume, along with mini fridges to store these skincare products. Driven by media and marketing that are targeting younger demographics, the trend is a marker of earlier engagement with adult consumer values and unrealistic beauty standards and growing pressures on girls to conform to adult norms.[1]

This development did not occur overnight, nor, as authorities like Jonathan Haidt and Jean Twenge suggest, is it simply a product of the digital age, including the impact of social media and social influencers (some of them children themselves). These have reinforced and exacerbated the trend, but they built on a larger development: the deregulation of advertising that occurred in the 1980s, which is a shift, at least in degree, unique to the United States. The development dramatically eased restrictions on marketing to children, exposing the young to intensified commercial pressures.

Other changes further contributed to this trend: an increase in children's allowances (averaging $30 a week by 2019)[2] and increasing parental concessions to children's pleas and whining—from a desire to promote happiness or simply minimize nuisance in busy adult lives. But the basic authors of change were not children nor parents; rather, they were the variety of commercial organizations that were finding new ways to reach them. To a greater extent than ever before, childhood became a market.

The results had profound implications for children themselves. Age compression is one: young children now encountered products and standards once aimed at teenagers. Barbie dolls, for example, initially aimed at young teens in the 1960s, now reached into much earlier ages: the average first Barbie for many became age three (and the 2023 Barbie movie was vigorously marketed to under-twelves).

In some cases—as with cosmetics and, arguably, many of the war-based video games—the process has gone further, breaking down previous barriers between childhood and adulthood, as regulations and norms that had shielded kids from the most extreme market penetration withered away. "Adultification" is a term initially applied to children who had to take on unusual responsibilities, but it now can refer to a broader process where children are treated as more mature than their actual age implies, exposing them to behaviors and standards traditionally considered appropriate for adults, including new levels of violence and sexuality. The result is an engagement with consumerist values and a self-consciousness about image—and often heightened levels of envy as well—from a young age.

The adultification of childhood raises several concerns about child development and well-being. It can lead to heightened stress and anxiety among children who feel pressured to meet adult standards without having developed the emotional, cognitive, and social skills to do so. It can also erode the space for childhood as a distinctive stage of life, where play and imaginative exploration occur freely and naturally.

The Background

Unlike golden ages that reside in a remote, shadowy past, many older adults are convinced that the golden age of American childhood existed within living memory, during the 1950s and early 1960s. Society, they believe, was more child-centered then and the postwar years were a much better time to grow up.

When older Americans consider the postwar era as a golden age of childhood, they wax nostalgic about specific foods, toys, movies, and TV shows that were emblematic of a simpler, more innocent time. These elements are not only remembered for their intrinsic qualities but also for what they represent about the culture and values of the era.

During that time there was a host of child-centered foods. Older adults associate TV dinners—those pre-cooked, frozen meals that can be reheated and eaten in minutes from an aluminum tray—with family gatherings around the television, blending mealtime with entertainment. They recall the sugary cereals marketed directly to children with cartoon mascots like Frosted Flakes' Tony the Tiger and the Trix Rabbit. They remember soda fountains and ice cream parlors, popular social spots for children and teenagers, which evoke nostalgia for a bygone era of innocence and community. They also recall a host of simple, inexpensive toys, like the Hula-Hoop, which encouraged physical play, in contrast with today's digital entertainment.

The movies too seemed more child-centered. The postwar years were a golden era for Disney animated films, with classics like *Cinderella* (1950) and *Peter Pan* (1953) becoming a beloved part of childhood for many. Family-friendly musicals like *The Sound of Music* and *Mary Poppins* were wholesome entertainment options that have stood the test of time.

Television shows also targeted children of every age. There was *Romper Room*, *Bozo the Clown*, *Captain Kangaroo*, and *Kukla, Fran and Ollie* for younger children, making childhood seem more innocent then. For somewhat older kids, *Lassie*, *Leave It to Beaver*, *The Mickey Mouse Club*, *Robin Hood*, and *Zorro*, with their emphasis on family values, adventure, and lessons learned, contrast with more recent fare, which emphasize more complex and often troubling themes.

The belief that the 1950s and early 1960s were more child-focused was the product of societal conditions unlikely to ever return. The postwar years were a time of rapid economic growth, with many families able to rely on a single breadwinner and many mothers staying home to look after their offspring. The growth of suburbia provided what many saw as an ideal environment for raising children, with a sense of closeness among neighbors that fostered a supportive environment for families along with greater freedom for unstructured outdoor play for groups of children themselves. With fewer sources of media and entertainment, children's exposure to commercial influences and adult themes was more limited compared to today's digital landscape. The shared experience of watching the same TV shows or listening to the same radio programs created a sense of unity and shared culture among children and families, contrasting with the highly fragmented media landscape of today. Though consumer culture was on the rise, the commercialization of childhood was not as advanced as it is today, leading to perceptions of a more innocent and less materialistic childhood.

While many older Americans cling to an idealized view of postwar childhood, it's important to acknowledge that nostalgia masks the complexities and inequalities of that era. It was also a time when as many as a third of young Americans spent part of their childhood in poverty, contradicting the era's image of universal prosperity. In addition, the social safety net was less developed than it is today. Programs specifically aimed at alleviating childhood poverty, such as food stamps (SNAP) and Medicaid, were not yet in place, leaving many children vulnerable. Diseases that are now preventable or treatable also made childhood a more precarious experience. The first half of the 1950s witnessed outbreaks of polio, which left thousands of children paralyzed and confined to iron lungs with life-long disabilities.

Further, the 1950s were marked by rigid gender roles, with societal expectations significantly limiting the aspirations and behaviors of girls. At the same time, legal and de facto segregation subjected African American and other children of color to inferior educational resources, recreational facilities, and health-care services.

In fact, a number of the challenges that children face today are rooted in developments that were just getting underway during that supposedly golden era. As with other crucial aspects of contemporary childhood, like increased schooling and inroads on play, the substantial transformation of children's culture began to take shape from the late 1950s onward, steadily accelerating even before the contributions of social media. Key changes included:

- The commercialization of childhood, that is, the targeted marketing to children, the creation of both more elaborate child-specific items and essentially adult fare, and the production of children's media, which contains integrated commercial messages or is tied to merchandise that children are encouraged to buy.
- The commodification of children's imagination, such as the development of children's movies, television shows, books, and digital content that are closely tied to product lines, encouraging children to extend their engagement from the screen or page to consumer products. Popular franchises, such as superhero universes or animated characters not only serve as anchors for extensive merchandise that includes toys, apparel, accessories, and even themed foods but also limit the scope of imaginative play to preestablished narratives and character roles, reducing input from children themselves.
- The digitization of childhood, the growing role of electronic and digital technologies in children's lives—from television to the Internet, streaming, video games, and social media—transforming how children play, learn, socialize, and engage with the world around them.

All of this enhanced the institutionalization of childhood, along with the rise of organized extracurricular activities, extended schooling, and formal day care. Though the motives of those eager to see children as a market differed from those of educational authorities, team coaches, or summer camp counselors, they shared in making a growing number of children, and children's socialization more generally, subject to adult guidance and manipulation.

The process of commercialization, commodification, and new media was fairly limited during the first three postwar decades, but the impact greatly intensified in the 1980s and 1990s, contributing to yet another important trend: the privatization of childhood. Access to commercially sponsored activities was heavily influenced by socioeconomic status, leading to deepening disparities in the benefits that children receive from these experiences. Quite generally, however, childhood itself came to be viewed as a private, rather than as a public, good, with children themselves a target market.

Unlike a public good approach that advocates for a collective responsibility and investment in children, regardless of their family's income or status, parents assumed primary responsibility for children's welfare, recreation, and development. Over time, there was an increasing reliance on market-driven solutions for child-related needs, making them accessible primarily to those with the means to afford them, exacerbating inequalities.

A fair-minded consideration must weigh gains against losses. It also raises significant questions about societal values and equity and how society can better support kids' well-rounded development while enhancing the joys and freedoms of childhood.

The Nature of Children's Culture

The children we live with also inhabit another world, a world that parents and teachers don't wholly control or amply appreciate. That parallel universe, children's culture, has its own values, styles, customs, tastes, interests, and traditions. Children's culture refers to the customs, practices, languages, forms of entertainment, and lifestyles that are shared, consumed, and created by children. It encompasses a wide range of elements, from toys, games, and playground activities to literature, music, television shows, and digital media specifically aimed at or emanating from children.[3]

Some of this culture's jokes, rhymes, games, and rituals are traditional, passed down from older to younger kids across multiple generations. Some are perpetuated by parents and teachers when they share fairy tales, nursery rhymes, folk songs, and games. Yet, while some aspects of children's culture remain relatively unchanged over time, others evolve or emerge in response to changes in technology, societal norms, and environmental factors. Popular shows, characters, songs, and franchises become integrated into children's play, inspiring new games, language uses, and imaginative scenarios. Kid culture reflects a complex interplay of tradition, commercial culture, emerging technologies, and children's agency in appropriating and transforming content to meet their needs.

Not just passive recipients of cultural forms, kids are active creators and innovators. They adapt traditional games to new contexts, invent new variations of rhymes, interact in shifting ways, and create entirely new forms of play that reflect their experiences and imaginations, ensuring that children's culture is a dynamic and ever-evolving space.[4]

In no domain can we better observe children's voice and agency than in children's culture—the meaning-making and expressive activities that include children's imaginative world, such as their folklore and humor; their social relationships, including their friendships and interactions with peers; their play, including games, sports, and computer and video games; and their consumption of commercial popular culture, whether books, television shows, or movies.[5] But for most adults, children's culture is terra incognito. Only a handful of scholars have investigated the secret spaces of childhood and systematically studied the dynamics and functions of kid culture. To a striking degree, the academy has left children's culture to poets and novelists.

There's the view associated with Lewis Carroll's *Alice's Adventures in Wonderland*, which depicts children's culture as a realm of fantasy, make-believe, magical thinking, and the fantastical—a dreamscape of untrammeled imagination. This view emphasizes children's creative potential, where magical thinking and make-believe play allow for the exploration of alternative realities and the stretching of the imagination beyond the constraints of the adult world. Carroll's depiction also suggests that through fantasy, children engage in a form of learning and discovery that is distinct from adult-led education. This imaginative exploration is crucial for cognitive and emotional development, providing a space for children to experiment with ideas, emotions, and identities in a relatively safe and boundless context.

There's also the perspective exemplified by William Golding's *Lord of the Flies*, which portrays children's culture as a Darwinian world marked by taunting, teasing, bullying, aggression, sadism, and the pursuit of status. Golding's narrative suggests that children's interactions can serve as a microcosm of human society that forces readers to confront uncomfortable truths about power and morality.

Then, there's the perspective represented by Mark Twain's Tom Sawyer and Huckleberry Finn novels, which depict a childhood culture of subversion and rebellion that revels in dirt, noise, and vulgar language and that demonstrates little regard for private property or the proprieties upheld by adults. This view celebrates childhood's independent spirit, where kids often resist adult norms and constraints, finding joy in disorder and disobedience. Twain's portrayal also serves as a critique of adult society and its moral and social conventions. By valorizing the freedom, ingenuity, and resilience of his young characters, Twain champions a more authentic, albeit unruly, form of living that challenges the pretensions and hypocrisies of the adult world.

Across history, adults have tended to treat children's culture dismissively or contemptuously, as a trivial, inconsequential world of fun and games that stands in stark contrast to the supposedly more rational, sensible, practical, and sophisticated world of adults. Yet we shouldn't be so flippant, for kid culture serves essential developmental and educational functions. Children's culture plays a pivotal role in kids' cognitive, social, and emotional growth, psychological well-being, identity formation, and socialization, including their understanding of gender roles and their sense of agency as well as the values and skills they acquire.

Children's culture is not static. It is, rather, dynamic, shifting in response to demographic and economic changes, transformations in technology, and equally important swings in social values. As we shall see, between the late 1940s and the 2020s, there has been a profound shift from regarding childhood as a time of innocence that needed to be insulated and shielded from adult realities to preparing children for the adult world, with a growing emphasis on educational achievement and an understanding of the risks that they might face, including the threats of bullying and physical and sexual abuse but also a growing eagerness to see childhood as a profitable market opportunity.

Children's culture is a critical arena for learning, socialization, emotional development, and identity formation. Engaging in make-believe play allows children to explore various scenarios, roles, and perspectives, fostering creativity, problem-solving skills, and cognitive flexibility. Through fantasy and imaginative play, children experiment with cause and effect, explore abstract concepts, and practice narrative construction.

Storytelling, rhymes, and games within children's culture contribute to language acquisition and literacy. Children learn new vocabulary, narrative structures, and communication skills through their interactions and play. Through games and exploration, children learn about the world around them. They develop an understanding of physical concepts (like gravity and spatial relationships), social concepts (such as fairness and cooperation), and abstract ideas (including time and change).

Children's culture is a critical context where kids learn how to interact interpersonally and negotiate, collaborate, compete, and empathize with their peers. Through their play, they practice social roles, discern norms, and learn about leadership, teamwork, and conflict resolution. At the same time, kid culture provides a safe space for children to express and manage their emotions. Pretend play, for example, can help children work through fears, anxieties, and frustrations, offering avenues for emotional catharsis and resilience building. Group play can encourage perspective-taking. By engaging with diverse characters and scenarios in stories and games, children learn to understand and relate to feelings and viewpoints different from their own.

In addition, children's culture encourages self-expression and the exploration of personal interests, preferences, and identities. Through their choices of play, dress, and media consumption, children express individuality and explore aspects of their identity. As children navigate their cultural world—making choices, solving problems, and creating within their play—they develop a sense of agency and competence. These experiences build self-confidence and a belief in their ability to influence the surrounding environment.

Most importantly, it's within children's culture that the next generation's sensibilities are formed and their identities are constructed. It's largely within children's culture that kids learn about gender roles and social hierarchies, which inform their understanding of their place in the broader social world and how they perceive right and wrong. Meanwhile, exposure to various forms of media and artistic expression within children's culture—ranging from literature and music to visual arts and digital media—shapes aesthetic preferences and sensibilities.

The social dynamics within children's culture, including peer groups and friendships, play a significant role in identity construction. Belonging to a group helps children define themselves in relation to others, developing a sense of self based on shared interests, values, and experiences.

Children's culture can also be a space of resistance against adult norms and expectations, where children assert their autonomy and individuality. This rebellion, whether through subversive play, humor, or adopting countercultural symbols, allows children to carve out distinct identities that challenge imposed roles.

The consumption of media and branded products is another avenue through which identities are constructed within children's culture. Preferences for certain brands, shows, or characters become markers of identity, aligning children with specific cultural groups or fandoms.

Children's culture is not merely a backdrop to childhood but an active, dynamic force in shaping how children see the world and themselves. By participating in this culture, children learn to navigate social relationships, develop personal and collective identities, and establish the sensibilities that will inform their future as adults.

Back to the '50s

Current nostalgia for the immediate postwar period, though often oversimplified, correctly reflects a framework for children's culture vastly different from that of the twenty-first century. In addition to wider opportunities for play, there was far less media saturation. Children's entertainment, beyond their own activities, was more limited to radio and print, plus some access to television sets almost entirely located in living rooms and centered around family viewing. Most media content was also heavily regulated, aimed at providing wholesome entertainment. Overall, despite some shared interest in family TV shows, with content that could be enjoyed by all ages without concern about inappropriate themes, there seemed to be a stronger demarcation between the world of childhood and the world of adults. Children were not targeted as aggressively by advertisers, and toys and entertainment were simpler, often non-electronic, less expensive, and seen as encouraging creativity and imagination in ways that contemporary digital entertainment does not.

To truly understand the nuances and texture of children's culture during the postwar era, firsthand accounts, such as memoirs and autobiographies are essential. These primary sources offer a window into the experiences, perceptions, and emotions of children from that period, helping us to comprehend how play and children's culture differed from today. They also remind us of the crucial disparities in postwar childhood, some of which have been reduced in more recent decades—again, nostalgia should not carry us away.

Vietnam War veteran Ron Kovic's memoir, *Born on the Fourth of July*, which later became a Hollywood blockbuster film starring Tom Cruise, provides a poignant and deeply personal reflection on postwar boyhood. Through his narrative, Kovic illuminates several defining characteristics of that era's boyhood experience, which offers insights into how societal values, physical landscapes, and cultural practices shaped their development and perceptions of masculinity and patriotism.[6]

Kovic notes the ready availability of large numbers of boys to participate in play, reflecting a time when community bonds were strong and neighborhoods teemed with children of similar ages. This abundance of potential playmates facilitated a culture of spontaneous, unstructured play, which stands in stark contrast to the more scheduled and supervised play activities common in contemporary children's lives.

His memoir highlights the significant amounts of undeveloped land where children could roam and play free of adult supervision. This freedom to explore and engage with the natural environment fostered a sense of adventure and independence among boys, encouraging imaginative play and physical activities that are often more restricted in today's more urbanized, litigious, and safety-conscious society.

Kovic also emphasizes the central role of team competitions in boys' sports and games, underscoring the importance of physical prowess, teamwork, and competition in shaping boys' identities and social hierarchies. This focus on competitive sports as a key component of boys' culture reinforces traditional notions of masculinity, emphasizing strength, stoicism, endurance, teamwork, and leadership.

The memoir vividly describes how patriotic parades, war movies, and Westerns hammered home a web of values and beliefs about patriotism. This cultural backdrop served to glorify military service and the ideals of heroism, sacrifice, and national pride, deeply influencing boys' perceptions of their roles and responsibilities within society. This pervasive sense of patriotism contrasts with the more diverse and questioning attitudes toward nationalism and military service prevalent in contemporary culture.

A particularly striking contrast with contemporary boys' culture is the prevalence of gun play in Kovic's boyhood. This aspect of play, normalized within the context of postwar America's fascination with military and Western heroes, reflects broader societal attitudes toward guns and violence. In contemporary society, concerns about gun violence and a greater awareness of its implications have led to a more cautious approach to gun play in children's games.

Homer Hickam's *Rocket Boys* offers another vivid and inspiring portrayal of post-World War II boyhood, particularly focusing on the impact of science and the space race on the aspirations and imaginations of young people during this era. The memoir recounts the true story of Hickam and his friends in the late 1950s in Coalwood, West Virginia, as they embark on a journey of amateur rocketry, driven by their fascination with the Soviet Union's launch of Sputnik.[7]

The memoir illustrates how the space race and advances in science and technology served as sources of inspiration for Hickam and his peers. The launching of Sputnik by the Soviet Union ignited a sense of wonder and possibility, motivating the boys to dream big and pursue ambitions beyond the expected paths laid out for them in a coal-mining town. This reflects a broader cultural moment in which scientific achievement became linked to national pride and personal aspiration.

Hickam's story reveals the complex dynamics between the boys and their families and community. The narrative shows how the boys' scientific interests created new forms of community engagement and dialogue, challenging traditional expectations and roles within their coal-mining town. For Hickam and the other rocket boys, science became a crucial part of their identity formation. Their engagement with rocketry set them apart and gave them a sense of purpose and belonging. This reflects a time when science and technology were increasingly seen as avenues for individual achievement and societal contribution, resonating with the broader optimism of the postwar era.

Susan Allen Toth's *Blooming* paints a vivid picture of girlhood in the 1950s in Ames, Iowa. Unlike narratives that focus on political events or technological innovations, Toth's memoir provides insight into the everyday experiences, challenges, and joys of postwar girlhood in a small-town American setting. In contrast to Kovic and Hickam, Toth's focus is indoors rather than outdoors. She describes the sibling rivalry between herself and an older sister, slumber parties, finding refuge in a local library, and trips to a family cabin.[8]

Her account underscores the prevailing societal expectations and gender roles that shaped girls' lives in the postwar era. Girls were often groomed for future roles as wives and mothers, with a strong emphasis on domestic skills and virtues such as modesty and compliance. Toth reflects on these expectations, exploring how they influenced her ambitions, relationships, and self-perception.

In her account of growing up female in the 1950s, *Young, White, and Miserable*, Wini Breines, a sociologist, analyzes the contradictions and constraints of growing up female in a decade often idealized for its economic prosperity and social stability, but which was also marked by rigid gender norms and a backlash against women's aspirations for autonomy.[9]

Breines discusses how the 1950s saw a reinforcement of the cult of domesticity, in which women's roles were primarily defined as wives and mothers within the nuclear family. This ideology was propagated through various media, including magazines, movies, and television shows, which glorified domestic life and pushed young girls to aspire to marriage and motherhood as their ultimate goals. The book lays bare the intense social pressure on young women to conform to feminine ideals that emphasized passivity, compliance, and physical attractiveness. Breines points out how these pressures were not only external but internalized by girls themselves, leading to issues with self-esteem and identity.

Young, White, and Miserable also addresses the role of education in shaping girls' futures. Despite improvements in educational access, there was still a strong societal expectation that women would not pursue long-term careers. Educational and professional aspirations were often sidelined in favor of preparing for a life of domesticity. This led to a situation where women were educated but with limited prospects for using their education outside the home.

Breines articulates a sense of dissatisfaction among young women, stemming from the narrowness of the paths available to them. This discontent sometimes led to forms of rebellion, though these were often private and personal rather than public or political. The book traces the roots of the feminist movements of the 1960s and 1970s to these feelings of dissatisfaction and the desire for a life beyond traditional roles.

Even though children's postwar culture was more homogenous than its contemporary counterpart, it is, of course, important to acknowledge its diversity. Ruth J. Simmons's *Up Home* recounts her extraordinary journey from Jim Crow Texas, where she was the youngest of twelve children in a sharecropping family to the presidencies of Smith College and Brown and Prairie View universities. Her description of a childhood in an isolated, rodent-infested, tin-roofed, clapboard shack with a wood-burning stove, without shoes, and with no running water, electricity, or store-bought clothes, coupled with regular whippings, is incredibly vivid and sounds more like the 1880s than the 1950s. She recalls that "there was never enough to eat," which led one of her sisters to try "to eat a raw bird; another ate lye from a can she found in the house." She also describes how growing up in a segregated society strewn with racial indignities, humiliations, and abuse left an impact on her childhood home—and how "racism had reduced my father to a shadow of the man he could have been, and he turned the demeaning arrogance that had victimized him on my mother, making her subservient to him in every way." However, thanks to a series of mentors and to the books that she read, she was able to acquire "an interior life that blunted the ugliness of my daily life." Still, she felt deep inner conflict and guilt "about leaving my familial culture behind."[10]

Her life provides a vivid reminder about the dangers of nostalgia. Hindsight isn't twenty-twenty and rose-colored memories invariably distort and sanitize past realities. Still, memoirs like hers remind us of the profound differences between the fairly recent past and the present.

Transformation Through Commercialization

Postwar children's culture was commercialized to an extent, particularly since the rise of television involved advertising that was targeted directly to children as well as the creation of more child-themed products. Even radio had featured appeals to a child market. However, the scope and scale were far more limited than what began to develop in the later twentieth century.

During the 1950s and 1960s toys ranged from simple, traditional playthings like dolls and trains to the first generation of electronic and battery-operated gadgets. Mr. Potato Head, which was introduced in 1952 and was the first toy advertised directly to children on television, originally sold for about 98 cents, which equates to approximately $9 or $10 in 2025. The wildly popular Slinky, a spring-like toy that could climb up or down stairs, sold for around $1 at the time, equivalent to about $10 or $11 today. The Hula-Hoop, a simple plastic ring that kids twirled around their waist debuted in 1958 and sold for approximately $1.98, which would be around $17 or $18 now.

Modestly more expensive toys began to appear in the late 1950s. The original Barbie doll, which appeared in 1959, sold for $3, which is about $26 today. The original G.I. Joe action figures, which were introduced in 1964, sold for around $4, which would be approximately $32 today. Etch-A-Sketch, a mechanical device that allowed kids to create images by turning dials, was introduced at a price of $2.99, equivalent to about $25 now. Meanwhile, a small, basic Lego set started at around $1.50 to $3, equating to about $13 to $26 today. Larger sets could cost significantly more, even up to $10 or $20 at the time, which would be roughly $85 to $170 today.

To be sure, given lower average household incomes, toys that seem quite inexpensive by today's standards represented a more significant expenditure for families at the time. Still, they were far cheaper than the new electronic toys that began to be introduced in the 1970s. Alongside inexpensive toys like the Nerf ball, a soft, safe ball that could be played with indoors and which cost around $4, and Uno, a now-classic card game that cost between $3 and $5 at the time, there were the first video-processor-powered toys that could speak and the first video game consoles. Speak & Spell, which was among the first handheld electronic devices to use a visual display and a speech synthesizer to vocalize words, was marketed as an educational toy that could guide children through spelling exercises and games. It originally cost $50 in 1978, which is about $200 today. The Magnavox Odyssey video game player, introduced in 1972, had a $100 price tag, equivalent to $600 today. Atari Pong, which appeared three years later, cost $98.95.

During the 1970s, there were concerted efforts by nonprofit organizations like ACT (Action for Children's Television) to limit children's exposure to ads and tie-ins—links among commercial products and television programming—much as European societies were doing. In 1978 the FTC (Federal Trade Commission) proposed a rule that would ban all advertising to children under age eight and require nutrition disclosures in sugary food TV ads to kids aged eight to eleven. The commission emphasized the inability of young children to distinguish ads from other sources of information and the resulting susceptibility to manipulation, either for direct purchases or, more commonly, to place pressure on parents by whining. The so-called Kid Vid regulations were strongly opposed by the advertising and broadcasting industries, which argued that such rules would infringe on commercial free speech and lead to a reduction in children's programming due to the loss of advertising revenue.

Indeed, a number of powerful lobbies formed aiming to reverse these regulatory efforts. Commercial television channels—which argued that the "very existence" of children's television was at stake—were joined by the food lobby, eager to sell sugared products to kids. By 1980 that lobby had a budget about a third as large as that for the whole FTC. The tide began to turn.

There was a sharp shift in the regulatory framework during the presidency of Ronald Reagan. Rather than viewing kids as a vulnerable demographic that needed to be protected, children were increasingly seen as market to exploit. In 1981 the FTC formally dropped its attempts to restrict advertising to children, citing concerns about the feasibility of enforcing such a ban and its implications for free speech. "While the rule-making record establishes that child-oriented television advertising is a legitimate cause for public concern," the agency declared, "there do not appear to be at the present any workable solutions which the commission can implement." Even a concern that sugared products caused cavities was put off with the claim that further study was needed. The year following deregulation, each of the top ten best-selling toys was tied into a television show, including Transformers, G.I. Joe, Care Bears, Voltron, M.A.S.K., Cabbage Patch Kids, He-Man, Super GoBots, WWF Figures, and My Little Pony.[11]

Today, advertising to children is governed by a mix of federal regulations, industry self-regulation, and various state laws. The approach reflects a sense that children, recognized as a vulnerable audience, should be protected from misleading and manipulative advertising practices. The Children's Television Act of 1990 regulates the amount and content of advertising during children's programming on broadcast television and requires broadcasters to provide educational and informational programming for children. The Children's Online Privacy Protection Act, enacted in 1998 and updated since, empowers the FTC to protect children under thirteen by restricting the collection and use of personal information from children by websites and online services, including for advertising purposes, and requiring parental consent for data collection. At the same time, the advertising industry, through the voluntary Children's Advertising Review Unit of the Better Business Bureau, has rules covering product placement, disclosures, and online privacy. However, the efficacy of these regulations and guidelines remains unclear, especially since many children consume media targeted at adults and because marketers have found loopholes, like reliance on social media influencers, to evade any restrictions.

Not surprisingly, the relatively free-wheeling American approach contrasted sharply with measures being developed in other affluent countries. While there were national variations, most European nations viewed advertising for children in a far more skeptical light, under overall direction from the European Union. Sweden banned ads to kids under twelve outright, in a 1996 law—not only during children's shows but immediately before and after. Spain, citing the "protection of youth and childhood," forbade any advertising in children's shows lasting thirty minutes or less. While this has not prevented some increase in marketing budgets directed at children, the growth is many times less than what occurred in the United States.[12]

For from the 1980s onward, American advertising budgets for child audiences soared. One estimate holds that where in the 1970s about $100 million targeted childhood, by the 2020s the figure was $17 billion—with much of the growth in the last two decades of the twentieth century. By the 2020s it was estimated that the average American child above infancy was seeing 40,000 ads each year. Not surprisingly, when contemporary children were asked what they wanted for a special occasion, like a birthday, the response almost always reflected that latest advertisement or online solicitation; the introduction of "wish lists" provided yet another opportunity to catalogue what children have been told to want, though filtered to some extent by different individual interests.

Colonization of Children's Imagination

Accompanying the increasing commercialization of childhood is what we might call the corporate colonization of children's imagination, with franchises and branded content increasingly dominating much of children's media. This shift toward heavily branded and merchandise-driven content may well limit the scope of children's imaginative play to preexisting characters and narratives. The rise of tie-ins is particularly striking: a product now featured in a kids' movie or TV show also shows up in a doll or some other item that "must" be purchased, sometimes along with a corresponding theme emphasis in one of the fast-food outlets. The children are surrounded.

In certain respects, mass media, especially television and movies, became more child-centered after the 1950s. Whereas children's television programming in the medium's early years was confined to Saturday mornings and a few brief after-school hours, programming for kids can now be found on a cable channel or a streaming platform like YouTube any hour of the day. Since the 1980s Disney-produced children's musicals, kid-oriented animations like *Shrek* and *Despicable Me*, epics like the Star Wars films, and the Lord of the Rings and Harry Potter series of movies aimed at children have become among Hollywood's most consistently profitable franchises.

Yet the pervasiveness of programing targeting kids, plus various commercial tie-ins, including branded toys and other products, has quite rightly prompted fears of the corporate colonization of children's imagination. Many adults also worry about the decline in certain realms of publishing for children. Innocent magazines like *Highlights for Children*, slow-paced TV shows like *Captain Kangaroo* and *Mr. Rogers Neighborhood*, and educational programming along the lines of *Mr. Wizard*, a science show, all disappeared by the early twenty-first century.

Strikingly, the widely hailed children's show that did manage to survive well into the twenty-first century was not as benign as its reputation might suggest. A growing concern has emerged that even nominally child-friendly and educational shows like *Sesame Street"*—which was celebrated since its inception in 1969 for its use of television as a medium to teach basic literacy, numeracy, and social skills—have had an adverse impact on kids. One criticism is its reliance on short segments and rapid editing, which can contribute to shorter attention spans in children. The show's fast pace, designed to keep children engaged, might condition young viewers to expect constant stimulation and, as a result, struggle with focusing on slower-paced tasks or longer narratives. Questions have also been raised about how the format of *Sesame Street* contrasts with the traditional learning environments children encounter in school. The quick cuts and variety of short segments are very different from the more extended focus required in a classroom setting, potentially leading to challenges when children transition to formal education.

But the biggest source of concern centers on *Sesame Street*'s extensive merchandising of character-related products, from toys and clothing to books and games. While these products can reinforce educational messages and provide additional revenue for the show's educational initiatives, there is concern that marketing these products to children can encourage consumerism from a very young age. The sale of character-related products has also raised questions about whether the need to maintain a marketable image for characters has influenced the show's educational priorities and content decisions. Clearly, the growing commercialization of children's culture has a long reach.

A balanced understanding of the changes that have occurred in children's media must also, however, recognize genuine gains as well as losses. To take one striking example, since the 1950s, feminism and a heightened sensitivity toward diversity have significantly influenced the Disney animated musicals, leading to more nuanced, empowering, and inclusive films. These influences have reshaped the themes, character development, and narratives of Disney's films, moving from traditional portrayals of gender roles and cultural homogeneity to more complex and inclusive representations.

While the 1950s are often considered part of the golden age of animation, featuring Disney classics like *Cinderella* (1950) and *Peter Pan* (1953), these films had little to no representation of non-white characters or cultures, except in stereotypical or marginal roles. They typically featured clear distinctions between good and evil, with gender roles often traditionally defined: male characters embarked on adventures, while female characters were often relegated to roles of damsels in distress or nurturing figures or else were portrayed as perpetrators of evil, like the Evil Queen in *Snow White and the Seven Dwarfs* (1937) or Cruella de Vil in *One Hundred and One Dalmatians* (1961).

As the feminist movement gained momentum from the 1970s onward, there was a gradual shift in how female characters were portrayed in Disney films. More complex and capable female characters appeared, challenging traditional gender roles. This trend accelerated in the 1990s and 2000s, with characters like Mulan (1998) and Merida from *Brave* (2012) embodying themes of independence, strength, and defiance against societal expectations.

Early Disney films often featured female protagonists whose stories revolved around finding love, with characters like Cinderella and Snow White fitting into traditional gender roles. Feminism's influence is evident in the evolution of Disney's female characters, who have become increasingly independent, strong, and complex. Modern Disney heroines, such as Moana (2016) and Elsa from *Frozen* (2013), are characterized by their determination and their focus on personal growth rather than romantic fulfillment. Feminist values have also encouraged Disney to emphasize themes of empowerment, agency, and self-discovery. Films like *Mulan* and *Brave* showcase heroines who challenge societal expectations and pursue their paths, highlighting the importance of courage, resilience, and the quest for identity. While earlier Disney films often culminated in marriage or romantic love, more recent films have focused on a broader range of relationships, including friendship, familial bonds, and self-acceptance. This shift away from the traditional happily-ever-after narrative reflects a feminist understanding of women's diverse experiences and aspirations.

Disney's approach to cultural diversity has also evolved significantly, with a deliberate shift toward more inclusive storytelling. During the 1990s Disney movies began to feature protagonists and stories from a variety of ethnic and cultural backgrounds, such as *Aladdin* (1992) and *Pocahontas* (1995), attempting to move beyond stereotypical portrayals and celebrate cultural richness and diversity. The corporation's more recent films feature characters from a variety of ethnic backgrounds and cultures and make a concerted effort to accurately and respectfully represent different societies. *Moana*, *Coco* (2017), and *Raya and the Last Dragon* (2021) showcase a much greater commitment to authenticity and sensitivity in portraying cultural stories, traditions, and values than did *Song of the South* (1946), *The Three Caballeros* (1944), or the original *Jungle Book* (1967). There has been a deliberate move toward more inclusive storytelling, featuring characters from a variety of ethnic backgrounds, cultures, and experiences. In response to criticisms of its past representations of race, ethnicity, and culture, its films have sought to promote understanding and tolerance.

In addition, there were attempts to tackle complex themes such as environmentalism, mental health, and the nuances of good and evil, moving beyond the clear-cut moral tales of earlier decades. Films like *Inside Out* (2015) and *Zootopia* (2016) explore emotions, identity, and social issues in ways that were intended to resonate with both children and adults, mirroring ongoing societal conversations around gender, culture, and identity.

While in some respects mass media has become more child-centered and offers many benefits in terms of accessibility, educational content, production values, and entertainment quality, it also poses challenges related to overcommercialization, the blurring of the line between entertainment and advertising, and the impact on children's creativity and imagination. With so much content produced and distributed by a relatively small number of large corporations, corporate-produced images and stories likely limit the diversity of creative thought and the development of independent imaginative capabilities. Also, the sheer volume of available content raises concerns about overexposure and the potential for passive consumption, where children become accustomed to being entertained rather than actively engaging their own creativity and imagination in play. For many children the limitations on imagination are very real—and another vital feature of contemporary American childhood.

The results are no mere abstractions. Studies of American children from the late twentieth century onward show a serious erosion of many earlier cultural staples. Reading for pleasure has declined markedly. So has knowledge of many traditional children's rhymes and jokes—much like the decline of customary forms of play. Play with dolls declined (though it did not disappear), as did tinkering with chemistry sets or building imaginary forts. This was not the children's culture of the earlier twentieth century.[13]

Electronics

Apart from childhood's increasing commercialization and the growing role of popular media in children's lives, there are other consequential developments that deserve more attention than they sometimes receive. The most obvious is the increasing role of electronics in children's lives. During the 1950s and 1960s, the main electronic influence was the television, which was becoming a staple in American households. Its impact was significant but limited by the number of channels and broadcast hours. But since the 1960s, the role of electronics in children's lives has expanded exponentially, initially with the advent of video game consoles and subsequently with personal computers, smartphones, tablets, and apps. This has transformed how children play, learn, and socialize, making digital interaction a central aspect of modern childhood.

With fewer siblings and fewer near-age peers living nearby, opportunities for traditional sibling and peer play declined and reliance on mediated forms of entertainment measurably increased. At the same time, the rise in dual-income families and single-parent households and parents often busy with work commitments, children spent more unsupervised time alone or, conversely, acquired more structured schedules that leave both them and their parents eager for easy distraction in the hours that are free. As a result, children are spending more time not only in day care, after-school programs, and other organized activities that shape their social and cultural experiences but also in front of a television set, a computer screen, a video game console, or a smartphone by themselves. With less time for unstructured outdoor play, engagement with digital media helps keep kids distracted and out of their parents' hair.

Many of today's worries fixate on the adverse impact of social media on children. It's noteworthy that the US government only began to survey Internet and smartphone access by children ages three to eighteen in 2016. What we have learned is that between 2019 and 2022 the amount of time that tweens between the ages of eight and twelve spent using screens and social media rose from four hours and forty-four minutes a day to five hours and thirty-nine minutes; the figure increased from seven hours and twenty-two minutes to eight hours and thirty-nine minutes for teens thirteen to eighteen. Some of that increase arose in response to the pandemic, but the use of social media and technology has remained high even in the pandemic's wake, with a quarter of teens saying that they use apps like TikTok, Snapchat, Instagram, and YouTube "almost constantly."[14]

The introduction of every new technology, from the movies and radio to the 45-rpm record, the transistor radio, and television, has prompted fears for children's well-being, but there can be no doubt that digital technologies are different, precisely because the gatekeepers that restricted what children could see or hear barely exist. According to a 2021 study, more than two-fifths (42 percent) of children have a cell phone by the age of ten. By age twelve, that figure is 71 percent and by age fourteen, 91 percent.[15] Access to information is much more unfiltered than in the past. We have come a long way from a time when a child had to climb a bookcase to catch a glimpse of *Fanny Hill* or their father's collection of *Playboy* magazines. Nowadays, pornography is just a click away with the advent of the Internet. Age compressions—the exposure of younger children to material that used to be aimed at teenagers—is one clear result, as in the growing passion for cosmetics among younger girls. And while the social media giants make some bows to self-regulation, they are notoriously lax in some of the materials they make widely available to children.

This is the age of screens, and children now spend more time with interactive electronic media than any other form of entertainment. Today's children have never lived in a world without apps, streaming, video games, and the Internet. Adults find it increasingly difficult to monitor and regulate what even young children see.

Video games, played by 80 percent of boys, have spawned many of the same criticisms previously directed at television and the movies: that these games desensitize children to violence, undercut their ability to distinguish between fantasy and reality, and diminish the development of their imagination. Video games have also been blamed for fostering hyperactivity among the young and diminishing children's social skills by isolating kids from one another. In addition, adults fear that video games give even young children ready access to imagery that is more sexually explicit, misogynist, and brutally violent than that which was available to preadolescents in the past. For example, in one of the most popular video games, *Grand Theft Auto*, players can rape prostitutes and beat them to death with baseball bats.[16]

Again, the situation is more complex than a simple declension model would suggest. In fact, video game playing is far more social and not nearly as isolating as detractors fear. Not only do video game players often compete against one another, but their game playing experiences provide the basis for many of their conversations with friends. At a time when individual households and neighborhoods have fewer children, cell phones, instant messaging, email, and websites like YouTube and apps like Instagram and Tik Tok provide ways that the young can form and maintain meaningful and supportive relationships and express themselves creatively.

There is also evidence that video games enhance children's cognitive development, manual dexterity, motor skills, and visual acuity. These games can be cathartic, allowing kids to release tensions and express feelings and impulses that must usually be repressed. Video games also give girls and boys a chance to master and manipulate reality and create and control a fantasy world in which they can exercise power or agency. And, further, the video game aesthetic is only one example of the highly stylized, hyperbolic forms of expression that pervade contemporary entertainment.[17]

Increasingly, it's social media that has generated the most anxiety, apprehension, and alarm. Critics point with concern to a correlation between increasing use of social media and a decline in many girls' mental well-being. Although it does appear that social media has had a negative effect on a significant subset of girls, caution is necessary. Some of the problems blamed on social media, like bullying, existed previously; social media has only made them more visible. Also, other factors, including social isolation and a culture that sexualizes even young girls and places a premium on popularity, are likely contributing to higher rates of anxiety and depression. Then, there's a point too often ignored: All of the problems attributed to social media are in fact worse among adults, who report even higher levels of anxiety and depression and who have much higher rates of drug and alcohol abuse, suicides, and other kinds of antisocial behavior.

There is no doubt that electronic media serve a compensatory role in a society in which children's freedom to roam has been constricted by nervous parents, allowing "home-bound children...to extend their reach, to explore, manipulate, and interact with a more diverse range of imaginary places than constitute the often drab, predictable, and overly-familiar spaces of their everyday lives." Video games and other digital media also give expression to new kinds of narratives that are becoming increasingly common in various cultural genres: narratives that "lack the focus on characterization, causality, and linear plot development which defines classical storytelling and instead focus on movements through and the occupation of narrative space."[18]

Kids are not passive receptacles of media but active agents who play with and reinterpret what they see. Since the early twentieth century, children have constructed their identities and formed their culture out of symbols, images, and stories that they have adopted from the raw materials provided by popular culture. While many adults assume that children's consumption of media is purely passive, mind-numbing entertainment, in fact many interactions with media are playful—spontaneous, unstructured, and exploratory. Much as Cold War children's culture sought to prepare the young for a particular conception of the future, so too does contemporary children's culture: a twenty-first-century world dominated by new technologies.

Children's increasing engagement with electronic media has heightened adults' awareness of aspects of children's play and fantasy lives—especially the violent, the sadistic, and the scatological—which have long existed but were previously hidden from view. Since no movie or video game rating system can automatically preserve children's innocence, it makes sense to give the young the visual, technological, and media literacy skills they need to use new media critically and safely.[19]

There can be no doubt that digital technologies have had a big effect, especially on the subset of children who are especially vulnerable to the negative impact on their self-image and to online bullying. Digital technologies have indeed transformed the landscape of childhood, influencing how children play, learn, and socialize. But it's essential to recognize that their rise and popularity are a by-product of and compensation for broader societal changes and that they accompany the other shifts that have increased exposure to commercial and corporate influence.

The Issue of Autonomy

Over the past half century, children's cultural autonomy has eroded. During the 1950s and 1960s children often enjoyed a high degree of independence, with unstructured outdoor play and neighborhood exploration considered normal. There was a greater societal tolerance for risk in children's activities and many stay-at-home mothers monitored kids' play quite casually. At the same time, children were freer to explore their own culture, independent of what advertisers might try to push on them—if only because they encountered far fewer ads.

Since the 1950s the autonomy of children's culture has diminished, with increased adult supervision and structured activities and with the growing importance of commercialized cultural fare. Concerns over safety, alongside changes in urban design and lifestyle, have led to the decrease in independent outdoor play, while the rise of digital media also contributed to more time spent indoors. At the same time, an increase in commercial inroads into children's imagination significantly reduced autonomy from yet another direction.

Another implication of these changes is the increasing tendency to treat childhood as a private, not as a public, good. The result is a growing disparity in access to quality education, extracurricular activities, and even basic health care based on family income. This shift reflects broader trends toward privatization and familial or parental rather than social responsibility, impacting how children grow, learn, and play.

In terms of children's culture, social inequalities are both blatant and subtle, as almost all families, except the very poorest, attempt to provide children with some commercial goods, from TV sets to expensive birthday presents. On the blatant side: richer families can simply afford more stuff for kids. While it is vital to remember that 71 percent of children have a TV set in their own room, 29 percent do not, and while some of this reflects parental reluctance it can also reflect poverty; the same applies to computer access. The rising costs of the most popular toys create an obvious and significant class divide in childhood. On the subtle side: wealthier families, with more access to quality childcare, more opportunities to afford lessons and camps, undoubtedly have more ability to mediate some of the commercial pressures on children than many other families have. They can more readily enforce rules about phone use and provide alternatives to TV viewing or even video games for young kids. There are some downsides to this kind of parental oversight, which can limit children's autonomy in its own way and which hardly insulates kids from all commercial pressure, but it does suggest another social differentiator for children themselves.

We cannot bring back the post-World War II landscape of childhood, with its abundance of kids and its many vacant lots, fields, and woods that provided places for free, unstructured, outdoor group play. Yet, while it's true that demographic, economic, and familial changes make it impossible to return to the kind of childhood experienced in the 1950s and early 1960s, there are actionable steps society can take to mitigate some of the negative effects of developments—including changes in the nature of play, media consumption, and commercialization impacting children's lives—that have transformed children's culture. These steps should focus on creating environments that promote face-to-face interaction, unstructured play, physical activity, and creativity, while minimizing commercial influences and reducing the ability to see childhood primarily in terms of market opportunities. The contemporary history of intrusions into children's culture suggest obvious targets for remediation.

Beyond Nostalgia and Decline

Today, many adults view the history of children's culture through a declensionist lens, and not without reason. This perception of decline is partly rooted in nostalgia but also in changes in the nature of childhood itself.

Certainly, many older adults nostalgically recall their own childhoods as a time of greater innocence, freedom, and simplicity. The 1950s and early 1960s are remembered as a time of postwar economic prosperity and strong community ties, which are contrasted with today's economic strain and social fragmentation. Rosy retrospection, a psychological phenomenon in which past memories are recalled as more positive than they might have been at the time, certainly contributes to idealizing the postwar era.

The dramatic rise in digital technology and media consumption are often cited as a primary reason for the perceived decline. Concerns about screen time, social media, and the Internet's impact on children's attention spans, social skills, and mental health contrast sharply with the more analog and outdoor play of earlier decades. But as we have seen, the embrace of digital technologies is, in part, compensation for broader demographic, economic, and social transformations. Changes in family structure, with nearly three-quarters of mothers, even of very young children, working outside the home, have presented parents with a dilemma about how best to care for children when they aren't available and electronic media and platforms have provided part of the answer. At the same time, declining birth rates have encouraged kids to spend more time indoors and online, with technology providing a vehicle for virtual interactions.

To understand contemporary children's culture, it's important to look beyond technology and focus on the longer-term historical transformations that have shaped contemporary American childhood. The most important is the increased targeting of children by advertisers and the proliferation of branded content, which have contributed to a more commercialized and less innocent childhood, fostering fears that children are growing up too fast too soon.

While a declensionist perspective highlights genuine concerns about contemporary childhood, it also oversimplifies the past and doesn't account for the genuine advances that have taken place or the ways in which children today are navigating and contributing to their cultural landscapes. Viewing the changes in children's culture in the United States since the 1950s as a narrative of decline oversimplifies a much more complex history of change. A more nuanced approach must acknowledge gains as well as losses, including the growing attentiveness to diversity, disabilities, children's psychological life, and at least some of the gross inequalities that have characterized American childhood. This said, there remains a distinctive contemporary challenge: Thanks to increasing commercial license as well as new technologies and family needs, we have allowed too many external and manipulative impositions on children's culture.

The problem is not that society has changed too much. It is that contemporary society has failed to adapt adequately to the changes that have occurred and that are almost certainly irreversible. Each era presents children with unique challenges and opportunities. Historical perspective can help us understand what has been gained as well as what has been lost and can therefore provide a more empathetic view of contemporary childhood while spurring efforts to address today's problems.

As a society, we need to restrain the commercialization of childhood and the impact of corporate interests on children's values, desires, and self-image. We must also combat the omnipresence of digital technologies in children's lives and promote more opportunities for the independent expression of children's imagination, which, in the final analysis, offers the most efficacious response to the stress and anxiety that too many children experience.

The American Child: The Transformation of Childhood Since World War II. Steven Mintz and Peter N. Stearns, Oxford University Press. © Oxford University Press 2025. DOI: 10.1093/9780197797112.003.0008

9

The New Neurodevelopmental, Emotional, and Behavioral Disorders of Childhood

The paradox of contemporary American childhood unquestionably applies to children's health. By many measures, children's well-being is at an all-time high. Infant and childhood mortality is at or near the lowest rate ever, while rates of teen smoking, alcohol and drug abuse, and pregnancy have dropped to levels unseen since the early 1960s, if not earlier. Granted, there's an increasing number of children diagnosed with various chronic illnesses, but this is due to the paradox of progress: as we continue to reduce infant and childhood death rates, more children living with these conditions survive.

Almost all of the most common, classic ailments of childhood—like chicken pox, conjunctivitis, croup, diarrhea, ear infections, measles, mumps, and strep throat—are now largely preventable or treatable. Nevertheless, apprehension dominates the public narrative surrounding childhood. From the time a child is in the womb, parents agonize over potential birth defects, miscarriages, stillbirths, and pregnancy complications. This anxiety is fueled by the power of prenatal tests to identify almost 800 conditions, many of which lack effective treatment options.[1]

Post-birth, the anxiety only escalates as parents become fearful about sudden infant death syndrome, previously known as crib death, along with a myriad of other worries: from vision and hearing deficits, to spina bifida, cerebral palsy, and hydrocephalus, often referred to as water on the brain. To be sure, parents also worried in the past about premature labor and high blood pressure (preeclampsia) to ectopic pregnancies and birthing complications like placenta previa. In the post-World War II era, concerns about gender identity also occupied many minds.[2]

But the fears that plague the public most deeply today stand apart. The public spotlight is firmly on behavioral, emotional, developmental, and

As a society, we need to restrain the commercialization of childhood and the impact of corporate interests on children's values, desires, and self-image. We must also combat the omnipresence of digital technologies in children's lives and promote more opportunities for the independent expression of children's imagination, which, in the final analysis, offers the most efficacious response to the stress and anxiety that too many children experience.

9

The New Neurodevelopmental, Emotional, and Behavioral Disorders of Childhood

The paradox of contemporary American childhood unquestionably applies to children's health. By many measures, children's well-being is at an all-time high. Infant and childhood mortality is at or near the lowest rate ever, while rates of teen smoking, alcohol and drug abuse, and pregnancy have dropped to levels unseen since the early 1960s, if not earlier. Granted, there's an increasing number of children diagnosed with various chronic illnesses, but this is due to the paradox of progress: as we continue to reduce infant and childhood death rates, more children living with these conditions survive.

Almost all of the most common, classic ailments of childhood—like chicken pox, conjunctivitis, croup, diarrhea, ear infections, measles, mumps, and strep throat—are now largely preventable or treatable. Nevertheless, apprehension dominates the public narrative surrounding childhood. From the time a child is in the womb, parents agonize over potential birth defects, miscarriages, stillbirths, and pregnancy complications. This anxiety is fueled by the power of prenatal tests to identify almost 800 conditions, many of which lack effective treatment options.[1]

Post-birth, the anxiety only escalates as parents become fearful about sudden infant death syndrome, previously known as crib death, along with a myriad of other worries: from vision and hearing deficits, to spina bifida, cerebral palsy, and hydrocephalus, often referred to as water on the brain. To be sure, parents also worried in the past about premature labor and high blood pressure (preeclampsia) to ectopic pregnancies and birthing complications like placenta previa. In the post-World War II era, concerns about gender identity also occupied many minds.[2]

But the fears that plague the public most deeply today stand apart. The public spotlight is firmly on behavioral, emotional, developmental, and learning disorders like ADHD, autism spectrum disorder, attachment disorders, anxiety disorders, conduct disorders, eating disorders, intellectual disabilities, learning disorders, and a spectrum of emotional and mood disorders. These include chronic depression, bipolar disorder, low self-esteem, and learning disorders such as dyslexia (reading difficulties), dyscalculia (mathematics difficulties), dysgraphia (writing difficulties), and dyspraxia (fine motor skill difficulties). In addition, concerns about food allergies and children's interpersonal relationships, such as abuse or bullying, also cause significant anxiety.

Here, we will delve into a series of childhood disabilities that have drawn significant public concern: ADHD, autism, childhood obesity, dyslexia, and food allergies. One might well ask what insights cultural and social historians can offer that wouldn't be better answered by a child psychologist, epidemiologist, medical researcher, neurologist, neuroscientist, or pediatrician. Our answer is straightforward: we will explain why certain disabilities began to gain recognition at specific periods in history, why particular symptoms became the focus of public concern, and why certain treatment strategies came to be preferred.

A historical lens can shed light on issues that might otherwise go unnoticed:

- Why a particular disorder or disability only comes under public scrutiny at a specific point in time.
- Why the prevalence of certain childhood disabilities varies across different eras, geographical regions, and socioeconomic classes.
- How and why the definitions, comprehension, diagnosis, and treatment of these disorders have evolved over time.

As we will see, the new disorders and disabilities of childhood need to be understood within the context of several wider trends, such as:

- "Risk awareness"—the growing adult sensitivity toward both physical and psychological threats to children's well-being.
- "The psychologizing of childhood"—the increasing tendency to interpret children's behavior from a psychological viewpoint, with an emphasis on understanding their mental state and creating therapeutic treatments informed by psychological insight.

- "The scientizing and medicalizing of disabilities"—the transition from attributing disabilities to environmental, cultural, and situational factors, to understanding them through biological, genetic, and neurological explanations and categories.
- "Concept creep"—the phenomenon of previously rigid categories of disabilities broadening and becoming more flexible over time.[3]

Also, in understanding these disorders and disabilities, another key concept—of a "symptom pool"—needs to be introduced. This is the idea that, at specific periods in history, certain culturally specific symptoms emerge as dominant ways for children to express or respond to distress.[4] A historical analog might help explain this concept. In the late nineteenth century, two conditions were popularly diagnosed, especially among women: hysteria and neurasthenia. These disorders were associated with a variety of symptoms, from fainting and uncontrolled emotions to chronic fatigue, nervousness, insomnia, shortness of breath, and a host of other physical and emotional manifestations.

A purely physiological understanding of hysteria—that it was caused by disturbances in a woman's reproductive system—gave way, under the influence of figures like Sigmund Freud, to a belief that hysteria was a psychological condition caused allegedly by repressed trauma or unresolved psychological conflicts, often of a sexual nature. Hysteria no longer exists as a diagnosis, although its symptoms are sometimes regarded as conversion, dissociative, or somatic disorders. In 1980 it was removed from the *Diagnostic and Statistical Manual of Mental Disorders*, the handbook used by healthcare professionals to diagnose mental disorders.

Neurasthenia, a term introduced in 1893, was thought to be a condition of nervous exhaustion, attributed to the demands of modern life. It was often diagnosed in both men and women who were engaged in intellectual work, contributing to the perception that weakness of the nerves or emotional exhaustion was a disease of the educated and social elite. Although neurasthenia is still sometimes diagnosed in China and Japan, in the United States it, like hysteria, is regarded a historical relic, a vestige of a nineteenth-century understanding of the human mind. Hysteria and neurasthenia reveal how social and cultural contexts can shape the interpretation and treatment of illness and the way distress is expressed. In the case of contemporary childhood, the rise of many new disease concerns unquestionably reflects a changing cultural context—along with some measurable new symptoms.

The challenge centers on discussing the balance between cultural construct and "reality."[5]

Historicizing the New Disabilities and Disorders of Childhood

Although the newly recognized disabilities of childhood discussed in this chapter have distinct etiologies and symptoms, they nonetheless exhibit several shared characteristics. For one thing, awareness of these disabilities is relatively recent. We can pinpoint the first instances of autism or peanut allergies, which we cannot do with enduring diseases like malaria or tuberculosis. None of these neurodevelopmental or behavioral disorders is timeless; each entered public consciousness at a specific moment in history. For instance, dyslexia was first recognized as a distinct disorder toward the end of the nineteenth century, autism in the 1930s and 1940s, attention deficit disorders in the late 1950s, and peanut allergies in the 1980s.[6]

Yet while these disorders are new, they are not very recent. Therefore, it is a mistake to overemphasize the role of very recent developments, for example, fixating on the rise of social media, in understanding causation. As we shall see, the contributors to the emergence, evolution, and diffusion of these disorders require a more complex explanation.

The childhood disabilities that cause the greatest concern today—ADHD, autism, childhood obesity, food allergies, and developmental and learning disabilities such as aphasia, dysphagia, apraxia, dyspraxia, and dyslexia—are largely behavioral, emotional, and psychological. The disabilities of yesteryear, in contrast, were physical, often arising from birth defects, infectious diseases, bacterial infections, and accidents, and included blindness, deafness, paralysis, and deformities. In each case, these "new" disorders have looser and more contested definitions. Some are attached to physical symptoms, while others are more clearly psychological.

Unlike many earlier disabilities, the prevalence of these disorders seems to be on the rise. This contrasts with previous disabilities, which generally declined in the early twentieth century. This upward trend results from several factors, starting with the tendency for definitions to broaden over time. The psychologist Nick Haslam coined the term "concept creep" to describe the loosening of criteria for harm, abuse, or disability, thereby expanding the group affected by the condition.[7]

Why have such concepts become more flexible and comprehensive? Partially, this reflects a growing recognition that human behavior lies on a spectrum rather than being strictly divided into normal and abnormal. Equally significant is a shift in incentives and a gradual reduction in the stigma associated with certain disabilities. As recently as the 1960s, disabled children were often hidden away and even institutionalized. As recently as 1970, about a million children with disabilities were kept out of school. Today, acknowledging a disability can lead to benefits such as an individualized education plan in school, despite the continued presence of stigma.

Another distinguishing characteristic of these disorders is that their incidence varies greatly across different countries that are at the same level of economic development. Gender too seems to make a difference not only in the pervasiveness of these disabilities, but in its expression.

The definition and diagnosis of these disabilities is subjective in ways that differ markedly from other diseases and disabilities. Detection largely relies on subjective observations, and the diagnostic criteria have changed significantly over time, complicating the accurate comparison of prevalence rates across different periods.

Without a widely accepted scientific consensus on the root causes of these conditions, there is considerable debate over their origins and treatment. Lacking a universally accepted scientific understanding, a host of speculative theories arose to fill the gap, such as the thoroughly debunked but persistent notion that childhood vaccinations or so-called refrigerator mothers cause autism.

A historical approach in no way undermines the reality of these disorders or disabilities, dismisses them, or implies that treatments are random or ineffective. Various disorders almost certainly have different causes and contributors. A disorder or disability can partly be a cultural construct and a product of specific sociological circumstances, yet still be very real. The new childhood disorders result from a complex interaction among biology, neurology, and cultural, social, institutional, and professional environments. Thus, it is not surprising that their incidence, expression, and treatment varies widely across cultures.[8]

From historical analysis, we can glean some key insights. One is that the rising emphasis on biopsychological, genetic, and neurological explanations has led to an underestimation of environmental, cultural, and contextual factors, including the impact of social class. While the bio-neurological-psychological focus has yielded significant benefits, it has also resulted in a narrowing of perspective. In understanding these disorders, society needs to strike a better balance between the biological and the contextual. In essence, culture and context play a critical, yet underrecognized, role in the new childhood disorders and disabilities.

Of equal importance, the scientific, medical, and psychological labeling of these disorders and disabilities can adversely affect the expectations of parents and teachers and the self-perception, self-concept, and self-esteem of children themselves. The past half century has witnessed the rise of a conception of children as deficient, fragile, and vulnerable, even as this society has repudiated earlier notions about age-appropriate learning and speaks a great deal about cultivating resilience and grit. Excessively broad and inclusive definitions of disabilities may make it more difficult for children with these labels to forge an independent identity, cut the umbilical cord with parents, and think of themselves as active and competent agents who are capable of mastering essential skills, overcoming life's inevitable frustrations and barriers, and control their own fate.

The Historical Approach to the New Diseases

The historical approach is a vital means of facilitating a more nuanced understanding of the formation, comprehension, and treatment of particular disorders and disabilities, fostering greater empathy for both parents and children. Whether one is a physician, psychologist, or historian, it is crucial to explore the various factors—neurological, physiological, social, behavioral, cultural, and environmental—that shape the understanding of these disorders and disabilities. The approach is all the more essential in a culture increasingly shaped, since the 1960s, by psychologizing assumptions.

Historians can shed light on these new disabilities, which have primarily been under the purview of medical and psychological professionals and researchers. Historians can provide a detailed analysis of the specific circumstances under which a disability was first recognized and how its diagnosis and treatment has evolved over time. This historical perspective complements views that focus solely on biological, physiological, and psychological factors.

History stands out among the social sciences for its emphasis on context, contingency, temporal change, and multicausal explanations. It views social phenomena dynamically, diachronically, and longitudinally, and rejects deterministic approaches, including those based on biology. In essence, history provides us with new lenses to view contemporary childhood disabilities and disorders and leads us to ask why a disorder is first recognized at a particular moment in time, how and why its incidence varies over time, and why specialists in different national contexts treat the disorder in distinctive ways. Thus, we need to understand why the United States stands out in the rates of issues like ADHD or peanut allergies, compared to other postindustrial countries.

A historical perspective inevitably raises several crucial issues. One is whether a condition that concerns us today, like dyslexia or autism, existed earlier in time but was ignored or otherwise defined. Thus, it is important to ask, for example, whether children that contemporary society defines as autistic or obese were previously regarded as timid or chubby. Another key issue is how much heightened interest and terminology explains the increasing incidence (or identification) of a disorder or whether a new factor, like school pressures, is an underlying cause of a measurable increase in diagnoses of dyslexia or attention deficit disorders.

Then, too, what are the new disorders' social and psychological consequences? Have parents, teachers, and school counselors begun to anticipate, or over-anticipate, such problems? Do kids themselves worry about these issues, even if they are not personally affected? Have they begun to look for problems in their classmates or themselves? In addition, there is the issue of social class: whether the prevalence of such disorders varies across social classes, whether certain disability labels are more likely to be attached to children from lower-income backgrounds or particular racial or ethnic groups, and whether middle-class and upper-middle-class parents are more adept at using disability labels for their own children's advantage.

Today, nearly a fifth of undergraduates reportedly has a registered disability—a development that has had far-reaching consequences for how faculty members teach and assess student learning and the support services that colleges and universities provide.[9] The current approach, to provide accommodations, is, of course, not just a legal requirement but an ethical imperative as well. But educational institutions, especially at the college level, currently do little to introduce students with disabilities to various strategies and tools that can help them better meet the challenges they will encounter in the workforce and in adult life.[10]

Childhood Obesity

Some of the new disorders of childhood have definite physical symptoms, like obesity, allergies, and asthma. Others fall more clearly into the psychological category, including attention deficit and autism spectrum disorders.

Public concern about childhood obesity is a relatively new phenomenon, only gaining recognition as a significant issue in the 1980s. In fact, the term "childhood obesity" didn't make its appearance in newspaper articles until 1991. From that point forward, the media, health organizations, and pharmaceutical companies consistently communicated that childhood obesity had grown into a "national health crisis" of "epidemic" proportions. From the early 1990s to 2001, *The New York Times* published more articles on childhood obesity than on AIDS, pollution, and smoking. According to the CDC 18 percent of children and 21 percent of adolescents are obese, and the rate continues to climb. As a result, health issues like heart disease, cancer, stroke, and type 2 diabetes are often linked to childhood obesity. Alarmist statistics, sensational media coverage, and public service campaigns using scare tactics have all contributed to increased parental anxiety. Yet the fact that the incidence of childhood obesity was largely concentrated among the poor was generally downplayed.[11]

In many ways, the portrayal of childhood obesity as a pressing social issue mirrors patterns seen in other emerging health concerns. During the 1980s and 1990s, the framing of childhood obesity leaned more toward diet and exercise rather than genetics or metabolic rate. The issue was largely seen as a result of an imbalance between caloric intake and expenditure, driven by high consumption of sugar-laden drinks and sweets, refined carbohydrates, processed foods, corn syrup, and fats. The spotlight typically focused on individual children who overate, spent too much time in front of screens, and didn't engage in enough outdoor play.[12]

However, this depiction of childhood obesity as a consequence of poor diet and lack of exercise is not universally accepted among nutritionists, public health specialists, or physicians. Some critics contend that the main gauge of childhood obesity, the Body Mass Index, is not a valid indicator of whether a child is genuinely overweight. These detractors also asserted that being slim didn't equate to being healthy and that a bit of extra body weight doesn't automatically translate to being unhealthy. Other critics point out that obesity wasn't always the result of unhealthy eating or lack of exercise, nor was it necessarily the fault of the child or the parents, since it can be a product of genetics, metabolism, stress, and food insecurity. As epidemiologists and sociologists of medicine have shown, it is not coincidental that children who live below the poverty line are 1.5 times more likely to suffer with being overweight and 1.6 times more likely to be obese.[13] At the same time, intense commercial promotion of certain foods—linked to the growing interest in seeing childhood as a market—contributes to the problem as well, with links to social class distinctions in food availability.

Many of those who criticize the focus on obesity and diet worry about the psychological effects of labeling children as obese or at risk of obesity. The term "obesity" implies laziness, lack of willpower, and diminished self-control. Even worse, many studies seemed to stigmatize African American and Hispanic children who, on average, displayed higher and more rapidly increasing obesity rates. Labeling children as obese could be psychologically damaging and stigmatizing, potentially leading to low self-esteem and harmful dieting behaviors.

Childhood obesity is undoubtedly a real issue. The most credible surveys show that obesity rates among children are on the rise, although the causes and future implications remain uncertain. However, it's also clear that the preoccupation with childhood obesity isn't solely about its frequency but is also a reflection of adult anxieties over perceived problematic aspects of modern childhood. These concerns include the decline in home-cooked family meals and the increase in time spent on activities like video gaming and television viewing. In a culture where pleasure and virtue are still seen to some extent as opposing forces, food becomes particularly contentious, associating sinfulness with self-indulgence.

There has been a growing recognition of the economic, environmental, and political factors contributing to childhood obesity, particularly its association with poverty. During the past two decades studies have shown a strong correlation between poverty levels and obesity rates, suggesting that low income, rather than race or ethnicity, puts children at a higher risk of becoming overweight or obese. This highlights class differences in access to healthy food and stress levels.[14]

Childhood Allergies

According to allergists and immunologists, it is indisputable that the incidence of childhood allergies has shot up in recent years and that allergies have become deadlier. Although the explanation remains uncertain, recent studies point to the role of environment, climate change, migration, child feeding patterns, hygiene, and epigenetics—the modification of gene expression (rather than alteration of the genetic code itself) due to environmental exposure, pollution, lifestyle, and methylation, chemical reactions in the body in which certain molecules are added to DNA and proteins.[15]

The incidence of asthma, after a sharp rise, has apparently stabilized, but other respiratory and food allergies continue to increase, perhaps the results of changes in pollen seasons, the introduction of new foods or plant life or foods raised or processed in new ways, food additives, mold growth, tick bites, dust mites, and more. There's also the "hygiene hypothesis," that children are too removed from natural immunities.[16] The World Health Organization estimates that nearly half of all schoolchildren are sensitive to at least one allergen.[17]

Over the past century, specialists have offered contrasting explanations of the increasing incidence of allergies. In the mid-twentieth century, during Freudian psychoanalysis's heyday, many allergies were deemed psychosomatic, while another influential group of allergists and immunologists claimed that many psychiatric symptoms were in fact the product of allergies, especially food allergies, that are aggravated by pollution, food additives, and highly processed foods that are high in fat, sugar, and artificial preservatives.[18]

It is food allergies, especially peanut allergies, that have elicited particular concern. A tragic incident that took place in 1986 brought the issue to public attention. An eighteen-year-old top-ranked squash player and Brown University freshman succumbed to an allergic reaction after consuming chili made with peanut butter. In 2005 a fifteen-year-old girl from Montreal, despite her known peanut allergy, died after sharing a kiss with her boyfriend who had eaten peanut butter. Symptoms of peanut allergies can range from hives, an itchy tongue, and swollen lips to sore eyes, dizziness due to low blood pressure, stomach cramps, vomiting, diarrhea, and a rapid heartbeat. In severe cases, particularly for highly allergic children, even minimal exposure to peanuts can trigger anaphylactic shock, resulting in throat constriction, lung collapse, drastic blood pressure drops, cardio-respiratory arrest, unconsciousness, and in some cases, death.

A study found that the prevalence of peanut allergies in children skyrocketed from 0.4 percent in 1997 to 1.4 percent in 2010. It remains unclear why a common lunchbox item from the 1950s has evolved into a potentially lethal allergen for some children or why these allergy rates seem significantly higher in Western nations compared to the Far East, where peanuts are a more frequent ingredient in meals.

Families dealing with peanut allergies face enormous challenges, as they must scrutinize every food item their child consumes, both at home and elsewhere. Dodging peanut exposure is a daunting task. Peanut oil is found in an array of products such as infant formula, chocolate bars, cakes, desserts, and ice cream toppings, and it can also infiltrate other foods through cross-contamination during manufacturing or meal preparation.

There are various theories attempting to explain the surge in peanut allergies. One hypothesis posits that reduced exposure to bacteria and viruses during early childhood may leave the immune system underdeveloped and hyper-responsive to allergic triggers such as pollen, cat hair, or peanuts. Another is that delayed exposure to peanuts is associated with allergic reactions. Still others insist that aversions or intolerance to certain foods are being conflated with full-blown allergies.

Medical historian Matthew Smith advocates for a historical perspective when examining the sudden spike in peanut allergy incidence. He believes that such a perspective could encourage a more comprehensive treatment approach that takes into account broader contextual factors currently overlooked, including diet, food additives, and potential environmental triggers.

Dyslexia

In recent years, dyslexia, like childhood obesity, has risen to prominence as a significant public concern. When children struggle with reading, it often results in feelings of guilt for parents and can lead to children developing a negative self-perception. Dyslexia, a term used today to describe a significant proportion of children who have difficulties mastering reading skills, is a genetically based, neuro-psychological condition that affects how the brain processes written language. In the United States, dyslexia represents the most common learning disability. As such, students diagnosed with dyslexia are entitled to certain educational supports under disabilities laws. However, the way reading disabilities are understood and addressed has evolved over time and varies across societies.[19]

The establishment of widespread schooling in the nineteenth century introduced the concept of the "normal" child and highlighted those who deviated from this norm. The recognition of a large number of students struggling with reading led to research into the causes and potential remedies for reading disabilities. Although the term dyslexia first emerged in English in the 1880s, it didn't become a widespread designation for reading disabilities until the 1970s. Initial research into the prevalence of children struggling with written language decoding led to the use of the term "word blindness," referring to a perceived defect in visual perception and memory, often associated with brain damage due to disease or physical trauma. Early intelligence testing in the twentieth century revealed that many students with significant reading problems performed adequately on IQ tests, differentiating these students from those with mental retardation or those considered mentally defective.[20]

By the late 1950s it was clear that brain injuries were not the primary cause of most reading disabilities. While one group of researchers focused on the neurological basis of reading difficulties through laboratory research on perceptual processing, another group, mainly educators, advocated for special education classes to provide intensive intervention for students with reading problems. However, by the mid-1960s it was evident that students placed in special education classes tended to remain isolated and often did not receive the necessary individualized attention. This led to a movement advocating for the "mainstreaming" of children with dyslexia into regular classrooms.

The 1970s saw the rise of psycho-neurological research into cognition and memory, resulting in a growing acceptance that dyslexia—a difficulty in decoding written language due to a phonological processing defect—was the primary cause of most reading problems. Concurrently, the enactment of legislation guaranteeing all children with disabilities the right to special education and related services changed the conversation and educational practice. For the first time it was beneficial to have reading problems medically or neurologically diagnosed as a disability. In times of tight budgets this classification secured access to certain supports and interventions.

Today, the concept of dyslexia is a subject of considerable debate among learning researchers. Critics question its scientific validity and usefulness in guiding effective educational interventions. From this perspective dyslexia is seen as a vague and imprecise term, conflating different types of reading difficulties and encouraging educational strategies, such as visual, visual-motor, and auditory training activities, that lack solid evidence of effectiveness. Furthermore, there is a concern that children who don't receive a formal dyslexia diagnosis might not receive the necessary help they need to become fluent in written language, which often requires intensive, individualized reading instruction. The debate continues, with some advocating for a neuro-psychological approach to reading problems, viewing them through a biomedical lens, while others argue for viewing these issues primarily as pedagogical challenges. In this context, it is noteworthy that specialists in Sweden, in contrast to their US counterparts, tend to treat dyslexia as a teaching and learning, rather than as a neurological, problem.[21]

ADHD

Today, about one in eleven American children, aged five to seventeen, is diagnosed with an attention deficit disorder, making this the most commonly diagnosed childhood psychiatric disorder. About 2 percent of three- to five-year-olds, 10 percent of six- to eleven-year-olds, and 13 percent of twelve- to seventeen-year-olds—two-thirds of them male—have been diagnosed with an attention deficit disorder.[22] Among those currently diagnosed with ADHD, 62 percent are taking medication containing methylphenidate, marketed under names like Ritalin, Daytrana, and Concerta. About 47 percent are receiving behavior therapy, and nine out of ten are receiving school accommodations.[23]

Naturally, children who exhibit inattentive, distractible, and highly active behavior are not a new phenomenon. However, the wide public concern for ADHD only emerged in the late 1950s, intensifying in the 1980s and 1990s. Looking at this issue through a historical lens can provide useful insights.

According to the medical historian Matthew Smith, psychiatrists in the past were mainly concerned with children who were shy, introverted, withdrawn, and nervous. However, several factors converged in the late 1950s that shifted the focus of educators, psychologists, and parents toward hyperactive children. One key event was the launch of the first satellite, Sputnik, by the Soviet Union in 1957, which sparked the heightened emphasis on academic achievement, especially in science and mathematics, amid fears that the United States was falling behind the Soviets. Concurrently, a new psychiatric disorder, hyperkinetic impulse disorder, was identified by child psychiatrists.[24] The focus on attention deficits, in other words, followed in considerable measure from the larger intensification of schooling.

Over time, the scope of concern evolved in what has been termed semantic enlargement, as the psychological concept of hyperactivity became increasingly expansive. Earlier terminology like "acting out" or "minimal brain dysfunction," which were used to describe aggressive or impulsive behavior in children, began to encompass both disruptive and distracted behavior. In 1980 the third edition of the *DSM* replaced hyperkinetic impulse disorder with attention deficit disorder. ADHD became widely recognized after it was included in the revised version of the *DSM-III* in 1987.[25]

Even as early as 1937 it was discovered that the stimulant Benzedrine could modify children's behavior and learning. This substance was initially used to treat depression, obesity, and fatigue. The synthesis of methylphenidate in 1944 further expanded the array of solutions to these problems. Particularly during the 1980s, as concerns about school performance escalated, the idea that hyperactivity and distraction could be best treated with medication gained rapid acceptance. This reflected a belief that hyperactivity and distractibility were brain-related, rather than influenced by environmental factors like strict school routines and teaching methods that promote passive learning. Alternative perspectives, such as the one proposed by allergist Ben Feingold in 1973, suggested that synthetic food additives and a diet rich in sugar, fats, and salts could trigger hyperactivity. However, this theory was never thoroughly tested.[26]

There can be no doubt that the increasing use of ADHD drugs is connected to ambitious or anxious upper-middle-class parents who are worried about their children's behavior and academic success, to school districts eager to manage classroom behavioral problems while receiving additional funding for students with a diagnosed learning disability, and to effective marketing by pharmaceutical companies—all of which also serve to explain the unusual incidence in the United States. There is also reason to believe that the increasing incidence of ADHD may be connected to increased exposure to food additives, excessive screen time, and a lack of exposure to the natural world.[27]

Presently, there is growing interest in understanding the developmental, contextual, and cultural factors that might influence ADHD, an increased appreciation for active classrooms and physical exercise, and new treatments involving behavioral therapy and longer-lasting medications. However, the kind of intensive research required to validate these approaches has yet to be carried out.

Autism Spectrum Disorder

Autism spectrum disorder and Asperger syndrome have seen a significant increase in diagnoses in recent years. The CDC estimates that about one in thirty-one children in the United States have been identified with an autism spectrum disorder. These conditions are characterized by impaired social interaction, communication difficulties, focused interests, physical clumsiness, and repetitive behavior.[28]

Autism was first recognized as a condition in the 1930s and early 1940s. In the United States autism was initially viewed as a rare distinct disease, rather than a spectrum of behavioral and communication traits, an idea proposed by Austrian pediatrician Hans Asperger and later popularized in the 1980s by English psychiatrist Lorna Wing. As late as 1957 psychologist Leo Kanner claimed to have observed only 150 true cases of autism. Autism was not included in the *DSM* until 1980, with autism spectrum disorder added in the revised edition of *DSM-III* in 1987.

Crucial changes in the criteria for diagnosing autism and Asperger syndrome partly explain the perceived increase in their incidence. In the past, many children who would now be diagnosed with autism spectrum disorder might have been labeled mentally retarded, feebleminded, cognitively disabled, schizophrenic, or in milder cases, introverted, shy, withdrawn, reclusive, or eccentric. Recognizing autism and Asperger syndrome as distinct conditions with a genetic component has been largely positive, emphasizing that these conditions do not necessarily indicate intellectual disability. However, the medicalization of autism also risks pathologizing autistic traits and damaging children's self-perception.

No specific causes for autism or Asperger syndrome have been determined, leading to a range of hypotheses. From the late 1940s to the 1960s, the blame was often put on so-called refrigerator mothers who were perceived as cold and distant. In recent years, several risk factors have been identified, such as family history of autism or older fathers. However, specific genetic or neurological markers remain elusive. The diagnosis still depends on clinical assessments using observation, interviews, and questionnaires, allowing for subjectivity.

The Medicalizing, Psychologizing, and Pathologizing of Childhood

Since the 1950s, attention has shifted from physical disabilities and a broad concept of mental retardation to behavioral, emotional, learning, neurological, and psychological disorders. These disorders have increasingly been seen as existing on various spectrums. The conclusions drawn from this historical perspective include the importance of understanding how disorders are constructed, the danger of conflating different phenomena, and the possibility that many childhood disorders may reflect adult concerns. Moreover, context may play a significant role in understanding childhood disorders. A comprehensive understanding of these conditions should consider biological, genetic, and neuropsychological explanations as well as environmental, social, and contextual elements. Such factors include parental fear, evolving diagnostic criteria, professional and corporate interests, and the societal definition of normality.

In our therapeutic culture, many disabilities have been psychologized and medicalized. This raises the risk of pathologizing normal childhood behaviors and distorting personal identities. We must be cautious about misrepresenting normality, promoting unrealistic parental expectations, and labeling children in ways that might make them feel inadequate or abnormal. In the "good old days" of diseases like measles and mumps, parents as well as health authorities rightly worried about contagion. In contemporary childhood, with new pressures and a new therapeutic vocabulary, there may be problems of contagion of another sort.

The American Child: The Transformation of Childhood Since World War II. Steven Mintz and Peter N. Stearns, Oxford University Press. © Oxford University Press 2025. DOI: 10.1093/9780197797112.003.0009

10

Anxious Children

The rates of children's anxiety—and particularly adolescents' anxiety—have become truly alarming, even if there is no agreement on the precise figures. And while the incidence was clearly exacerbated by the Covid pandemic, words like "epidemic" were already being applied to the phenomenon as early as 2001. Here is a major, and deeply troubling, example of the new kinds of diseases—or the newly identified diseases—afflicting American childhood from the later twentieth century onward—a particularly complicated instance of the general rise in psychological disorders.

During the years 2016–19, before the pandemic added its stress, 9.4 percent of American children between ages three and seventeen had "diagnosed" anxiety, according to the CDC. But another 30–40 percent were estimated to be suffering from some harmful level of anxiety, even if it fell below the most formal clinical levels. Possible symptoms ranged from panic attacks to unusual separation anxieties when away from parents, to phobias including fears about school or other social settings, or to more generalized worries about the future and "bad things" happening.[1]

The somewhat fluid line between severe and measurable anxiety contributed to the growing sense, among experts and the general public alike, that a crisis was involved. Even professionals frequently used the 30–40 percent figure rather than the significant but obviously more limited evidence of clinical problems. And lay commentary could range even more widely. Thus, a self-styled parenting expert could claim, in 2019, that virtually all contemporary American adolescents are anxious and the most are acutely aware of their condition: "They are anxious about everything we are anxious about, and more."[2] It is vital to incorporate the rise of anxiety into a history of contemporary American childhood as one of the most troubling new disorders of the era—but vital as well to remember that it is not quite as severe or generalized as is sometimes portrayed.

Statistical fuzziness aside, there is considerable agreement on a number of features of anxiety among American children. It is far more severe among adolescents than among grade-schoolers, though rates for the latter are not insignificant, at 4–8 percent of the total around 2019. In contrast to many other children's issues, females suffer far more acutely than males, particularly during (and after) adolescence. Again, before the pandemic, rates of 38 percent for female teenagers contrasted with 26 percent for males—high for both groups, but clearly more severe for females.[3]

On the other hand, race and social class correlated more weakly with anxiety data than was true for many other children's issues, though there were exceptions and, predictably, considerable dispute. Native American children definitely displayed the highest rates. Poverty had an impact, particularly when associated with trauma. But distinctions between whites and African Americans were not very significant. African American kids exhibited higher levels in grade school and middle school, but this may have been due entirely to the fact that they had less access to treatment and (according to some reports, which may well have reflected racial bias) were less amenable to treatment when available. But in high school, when overall levels soared, whites suffered more acutely than Blacks. Children's anxiety was, clearly, a rather elusive phenomenon.[4]

Children's anxiety was not, of course, a uniquely American issue. Many countries reported significant problems, including the characteristic gender distinctions but also a measurable increase over time. Furthermore, triggers like social media (for some children) and the pandemic had impacts in many places. However, there are indications that, as with issues like ADHD, rates of American anxiety—or at least adult awareness of children's anxiety—ran higher in the United States than in a number of comparable countries. Comparative studies suggested that anglophone countries suffered more than countries in the European Union, possibly because of a greater emphasis on competition, though possibly also because of structural distinctions in systems of education and their funding base. In Sweden, for example, rates of severe anxiety among children ran lower than those in English-speaking countries, and (at 20 percent of the total even after the pandemic) rates of more general anxiety were lower still.[5] But even in the anglophone world, the United States stood out to some degree. Thus, rates of children's anxiety in the United States ran about 40 percent higher than those in Britain and Canada in 2019—though they had been rising in all three countries during the two previous decades.[6] As with so many aspects of contemporary children's history, anxiety was both a global phenomenon and one with a probable American twist.

Despite some distinctive features—like the gender ratios—and a particularly acute sense of crisis by the twenty-first century, anxiety among American children displayed many of the characteristics common to the range of new ailments, in addition to the balance it highlighted between global and distinctively American features. It was genuinely troubling, but it joined with other disorders in a diagnostic fuzziness, particularly beyond the minority of clinically severe cases. Defining the distinction between a normal level of anxiety and a troubling one is notoriously difficult, despite the current tendency to emphasize the problematic. As several students of the phenomenon have noted, anxiety at a certain level can be positively constructive in motivating better performance.[7]

Definitional issues bleed into the challenge of distinguishing anxiety from other descriptors, like nervousness, that were common in the past but measurably less dire. Thus, did applying the label anxiety increasingly overtake references to nervousness because basic tensions became more acute, or because both experts and a wider public became entranced with a more ominous terminology? The relation between anxiety and more traditional nervousness warrants comparison with issues like obesity/plumpness or autism/shyness that were discussed earlier. As with the other new diseases, explaining the surge of anxiety raises some complicated analytical issues.

Finally—again like most of the other contemporary ailments—children's anxiety, or the growing insistence on using the term, is a phenomenon of the past seventy years of American history. Relatively unknown in the 1950s, it began to increase—or to draw greater comment, or both—from the middle of that decade fairly steadily into the early twenty-first century, when it would surge forward even more markedly. Anxiety is an important aspect of evolving American childhood, and while a brief historical survey hardly answers all the questions about its emergence it certainly contributes, both in pinpointing the trends and in inviting more careful inquiry into the causes involved.[8]

Context

Anxiety of any sort began to draw attention from the late 1940s onward, among relevant experts and soon amid a wider public. Postwar tensions prompted frequent references to a new "age of anxiety"—the term used by W. H. Auden in a poem that won the Nobel prize—that sometimes was assumed to account for new issues without further explanation.[9]

The advent of new drugs had even more obvious impact, though some were initially introduced with real concern about whether they would find an audience. Milltown was the first entrant, in 1955, and it was followed by a procession of FDA-approved medicines, including Valium and Prozac. Sales quickly soared: by 1971, 20 percent of all adult women and 8 percent of men were on Valium alone. Attention in the public press mounted as well, along with slick advertising campaigns that highlighted a growing list of specific issues, including social anxiety disorder.[10]

Medical attention surged as well. The initial edition of the *DSM*, in 1952, discussed anxiety as a "psychoneurotic disorder," while the *DSM-II* detailed a wider range of symptoms, including panic attacks. Commentary initially emphasized a rather small patient population, but later psychiatric and psychological manuals expanded the range, using figures like 30 percent of the adult population along with references to the "overabundance of tensions, fears, worries and anxiety that confront mankind today." Several professionals even formed an Anxiety Disorder Association in 1980. While concern about depression quickly rivaled anxiety among psychiatrists, there was no question that a major new issue had emerged that linked relevant experts, a lively pharmaceutical/commercial contingent, and an active public audience.[11]

Children in the 1950s

Concerns about adult anxiety did not immediately carry over into discussions of childhood. To be sure, a small number of children in the 1950s were receiving therapeutic treatment for acute anxiety, but this drew little comment, for anxiety levels among children more generally were quite low. Pharmaceutical attention did not focus on children at this point (except for some claims concerning ADHD); *DSM* comments on anxiety began to include children only in the third edition, in 1980.[12]

Student services at many colleges and universities were beginning to expand beyond the career guidance emphasis that had predominated since the 1920s. Even here, however, there was no focus on anxiety and also no sense that student mental health problems of any sort were increasing.[13] Conventional wisdom held that about 10 percent of most college populations had serious mental health issues, with a larger number potentially benefiting from some professional advice; and there was concern that at least half of the needy segment were not taking advantage of available services.

Beyond this, commentary was often rather vague, referring for example to "neurotic" difficulties, with a good bit of attention to worries about sexual orientation, particularly among male students. It was true—and relevant—that many students reported "nervousness"; loneliness was another common issue. Anxiety, however, was not explicitly involved.[14]

Commentary on anxiety issues for younger children was equally lacking, and even nervousness drew no particular attention at this level. Absence of relevant conceptualization combined with the absence of any evidence of significant issue.

There was, however, one exception for schoolchildren and college students alike: a variety of eager experts were beginning to identify young people's anxiety in facing or taking examinations. Some studies in fact began in the late 1940s, but it was in the following two decades that inquiries mounted, becoming something of a cottage industry among psychological researchers. Probes of levels of test anxiety combined with experiments that resulted in a variety of approaches to remediation, from individual counseling to group exercises to practice sessions—there was no agreement on what, if anything, worked best. There was, however, wide consensus that about 25–30 percent of all students, from grade school on to college, suffered from debilitating levels of test anxiety and that the results seriously affected their academic performance. No sense of crisis was yet attached, nor any belief that the problem was escalating; however, given the growing importance of academic success from the 1950s onward, the test anxiety category could prove increasingly significant.[15]

Finally, it was in the 1950s that a number of psychologists began to introduce anxiety scales and probes relevant for children of various ages (again, from grade school on up). A "children's form" of the Manifest Anxiety Scale was generated in 1956 and gained wide acceptance: between the 1950s and the 1990s, ninety-nine tests along these lines were administered to younger American children (variously aged, but with the largest number being eleven years old) and 170 tests were given to college students. Anxiety was increasingly being appraised in childhood, at least by a set of relevant experts.[16]

Results in the 1950s, however, simply confirmed the common impression: among all the age groups involved, anxiety levels were quite low. Only the specific issue of school examinations warranted any concern. Yet it was in this decade that the situation began to shift, though it would still take some time for anxiety to enter overall assessments of childhood with any frequency.

The Later Twentieth Century

Signs of change emerge most directly from two sources: evaluations of mental health problems among college students, including some issues that were clearly imported from earlier adolescence, and the steadily increasing anxiety scores of the children tested according to the Manifest Anxiety Scale. Commentary applied to grade school and high school students enters in as well, though a bit later on.

Tallies of the anxiety tests over time are the source of the striking finding that average anxiety levels among children by the 1990s were higher than those of the few children in the 1950s who had been receiving psychiatric care for the problem. Not surprisingly, averages aside, growing numbers of the young people taking the anxiety scale tests revealed serious mental health issues centered on anxiety.[17]

Psychologist Jean Twenge was the first to systematize the anxiety scale data, in an ambitious article over two decades ago. Her findings emphasized a steady buildup from the 1950s onward. No significant interruptions intruded, but the rates of change clustered in two subperiods—again, for schoolchildren and college students alike. The most substantial increases occurred between the 1950s and 1967, with a 27 percent jump for female children and 23 percent for male. (It may be relevant to note that this was the period when children's suicide rates began to mount as well, only to decline later on until a renewed increase after 2007). From 1968 to 1993 the additional surge was 22 percent among females and 12 percent among males. The big finding was the overall result, with the average child, by the century's end, suffering from troubling levels of anxiety when assessed by 1950s standards. But the internal periodization was interesting as well, as the relative mental health calm of the early 1950s was rather quickly shattered.[18]

College counseling services picked up the same trends from the 1960s onward, though with less initial focus on anxiety explicitly and with less precision concerning decade-to-decade shifts. The big news was the growing number of students—particularly freshmen—who were seeking psychological help but the even larger number who were now seen as needy. A Yale study in the 1960s noted that 10 percent of the student body was using the mental health clinics—the standard percentage—but the study now went beyond the common figure in claiming that 75 percent of students who tested positively for significant problems were staying away. And among those with problems, experts themselves now began to claim that anxiety was a major factor for the vast majority (80 percent). And while students themselves were not yet widely using the word anxiety explicitly, 35 percent of those seeking counseling at Harvard in the late 1960s were citing "anxious agitation." Dartmouth, which found 7 percent of its students "mentally impaired" in the class of 1962, saw the percentage soaring to 16 percent just five years later.[19]

By the 1970s the traditional 10 percent figure for students with serious issues was increasingly jettisoned, as college counseling personnel and students themselves reported growing problems and rapid growth in the numbers seeking formal help. It was at this point also that references to magnitudes began to vary widely, with claims of serious distress sometimes embracing the majority of the student body, as in a Boston University study. Certainly, the sense that anxiety and related problems were mounting was widespread. The University of Missouri, for example, reported a 300 percent increase in mental health complaints brought to the student clinic by the early 1970s, though anxiety was not the only culprit. By this point, and literally for every decade thereafter to the present day, a growing number of institutions saw the intensification of student demand for counseling assistance regularly outstrip the services available.[20]

The problems of college students admittedly go beyond a focus on childhood, and it remains true today that anxiety seems to increase from adolescence into young adulthood. Clearly, however, many college students and young adults were importing anxiety issues that had begun in their childhood years. And the surges in anxiety levels among children themselves, as evidenced in the anxiety test scores, show that rapid change was affecting childhood at many levels. The end-of-the-century child, according to all available data, was measurably more anxious than their counterpart of fifty years before.

Correspondingly, from the 1980s onward, reports of growing anxiety among grade- and particularly high school students, though less elaborate and precise than those derived from the college group, mounted steadily. Teachers as well as school counselors were urged to be aware of the problem. Referrals to mental health programs became increasingly common at this level. The changes that can be inferred from the scores on anxiety tests were beginning to draw serious attention from authorities dealing with children at all ages, though particularly during adolescence.[21]

The situation for school-aged children was admittedly complicated by the fact that, unlike their specialist counterparts in college centers, counselors were not expected to be able to diagnose and treat anxiety directly. They were, however, being urged at the end of the twentieth century to be alert for signs of anxiety and ready to recommend referrals to therapists. "With schools often serving as the first line of defense in addressing anxiety, it becomes imperative for professional school counselors to be aware of research on the effects of anxiety on children." And while children themselves might report problems, it was also noted that parents were sometimes more eager to point to anxiety symptoms than their offspring were. Clearly, and predictably, concerns about anxiety were mounting for children at every level of the educational system, and young people themselves were becoming more sensitive to the issue as well.[22]

The Challenge of Causation: Part I

While the sense that anxiety was a growing problem was increasingly widely shared, at least by the end of the twentieth century, not everyone involved, even at the specialist level, was particularly interested in the sources of change. For many, the larger sense that mounting anxiety was simply inherent in modern society was explanation enough. The growing tendency to expect frailties and vulnerabilities in children—that crucial element in helicopter parenting—often entered in as well.

Yet, as with other new diseases, the question of causation is a crucial aspect of contemporary childhood history, though it is far easier to raise than to resolve. And at least a few of the relevant specialists, including Jean Twenge, were eager to venture a few claims well before the avalanche of twentieth-century commentary that would increasingly point to social media and ultimately the pandemic.

The clearest twentieth-century finding, and it was an important one, was that the surge in children's anxiety did not correlate with larger economic trends. For American children generally, economic conditions improved even as anxiety mounted. This did not exclude the role of poverty for some children, and it certainly did not prevent troubling inequality. It was also true that, by the twenty-first century, mounting college costs and student debt muddied the picture, at least for older adolescents. Overall, however, economic trends may not figure prominently in dealing with children's anxiety levels.[23]

Other worries, however, were undoubtedly involved. Twenge was fascinated by the potential role of fears about nuclear war and mounting crime.

She rightly pointed to the possibility that war fears, particularly, might explain the particularly rapid anxiety surge during the 1950s and 1960s when, after all, many children were directly exposed to duck-and-cover exercises. The slower rate of growth after the 1960s might in her view reflect the reduction of acute war fears—along, ultimately, with the decline of the crime rate. Then, if this argument were extended to the twenty-first century, new fears about environmental collapse and school shootings might have replaced the 1960s concern about war and the crime rate with eerie precision.[24]

Yet there are some problems with the current events argument, though it is important to keep in mind. The argument does not clearly explain the continued increase of children's anxiety in the later twentieth century (at admittedly a possibly slower pace). It may apply less tellingly to the heightened anxiety of grade-school children, whose exposure to current events was less extensive.

Family issues were an even more obvious candidate. Twenge noted the possible link between the divorce surge and children's anxiety levels. The easing of the divorce rate by the 1990s might help explain why rates of increase in anxiety slowed a bit. Here too, however, there are problems. In the first place the divorce surge remained in full force in the 1970s and 1980s, when the rate of increase in anxiety levels dropped—though it is possible that adjustment mechanisms improved. Further, more recent studies point to complexities in the family instability/children's anxiety relationship, though there is much debate. Children of single parents are not predictably more anxious than others, and the same applies to children of divorce. The clearest linkage centers on children of middle-class families, where divorce or (in the case of unmarried couples) sudden exposure to single parenting shatter expectations and do generate heightened anxiety levels on average. This is not true, however, for children in many groups where single parenting looms larger. Other important changes in family patterns are equally elusive when applied to anxiety: thus, there has been some debate over anxiety amid the growing number of only children, but the results are inconclusive at best.[25]

The Challenge of Causation: Part II

Without dismissing the shifting tides of current events and the major changes in family structure, three other intertwined factors deserve particular consideration in addressing the increase in children's anxiety in the later twentieth century and even into the twenty-first: changes in schooling, the inadvertent role of experts themselves, and the diffuse implications of anxiety among adults.

The schooling point is the most obvious, though interestingly it was not included in the otherwise admirable Twenge analysis. As school performance became more important, as levels of testing increased, and as more children were expected to complete high school and even college, academic worries became more prominent—including a pervasive concern about disappointing eager parents and the competitive drumbeat in interacting with peers. The research on test anxiety picked this up implicitly. Most studies of anxiety among high school and college age students highlighted anxiety about school performance as a key component in the overall trend—indeed the most important single ingredient at the college level. For ambitious high schoolers, "admissions anxiety" about getting into the right college also figured prominently. Some of the gender and social class differentials in children's anxiety probably reflected the academic factor as well.[26]

The role of therapeutic expertise in promoting assumptions about anxiety is more difficult to chart but is inescapable. As well-meaning specialists increasingly probed for anxiety, they helped teachers, parents, and ultimately children themselves become accustomed to the term and increasingly ready to apply it in place of more traditional and milder labels like nervousness. As some mental health authorities themselves noted, the gradual growth of psychological and counseling services, the soaring popularity of terms like "test anxiety" and even "trauma," and the mounting publicity to the claim that a host of needy students must be steered toward therapy all helped promote the surge in anxiety self-reports.[27]

Nothing highlights the complex combination of school pressures and the role of therapeutic intervention better than the introduction, in the 1970s, of two new terms: math anxiety and writing anxiety. (A 1950s effort to popularize the neologism "mathemaphobia" mercifully came to naught.) The terms did not necessarily denote actual mental illness, though there were experts and popularizers who came close to making this claim. But they certainly focused more attention on a need for help than earlier, diffuse ideas about "nervousness," making it easier (for children and adults alike) to claim and feel a certain sense of disability. Was the problem really increasing? Probably yes, given the growing importance of grades and academic performance and growing rigor in some high school math courses. Was the problem also the result of the replacement of traditional but modest uneasiness with more troubling psychological language? Also almost certainly yes. Figuring out the balance between the two prods—new problems and new language for older patterns—is an impossible task, but it is the combination that warrants attention.[28]

Into this mix, finally, come the diffuse results of larger adult anxieties, which themselves may reflect current events (including exaggerated beliefs about crime), economic pessimism, and other, larger changes in turn-of-the-century American culture. If partly in response to new medication, adult anxiety began to surge, in the 1950s, before children's levels began to mount very significantly. Some adult anxieties would soon be picked up, for an important parent minority, in the paraphernalia of helicopter parenting. Other adult concerns, like the attention to children's (and particularly girls') appearance, might apply as well. Impossible to trace with any quantitative precision, the role of adult anxieties in spilling over to children, through protective warnings or larger ambiance, surely enters into the phenomenon. New behaviors—like decreasing interest in getting driver's licenses or teenage sex—certainly suggest that worries from the adult world were reaching young people quite directly, making them less venturesome on average. Yet adult discomforts may play an even greater role in the otherwise surprising increase in anxiety levels among children of grade-school age. Here, school performance factors, though not absent, play a lesser role, and concerns about social contacts, such as fitting in with peers, figure more prominently—along with integrating the warnings from parents.[29]

As with other features of the contemporary history of American childhood, the steady increase in anxiety—now over seven decades old—is in some senses surprising. Children have less reason for anxiety in many ways, beginning with declining rates of death and (until Covid) contagious disease. Yet the surge in anxiety is incontestable, as it responded to a complex mixture of factors. By the twenty-first century, if not before, it would embrace not only the growing minority of children who suffered directly but a larger number who worried about the health of their peers and, in some cases, wondered if they might be next.

The Twenty-First Century

The further increase in children's anxiety rates, particularly from the second decade of the new century onward, is a relatively familiar story, reflecting new factors and tensions but also clearly building on established trends. As before, children's problems mounted at the same time relevant adults became increasingly eager to label them. Among other things, by this point many students were children of adults whose own childhoods had featured mounting anxiety. Even now, however, as a 2019 report suggested, it remained difficult to determine the balance between new issues and the greater readiness to feel the need for and seek out help.[30]

Acceleration in children's anxiety continued to reflect tensions over school success and college admission but also included new fears responding, among other things, to school shootings and the even more pervasive shooter drills. For older adolescents, anticipation of issues in financing college and dealing with debt provided another novel angle that had been largely absent in the twentieth century.[31]

A steady increase in the number of "first-generation" students hoping to enter and then actually entering college furthered school anxieties from yet another direction. Interestingly, first-gen students had also figured prominently in the 1950s and 1960s, when college ranks and children's anxieties first surged. The group had not been explicitly labeled during this initial surge, but the relationship between new sources of college entry, and anxieties in high school and college ranks, was not an entirely unprecedented phenomenon. By the twenty-first century, however, students themselves, and those who served them, were much readier to identify the problem.[32]

Growing use of social media, beginning in 2006 when Facebook began to take hold, made its own contribution, particularly affecting some girls in the thirteen- to fifteen-year-old range who were already particularly vulnerable to certain types of anxiety. The anonymity of social media interactions, along with an intensification of feelings of inadequacy given the images of happiness and success now available, could leave a strong mark.[33]

The combination of new factors and old, along with some probable hyperbole, explain why accounts of children's anxiety levels soared beyond any precedent, even before the pandemic began to move reported levels off the charts. Sober experts by 2016 could thus claim that up to 60 percent of all students entering college were suffering from serious anxiety. Though depression remained a serious issue, and though students also still sometimes commented on stress, anxiety had become the focal point for many troubled children from high school onward, and a growing minority even before that point.[34]

Responses

Efforts to deal with the increase in children's anxiety have not kept pace with the rates of change, but they have had a significant impact on some children's lives over the past half century or more. Therapy of several sorts has been the primary component, but in more recent decades other experiments have added in as well.

Various forms of therapy were urged in response to the growing concern about test anxiety in the 1950s and 1960s. In some cases formal psychological treatment was recommended, but more generally group discussions and both individual and group practice sessions won the greatest attention, both at the college and high school level. Many of the ventures were experimental, and it is not clear that the results reached large numbers of children or adolescents. A few specific projects targeted selective groups, like students with physical disabilities.[35]

Growing awareness of wider anxiety issues by the 1970s prompted the rising interest in expanding formal counseling services on college campuses, or referrals to private therapists by school authorities. A few institutions had offered psychological care earlier—West Point had a psychiatrist on staff as early as 1921—but as late as the 1950s only 10 percent of all colleges, most of them private, offered any professional counseling. Expansion was steady thereafter, with additional staff hired every decade. As early as the 1980s, however, there were complaints about inability to keep up with growing student demand—quite apart from the older concern about troubled students who were trying to cope on their own. By 1986, 16 percent of all college counseling services stated that they were "overwhelmed," a figure that jumped to 27 percent by 2002 and would only continue to spiral. Anxiety issues were not, of course, the only factor in the expansion of therapy, but they played a major role.[36]

Therapy in turn featured two components. The array of pharmaceuticals relevant for the treatment of children's anxiety was considerably narrower than that available for adults, but Prozac or Zoloft (sertraline), particularly, could be both safe and often effective. Cognitive behavioral therapy (CBT) was the other pillar. Growing numbers of hospitals and campus clinics offered focused treatment for anxiety, some specializing on issues among children and adolescents.[37]

There were two problems, despite growing confidence among professionals, that some effective response was possible. Poverty and race severely limited access for many children, and even more affluent whites had challenges finding available treatment given growing demand. Beyond this, the treatments, while promising, did not always work. According to one study, serious involvement with CBT produced improvements for 60 percent of the young people involved, and when Zoloft was added the figure rose to 80 percent. Buoyed by these results and the growing incidence, some professionals by 2022 were recommending that all children be regularly tested for anxiety, an interesting extension of the therapeutic approach. At least for the moment, however, a gap remained between need and solution.[38]

Efforts at prevention in advance of a need for therapy were far more scattered, beyond some of the group work applied to anxiety about examinations. Occasional experiments occurred in schools from the 1980s onward to acquaint grade-schoolers with problems of anxiety in hopes that they might be prevented. Interestingly, Germany, Canada, and Australia invested far more in this kind of preventive effort than did the United States. In response to the pandemic, a growing number of high schools began allowing students to take mental health days, a venture blessed by law in at least twelve states.[39]

On college campuses, student services programs, beyond urging expansion of counseling staff, tried increasingly to promote a "fun" atmosphere from the late twentieth century onward, for example in greatly expanded orientation sessions for new freshmen. Abundant offerings of free pizza and donuts were a common response to stressful periods during the academic year. Promotion of fitness facilities and yoga programs contrasted with the reduction of exercise opportunities in the schools. In 2005 Kent State University pioneered the use of puppies to help students through examination periods, an experiment that spread widely.[40]

Ventures of this sort, worthy and surely sometimes useful, combined with growing efforts, often by individual instructors, to curtail reliance on examinations, offer greater flexibility on due dates, or reduce the length of assigned papers. Here, instructors were trying to adjust to the challenges many students seemed to be facing, whether formally diagnosed or not.[41]

* * *

It remained true that efforts to supplement therapy with prevention in advance remained unsystematic at all levels of the educational system. And even with therapy added in, the stark fact was that responses to student anxiety, and its diffuse sources, were failing to stem the tide. This new—though no longer brand new—feature of childhood experience, and of the list of relevant concerns among adults dealing with children, continued to grow. It might be hoped that the particular surge prompted by the pandemic would recede, but the fact was that, Covid aside, by the 2020s children's anxiety had been mounting fairly steadily for over seventy years. The same applied to the broader range of childhood disorders; and of the rather long list, only allergies had generated successful preventive treatments.

11

The Impact of the New Disorders

The shift from contagious diseases, the traditional bane of the early years of life, to the range of new ailments, from obesity to ADHD and anxiety, has been one of the most striking changes involved in the emergence of contemporary American childhood. Parents, teachers, and to an extent American society more generally have been taken aback by the extent and severity of the new disorders, which, only partly because of their novelty, may seem more troubling than the older threats.

This is because the bulk of the new ailments highlight a number of distinctive characteristics. They are for the most part harder to explain. Polio or measles, though frightening, had fairly clear causation compared to the spread of autism or ADHD or even obesity. Adults dealing with the new diseases among children may also face a greater sense of guilt and responsibility, particularly when the psychological dimensions are highlighted: did the problems result from poor parenting? The tendency to seize on a single factor—like social media or the pandemic in dealing with mental health issues—also reflects both the unfamiliarity with the problem and a hope that some simple target might be at hand.

Diagnosis is also more difficult. Chicken pox was chicken pox, though cases might vary in severity. But at what point is a nervous child actually ill? At what point is it essential to worry about a child who is somewhat overweight? Almost certainly, the eagerness to identify mental health issues and remove the stigma from therapy has increased the possibility of overdiagnosis, pulling some children into a disability category, sometimes with attendant medication that may not be desirable. On the other hand, as with severe autism, the contemporary approach has enabled some children, previously simply isolated, to gain considerable functionality and inclusion. But the boundary line between sickness and well-being in children has become harder to pinpoint—which can worry children as well.

Not surprisingly, given the fluidity of diagnosis, different groups take different positions on the new set of challenges, though there has been a measurable increase in overall recognition. Affluent families, for example, are much more tolerant of the need for mental health days than families in lower-income brackets (91 percent to 45 percent in one post-Covid survey)[1]—partly, of course, because the affluent have more resources to provide supplemental childcare.

Most of the new diseases also have durable qualities that were less common with the classic ailments, another important shift. Polio, to be sure, could lead to lifelong paralysis and was accordingly frightening, but most children who contracted polio were feverish for a week or two and then recovered. Mumps and measles were even more transitory, with rare if troubling exceptions. In contrast, anxiety or the new allergies might be lifelong, potentially prompting different kinds of reactions from children and adults alike. Here was one reason that so many Americans have been tempted to turn to the array of new prescription drugs in hopes of gaining relief.

Finally, at least to date, most of the new diseases continue to gain ground, in contrast to the traditional ailments that, by the mid-twentieth century, seemed increasingly open to new forms of prevention and treatment even before their largely definitive removal through inoculations. The Covid pandemic exacerbated the trends, at least on the mental health side, but this built on an established trajectory. American society is still groping for an effective pattern of response.

It is vital to remember that many contemporary children are not directly involved with most of the new ailments, though the numbers are substantial and clearly growing. Shock at the new disorders, and in some cases efforts to capitalize by promoting new services, often lead to considerable exaggeration, as with some of the claims about pervasive anxiety and use of terms like "epidemic."

The problems are severe, however, and they have affected children more generally who almost certainly, among other things, obsess more about their own mental health or their body contours than their counterparts did a few decades ago. The pressure on states like Oregon to offer "mental health" days thus came directly from teenagers, the vast majority of whom sought the option whether they themselves planned to use it or not. Even before Covid, in 2018, a Pew report indicated that 70 percent of all teenagers believed that serious mental health problems were increasing among their peers, again whether they themselves were implicated or not.[2] Here also was one other area where "adult" language and concerns widely penetrated children's culture; thus a nine-year-old, after a crying jag that was not necessarily novel, could offhandedly note that "I have emotional problems." High school and college students, again picking up cues from American society more generally, routinely refer to family setbacks, such as parental separation, as "traumas." Homesick summer campers increasingly talk of trauma and even PTSD. Rumors about mental problems have also formed one of the categories in which a substantial minority of teenagers were victims of harassment on social media.[3] The new diseases, and the concepts that have accompanied them, gained impact beyond their diagnosed incidence, another definable and troubling new feature of contemporary American childhood.

Numbers

Rates of explicit involvement in the new diseases are substantial, though precision is difficult. The fact that between a tenth and a quarter of all students in some colleges have some recognized disability, disproportionately on the mental health side, is striking, and the steady expansion of the numbers and percentages involved has brought huge changes to college campuses over the past several decades, as well as to the young people involved. Adjustments at the high school level have been at least as great.

The incidence of obesity and being overweight stands out numerically. Around 19 percent of all American children fall in the obesity category, and while the problem increases among adolescents, already 12 percent of all two- to five-year-olds are deemed obese.[4] But calculations of children who are noticeably overweight range higher, up to 33 percent of the total in all age groups. Some of the children involved may not perceive a problem, particularly in sectors that cannot afford regular medical visits, but some sense of stigma is widespread—as the use of social media to "fat-shame" suggests. This is one of the many categories where a significant minority of children gain some sense that they have a troubling, and often durable, problem.

ADHD diagnoses are more systematic than those for obesity since they affect school performance, reaching 10 percent of grade-schoolers, 13 percent among adolescents, again particularly among boys. Diagnosed depression hits 2 percent of grade-schoolers, 6 percent of adolescents ages twelve to seventeen; anxiety, 7.6 percent and 10.5 percent; and behavior disorders (which alone decline a bit among teenagers), 9 percent and 7.5 percent. Autism and Asperger syndrome figures are lower, but not insubstantial: slightly over 3 percent of American children are autistic, and another 2–4 percent have some level of Asperger's. Figures here reflect a particularly rapid rate of increase during the past decade.[5] The figures also assume some formal medical identification, raising the probability that, particularly in the lower socioeconomic categories, actual levels may well be higher than the official figures indicate. Further, as with anxiety, they assume some degree of severity; larger numbers of children may display milder symptoms, which might affect both their performance and their self-perception given the growing awareness of mental health issues.

Even with the caveats, and recognizing that some children may fall into more than one category, the totals are impressive. Compared to 1960s expert estimates for college students—which assumed about 10 percent affliction with some serious mental issue—they may suggest a doubling over half a century, though the comparison is shaky because the earlier diagnoses claimed far less precision. By the early 2020s the CDC was reporting that almost 20 percent of all American children would be identified with some mental health disorder every year, making it probable that an even larger segment was encountering the diagnosis at some point during their childhood. While treatment lagged behind reported rates, particularly among non-white children, about 15 percent were receiving some kind of therapy, with almost 10 percent on some kind of mental health medication.[6]

These trends had of course been building for several decades, though they accelerated after about 2005. By the end of the first quarter of the twenty-first century they added up to a substantial segment of American children who were encountering some impairment and who were being told that they had a mental health condition. In turn, despite a lingering sense of stigma, a growing segment of teenagers defined themselves at least in part in terms of their disability, sometimes even in cases where actual symptoms were fairly mild. This could in fact form part of the rising quest for identity. And a far larger number were aware of mental health struggles among their peers and might worry about their own futures in this regard.

The Causation Challenge

Efforts to explain the new patterns have shifted over the years. Generalized references to the troubles of "modern society," for example, have faded, though they may still hover in the background. The same applies to references to global problems, though environmental concerns are sometimes evoked (just as nuclear fears loomed large in some earlier assessments). The current tendency to focus on a single factor in analyzing trends in anxiety, depression, and obesity, like social media or cell phones, may go too far in the other direction. This risks oversimplifying analysis by neglecting the earlier stages of the new trends (and also bypassing the question of why some of the new ailments seem unusually prevalent among American children),[7] even as they help explain why some of the trends have worsened. Clearly, a more holistic approach is called for, but even here some difficult issues remain.

Several strands of contemporary childhood, taking shape from the 1960s onward, have contributed to the new normal, beyond the more familiar recent villains like the Internet or the pandemic. Heightened emphasis on schooling and testing created new pressures while also facilitating the identification of problems that might otherwise not have existed—with ADHD being the most obvious case in point. The decline of play, enhanced by growing commercialization, undoubtedly created or exacerbated other issues—certainly including obesity.[8] The new forms and levels of inequality affected diagnosis, incidence, and treatment alike. Some of the changes in family life surely factored in, though the relationship to problems such as anxiety is complex. Even the rise of one-child families has come in for discussion, though with inconclusive results.[9]

At the same time, growing emphasis on children's fragility, often with psychological overtones, heightened the tendency to elevate conditions like nervousness or sadness into disease categories. And the American embrace of a therapeutic approach has been more enthusiastic than that in countries such as Britain or Germany, with a smaller minority believing still that any stigma is attached—suggesting that Americans have become particularly open to identifying (and possibly exaggerating) the new disorders and assuming that professional help, and often medication, is essential. Certainly, increasing acceptance of the culture of therapy has proved doubled-edged in the United States: providing much-needed assistance to some children who are seriously ill but also encouraging children and adults alike to convert some traits into more serious, psychological categories. The fuzzy boundary line between new pressures and constraints and new perceptions complicates both diagnosis and response. The combination also helps explain why the incidence of the new disorders in the United States trended higher than in otherwise comparable societies elsewhere.[10]

Responses and Questions

Reactions to the new disorders have taken several basic paths, some of which—particularly the unusually heavy reliance on medication—reflect a somewhat distinctive national choice. The fact that no combination to date has succeeded in reducing the growing sense of crisis or the rising rate of reported illness suggests a variety of open-ended issues.

Extensive embrace of therapy—from relevant counselors and social workers, child psychologists, and child psychiatrists—was the predominant response to most of the new cluster of childhood ailments, from the later twentieth century onward. The emphasis was obvious not only amid the growing concern about anxiety but with learning disabilities and depression as well. Beginning in the 1970s, though with scattered precedents previously, colleges and universities steadily augmented their in-house professionals, along with relying on some private consultants, and public school districts did the same. By the 2020s an affluent and progressive school district, namely, Fairfax County in Virginia, boasted 588 professional counselors, 184 social workers, and 184 psychologists for a population of 188,000 students. The services provided involved more than diagnosing and treating student illness, but the latter loomed increasingly large. At the same time, from the late twentieth century onward, primary-care pediatricians were also increasingly urged to be ready to identify and at least partially address mental health problems among their charges.[11]

Rates of professional expansion were considerable. Simply between 2007 and 2016, for example, the number of child psychiatrists in the United States surged by more than 21 percent, significantly advancing their ratio compared to the total number of American children.

In the schools alone (and to a lesser extent at the college level), the growth of professional counselors was not simply a matter of numbers. It could affect both parental and teacher authority. While counselors offered vital assistance to some students, they also often gave some others a place to vent a variety of lesser grievances—from a slight by another student to annoyance that a parent had taken away a cell phone because of poor grades—that might better have been handled more independently by the students themselves. In some cases, after one or two sessions, counselors in many school districts by the twenty-first century gained the option of issuing students "flash passes," allowing them to miss entire classes on the grounds that they were upset while urging the teachers involved to "be sensitive to the student's feelings because they are going through a lot outside of school right now." The balance between essential support and tolerance of immaturity was complex, and counselors played a mixed role in the whole process, responding but also activating. The surging fear of mental distress among children prompted many school and college authorities to attach health warning labels to simple student malingering—though in fairness some of the students involved, convinced of their own fragility, were not necessarily consciously manipulative.

The rapid expansion of counseling was accompanied by growing efforts to counter the traditional stigma attached to seeking mental health support. Particularly in the twenty-first century the very open struggles of many leading athletes and movie stars were widely publicized, with a youth audience clearly in mind. For better or worse, admission of mental health difficulties was increasingly seen as a positive character quality. The message was not uniformly successful—some cultural groups, such as Asian Americans, still held back—but there was a measurable shift in the overall culture.

The mental health focus was not entirely inevitable, though it certainly responded to many rising problems. Some European countries resisted the move to put some clear learning difficulties in a mental health category. Sweden, for example, addressed issues of dyslexia through intensive help with reading, rather than psychological treatment.[12] Other possible factors in certain problem areas, such as deterioration in children's nutrition, received little attention outside the explicit obesity category.

Further, the rising American mental health concern directly advanced the number of professionals and school and college agencies eager to uncover any valid target—a standard result when a new disease emphasis is established. One of the reasons for the growing incidence of some of the new diseases reflected the clear incentives to identify students with mental problems.

However, the most obvious result of the focus on the mental health basis of the new disorders was an increasingly impassioned emphasis on the stubborn gap between available resources and the magnitude of the problems involved—a consistent theme from at least the 1970s. Though the figures steadily rose, a standard conclusion among professionals was that half, or slightly over half, of all needy children were actually getting help—that growing investments were falling dramatically short of need.

Thus, by the 1990s it was widely reported that only 47 percent of children in need were receiving any kind of assistance—and some claims ranged even further, citing the millions of young people involved. Problems that showed up behaviorally received the greatest attention, leaving vaguer but troubling categories like anxiety particularly bereft. Adolescents won greater attention than younger children, partly on the same basis. Culture and resources clearly factored in. Hispanics and Asian Americans used, or had access to, mental services less than whites. White-Black differentials, however, largely reflected differential poverty: poor whites were actually served less than their Black counterparts. The emphasis on unmet need was a compelling staple. The issue was further complicated by a gap between high school and college levels. Schools were legally required to register students with disabilities, but colleges could identify only those students who came forward, creating legitimate concerns that many, for whatever reason, were holding back. In response, at least by the twenty-first century, college students were increasingly bombarded by reminders to seek help.[13]

Emphasis on the therapeutic response also showed up in a variety of federal policies, which sought to offer new levels of protection and support for children with identified disabilities, while in the process also promoting expansion of the numbers of children involved. Classifying students as disabled has allowed schools to access higher levels of state and federal funding, supporting more individualized instruction, services such as speech therapy, and a variety of special accommodations. Under laws such as the Individuals with Disabilities Education Act (1990, replacing a somewhat similar law introduced in 1975), schools are legally required not only to identify but to assist students with disabilities, and failure to do so can lead to litigation and loss of funding. The result has unquestionably improved conditions for many students with mental disorders or other challenges, reducing though not eliminating recourse to a more punitive approach. Yet—out of concerns about funding or potential legal challenges—the same policies have encouraged the application of a "disability" label to children for school behaviors that might be categorized and treated more subtly. This result risks negative consequences, including stigma and self-doubt for students who might be erroneously categorized as well as inflation of the numbers involved. Here was arguably another source of the unusually high rates of reported mental distress among children and youth in the United States—and another sign of the double-edged quality to the therapeutic emphasis, providing both much needed help and potential overemphasis.

Beyond the therapeutic response, options have seemed more limited. The twenty-first century saw some limited efforts to attack sources of stress in schools: hence the slight reduction in the emphasis on tests, some interest in restoring recess for younger children, and of course the new fascination with mental health days. At the policy level, particularly after the pandemic exacerbated so many issues, attention focused particularly on proposals to rein in social media, though without much measurable result amid political polarization and the power of the giant corporations involved.

The rise of positive psychology after 1998 generated another alternative. A number of colleges and some schools established well-being centers aimed at encouraging individuals to take their own steps toward assuring mental and physical soundness instead of waiting for a need for therapy. The centers promoted constructive behaviors that ranged from good sleep and exercise habits to more frequent expressions of gratitude to the practice of meditation. Their impact, however, remained somewhat limited: few young people practiced meditation, for example, which drew a much larger number of college-educated adults. And the movement was criticized for overemphasizing individual ability to overcome obstacles and neglecting more structural issues. Certainly, to date, the well-being approach has not rivaled the reliance on expanded facilities for therapy.[14]

A further response, increasingly popular in schools and colleges, has involved the variety of "accommodations" for students identified with and claiming some kind of disability: where therapy and medication seem inadequate, allow affected students to take extra time with assignments and tests. By the 2020s, 10–25 percent of all college students were receiving designations of this sort. The approach raised its own set of questions. Were some students seeking the designation despite relatively mild or intermittent symptoms that might be handled in other ways? Particularly at the school level, were some middle-class parents becoming especially adept at winning extra time for their offspring as part of their strategies in overcoming what they saw as an intensely competitive environment? Were some students being encouraged to develop unreasonable expectations of flexibility on the part of teachers (and perhaps employers) instead of being provided with learning strategies that might obviate the need for special treatment? Revealingly, disability services experts, eager to get college students the help they believed necessary, explicitly worked to disabuse students of any notion that their disabilities were transitory—thus contributing to the sense among many adolescents that they were substantially and probably permanently defined by their ailment. Or, on the flip side, was the crucial problem the gap between students in need and the willingness to grant special treatment a common claim consistent with the urgent emphasis on inadequate therapeutic services. During the pandemic, for example, many student activists pressed instructors and administrators to suspend normal grading procedures, convinced that fragile mental health was near the brink with the Covid threat added in—an appeal that left some (older) authorities cold, convinced that there was no reason not to buckle down.[15]

Conclusion

Overall evaluation remains difficult, in part because many of the key problems, though not brand new, are relatively recent. The core issue, in diagnosis and treatment alike, remains defining and addressing the range and severity involved. The increasing interest in defining problems and seeking therapeutic response has undoubtedly benefited many children with major problems—many of whom, in decades past, would have been institutionalized and permanently marginalized. On the other hand, some children with milder challenges have been convinced of a level of need and deficiency that can actually work to their disadvantage. A new cultural symptom pool is available that is proving increasingly attractive to many young people themselves, reducing the capacity to overcome setbacks independently. The challenge is figuring out how better to define the boundary lines involved among the various categories, including some willingness to rein in the expansionist impulse.

It is also important to remember that current approaches, however vital for many individual children, have distinct limitations, for the levels of reported distress continue to surge. There is no question that attention to the need for therapy has overshadowed consideration of other possibilities—such as extending recess periods and physical education requirements that might have greater preventive potential. The urgent plea to expand on more of the same when it comes to therapy, however understandable, may not be the best path, or at least is unlikely to prove adequate. While many key issues are widely shared among advanced industrial nations, American levels, combined with inadequate coping mechanisms, seem to pose particularly acute problems. The invitation to explore additional and more preventive remediation is both obvious and pressing.[16]

The American Child: The Transformation of Childhood Since World War II. Steven Mintz and Peter N. Stearns, Oxford University Press. © Oxford University Press 2025. DOI: 10.1093/9780197797112.003.0011

12
Facing Up to Contemporary Childhood

In 1938, back in the day when overall child welfare was a more popular topic than it is currently, leading social worker Grace Abbott staked out a bold proposition: "The progress of the state may be measured by the extent to which it defends the rights of its children."[1] The claim, focused on the weakest and most vulnerable members of society, may have a somewhat anachronistic ring today. We have so many other things to worry about, so many other groups to consider. When we do think of children, we prefer to focus on a specific issue—like cell phones—not childhood's wider scope. Yet the core goal that Abbott urged, a product of the Progressive and New Deal eras, remains valid: assuring, to the greatest extent possible, a healthy and constructive childhood is vital not only to children themselves but to the adults they will become and the society they will shape.

For childhood is a public as well as a private good, a balance that has been threatened in recent decades. The United States has downplayed public support for children in favor of emphasizing private, parental responsibility—an imbalance that shows up in policies ranging from limited parental leave for newborns to spotty medical and day-care coverage. Yet even as the nation emphasizes private responsibility, external forces, bent on seeing children as a source of profit, complicate both child-rearing and the experience of childhood in novel ways.

The history of contemporary American childhood, in all its major dimensions, makes two points abundantly clear. First, over recent decades contemporary conditions have introduced serious problems for many children, with rising rates of mental distress the most obvious symptom, though not the only one. Second, dealing with these problems will be no easy task, requiring new thinking not just at the policy level but in the broader national culture. There is no simple fix.

Take, for example, the case of play. Contemporary history makes it quite obvious that play, including outdoor play, has declined to an undesirable extent. Many experts have pointed this out for some time. Quite recently Jonathan Haidt, along with recommending cell phone bans for younger children, urges a restoration of more unstructured play as the essential remedies for the deterioration of childhood.[2] And there's no question he is pointing in the right direction, though oversimplifying what must be done. But recognizing the goal of greater play and putting it into practice are two different things. Implementation involves new investments that would provide enriching opportunities for the large minority of children in or near poverty; new policies that, for example, would generate more abundant park space and reduce the emphasis on time spent in classrooms (think of the resistance to this essential move alone; how can we shake off the belief that more classroom sitting equals more learning, despite foreign examples to the contrary?); curtailing the corporate commercial pressures that have cut into independent child culture; reversing the trends toward excessive safetyism that have afflicted both parents and the wider society; even cutting into the rigors of organized sports—in other words, reevaluating many of the components of contemporary childhood at a variety of levels. All of this is desirable, and all are potentially doable, but it is a tall order that requires rethinking a number of national priorities.

There are grounds for hope. The fact that a number of recommendations are on the table—like restricting some aspects of social media—is a positive development, even if the suggestions sometimes seize on only one slice of a larger set of problems while corporate resistance looms large. The flurry of activity in 2024 toward restricting cell phone use obviously reflects constructive concern, though it is not clear how the efforts will pay off in practice and there is real danger in overinvesting in a single policy fix. A better comparative sense can be helpful for some of the broader policy issues affecting childhood. Other affluent societies, faced with similar basic challenges like a falling birth rate and rising educational requirements, have developed constructive approaches that might inform American efforts, from greater support for parents with new children to more rigorous limitations on classroom time in favor of more independent activities. American conditions argue against some mindless imitation of Finnish or German childhood, but there are things to learn. Finally, contemporary American childhood is the product of change; it is not immutable; change can be changed, though there is effort involved.

For it is past time to face the crucial challenges essential for improving the experience of contemporary childhood, under the broader umbrella of restoring children to a higher national priority. Historians dealing with contemporary patterns are understandably leery of moving from analysis to recommendation, worrying about getting out of their depth. In the case of childhood, at least, the relevant history virtually compels some response while also suggesting many of the directions that response should take.

A host of actors need to be engaged, as the play example already suggests. Parents, teachers, and educational policymakers must be involved. Colleges also have their role, particularly the elite institutions: we must cut back on the unnecessary inducements to competitive stress; the elites can easily fill their ranks with qualified students without encouraging applicants to take every AP course on the books or max out on extracurriculars. Federal, state, and local officials must be drawn in, as well as the judicial branch, given our proclivity for endless litigation. Corporations have become major players, and not just the social media giants. Doctors and mental health professionals loom large. The list is a long one, not to mention that amorphous entity, the broader culture.

Targets for change or reconsideration are at least as numerous, ranging from cutting back on mindless testing to (possibly) reconsidering the timing of American toilet training to providing greater support for the variety of contemporary American family forms. Rather, however, than offer a laundry list of worthy suggestions, six categories call for concerted attention. Two involve unavoidable challenges, two suggest the need to rebalance current approaches, and two highlight the most important additional measures. The goal is an American childhood less burdened by inequality; less open to unnecessary levels of therapeutic intervention and less troubled overall; and, within boundaries, more independent, offering greater opportunity to gain and demonstrate competence.

The Challenges: Inequality Plus

Priorities among fervent advocates for childhood reform vary, with two different emphases. For one group, inequality is the besetting problem of contemporary childhood, overwhelming any other concern. For the other, different issues affecting children more generally, like the impact of social media, take pride of place. Mutual conversation is not always easy. Thus, many recommendations for compensating for poverty ignore issues like play almost entirely, urging more rigorous classroom and homework assignments to offset the limitations of the home environment. In contrast, advocates who pin their hopes on measures like reining in social media are concerned with different, largely regulatory issues.

Yet any effort to restructure contemporary childhood must address both priorities. We need to provide more opportunities for imaginative play to poorer children, through funded summer camps and after-school programs. Day-care facilities must be extended to match what affluent families can afford on their own, both for basic oversight in relief of burdened parents and for opportunities for creativity and informal social learning. At the same time we need to work on the play needs of the middle- and upper-middle-class groups, to reduce over-regimentation and premature specialization. The play priority, in other words, is widely shared, but implementation must address inequality as well.

Some goals, of course, focus on inequality alone. The United States stands thirty-first, comparatively, in rates of child poverty, well below its standing in Gross National Product. Child homelessness is a huge problem, and the same applies to food insecurity, again with children disproportionate victims. Stubbornly high levels of infant mortality—here the nation ranks fifty-first, tied with Croatia—primarily burden the poor, and differential health conditions and medical support affect poorer children generally, including impacts on school performance. There is no question that developing a better model of contemporary childhood involves addressing these inequities head-on, and this means some serious changes in funding levels and government priorities. Shifts in the approach to schooling must also grapple with inequality, beginning with basic facilities and teacher compensation.[3]

Other targets, however, range more widely. Greater protection against corporate commercial exploitation applies to children generally, to take an obvious example. So does reduction of classroom time and the mania for frequent testing. Even the goal of matching other countries in providing parental leaves to tend to newborns has some implications for promoting healthy childhoods across the social spectrum. Similarly, greater attention to the woeful day-care situation, while it most obviously targets poorer parents, has some implications across the board.

The point is clear. Inequality, and its particular impact on contemporary childhood, is a vital issue, never to be neglected amid efforts to deal with some of the burdens on more affluent children. But there are other targets as well, some combining fairly readily with attention to inequality, some involving additional effort.

The Challenges: Partisanship and Advocacy

Given the importance of childhood and the magnitude of contemporary problems, it would be nice to talk beyond partisanship and apart from the frenzy of the culture wars. But that's impossible. At the same time, desirable reforms do not entirely fall in one camp or the other, and although conservatives may find less to like than liberals, there are adjustments for liberals as well.

A 2024 controversy suggested some of the complexity involved. A new federal program, from the Democratic administration, offered funds for summer food aid for poorer children to replace the meals provided by schools during other months. About half of the Republican-led states accepted the program, recognizing that it filled a need for children. But the other half balked: one governor cited the risks of childhood obesity, others objected to "welfare" or to the modest additional costs to the states or to anything the Democrats did. One governor, interestingly, having initially turned the program down, claiming, "I don't believe in welfare," reversed course after hearing from some persuasive low-income teenagers about the problems involved. Partisanship was inescapable, but at the same time it was not complete—childhood can cut across lines to some extent. There may be some joy as well in the fact that both sides in the 2024 presidential campaign discussed more resources for families with children, though the precise recommendations *and* their rationale differed; it remains to be seen if any action will result given deep divisions and competing priorities.

It's no secret that most of the measures needed to address childhood inequalities, particularly with funding involved, will not go down well with conservatives. Thus, a pandemic-inspired measure to provide some money to the lowest-income families—similar to programs that are standard fare in most affluent countries—simply did not survive the return of a Republican-majority House of Representatives in 2022, though a few Republicans showed interest. But partisan claims must not be overdone. The interest some Republicans show in promoting a higher birthrate might allow discussion of some of the changes in family support that must almost certainly be involved—again potentially creating some collaborative possibilities with welfare-minded Democrats. Serious conversation is unlikely at least in the first years of Trump II, where cost cutting reigns supreme, but there is no reason to abandon hope entirely.

On a related front: Both parties have done more talking than doing about parental leaves for several decades. Both parties have failed to come up with assistance for the flailing day-care industry, though Democrats have been more interested than their conservative colleagues, some of whom continue to believe that the solution lies in keeping mothers home. Democrats as well as Republicans have contributed to the testing mania in the schools, as in bipartisan support for No Child Left Behind. Perhaps most importantly, both parties are beholden to corporate lobbies bent on protecting commercial access to children. There is work to do in both camps.

Both parties contribute to excessive efforts to protect children from uncomfortable ideas—they just differ widely on what defines uncomfortable. The need to free contemporary childhood from excessive supervision will raise issues for conservatives and liberals alike—though liberals may turn out to be particularly uneasy, particularly reluctant to undo excessive safetyism, and particularly nervous about pushing back against undue psychologizing. The need to recast part of the cultural framework for contemporary childhood is not necessarily a partisan issue, though the culture wars will unquestionably complicate the process.

Compounding the challenge of partisanship is the decline of adequate child advocacy, another shift from the earlier twentieth century. It is troubling that, even as problems in American childhood have become increasingly apparent, no advocacy group has gained an ascendant role amid the welter of interest groups and lobbyists that populate national policy space. In contrast to the earlier twentieth century, when the National Child Labor Reform Committee won massive public attention and support from a range of celebrities until its demise in 2017,[4] a variety of organizations, such as the Children's Defense Fund (1973), now compete for attention. Most of them are sincere and worthy, but none has the influence of other contenders like the American Association for Retired Persons or the food lobby. Some have also struggled to find a compelling basic focus. Many important groups, like Parent-Teacher Associations, while persisting, have fallen victim to adult distractions and the rise of partisanship, with a 50 percent decline in membership in recent decades.[5] Relative weakness of organized child advocacy is particularly important since—as politicians well know—children don't vote, and even young adults don't do their share.

This is an issue that must be addressed. Might child health, broadly construed, command the attention that child labor once did? Can parents and grandparents, mostly sincerely concerned about their own progeny, provide greater support for initiatives affecting childhood more generally? A society in which far fewer adults have much contact with kids than ever before needs to find ways to compensate, and compensate dynamically. But this is a step not yet taken.

Rebalancing: The Issue of Regulation

Children need protections that adults don't require to the same extent. This has always been true, and it certainly applies to contemporary American childhood. But as this childhood has unfolded over several decades, it has become clear that the United States has approached the issue of protective regulation in the wrong way, devoting too much attention to the anxious, safetyist monitoring of children's daily activities and far too little to moderating the pressures on children that come from sources well beyond their control—notably, the new forms of media and the increasingly insidious, manipulative forms of corporate advertising. It is, of course, easier to tell children what to do than to call Meta or Kellogg to account—but the latter is essential if children are to gain the kind of cultural space needed for a creative, constructive childhood.

There are moves afoot to deal more firmly with the ways the social media giants target children, though so far there is more talk than action in an admittedly difficult area. Online sexual exploitation of children is likely to get worse with artificial intelligence. Cyberbullying adds troubling dimensions to an old problem. Social influencers expose children prematurely to adult realities. But new media are not the only challenge. It is vital to revisit the removal of most restrictions on children's advertising that has so deeply affected the childhood experience over the past forty years—there are earlier regulatory precedents we can turn to. Policymakers must work to enact and enforce regulations that limit the types and amounts of advertising directed at children, particularly for products that exploit their vulnerabilities or contribute to unhealthy lifestyles. We can also work to promote intelligent media literacy through school efforts to help children better understand content and distinguish advertisements from other sources of information and by developing more quality children's programming free from commercialization. We might even try to revive some traditional games and stories that beguiled children in the past, but these measures will not replace the need for new forms of regulation.

This is not a simple plea. Quite apart from the power of lobbyists, American legal traditions, particularly freedom of speech, pose limitations—though some of these had been addressed until 1981. But the broader need, to recalibrate our approach to regulating children—beefing up areas that kids simply can't control, relaxing strictures that have proved damaging, goes beyond the policy arena to the need to review the cultural framework that has come to define childhood, particularly in the contemporary era.

Rebalancing: Recognizing Changes and Gains

Given the various signs of deterioration in contemporary childhood, the temptation to conclude that the nation needs a vigorous push backward is hard to resist—and it looms large in some political formulas, particularly on the right. Around the edges the approach makes sense. It would be fine to restore 1950s-level recess in the schools, as some policymakers are realizing. It would be great to delay serious, specialized sports commitments, for most kids, until high school, as was the case before the rise of travel teams. And the list can be expanded.

However, a nostalgic, turn-back-the-clock approach is unrealistic for two reasons. First, many of the structural changes that set the framework for contemporary childhood are unlikely to reverse; and second, we don't want to throw the good stuff out with the bad.

This society's emphasis on the value of education corresponds to the new economic reality. To be sure, there are legitimate debates about alternatives to college, like apprenticeships in relevant skilled trades, but the demands of a knowledge-based economy are not likely to yield anytime soon. Schooling can and should be done better. More opportunities for high school completion and less burdensome access to college deserve continued attention. Young children need more relief from unrealistic expectations of educational performance, more opportunities to adjust gradually to fixed standards. There are opportunities to learn from the unusual success of some existing systems: thus, schools run by the American military for the children of service families already do a well-above-average job in learning results and greater (though not complete) equality among students of different ethnic groups. More generally, we must obviously cut back testing and work to make schools more inviting places to learn. But a restoration of 1950s educational patterns, with far fewer years on average devoted to schooling, makes no sense. Despite major problems and troubling disparities, educational advances for many children have brought measurable benefits in the economic sphere and beyond.

Contemporary demographic trends also are unlikely to change anytime soon, though there can and should be serious efforts around the edges to reduce some of the special burdens of American parenting. More might be done to counter the unrealistically adverse images of contemporary parenthood. Attention to the growing volume of happiness literature can come into play: while there are problems with American parental satisfaction, most research suggests parenthood and happiness still correlate strongly. We can talk more about the new roles fathers might take (and in some cases have taken) to ease maternal burdens. But all the evidence, American and international, suggests serious limitations to policy innovations that will raise the birth rate. At best, as one exceptionally active Italian region has demonstrated, abundant and prolonged parental support can stabilize existing levels. And all this means a need to adjust to the smaller percentage of children in the overall society and the many competing demands on adult time. Nor is a reduction in the average age of first parents very likely. A child-friendly contemporary American must focus on doing better with the children we have.

By the same token, diversity in family forms will probably not yield to a more standard model in the foreseeable future. Policy changes—for example, reducing the disincentives for fathers on welfare to live with their partners and offspring—are desirable. But a full return to predominantly two-parent, stable family households is not a realistic goal. Nor are most married women likely to abandon the labor force. Nor are girls likely to rein in their ambitions in order to make things easier for boys. And all this means two things. First, we need policies that support and recognize all types of families. Part of the fight against inequality must involve reducing some of the drawbacks of single parenthood. Second, we must recognize that in many cases a number of different family forms can work out fairly well for children, in some cases highlighting devotion to the child's welfare.

The penchant for psychologizing normal childhood behavior does warrant new debate, toward making firmer distinctions between problems and disabilities and cutting back the temptation to pathologize so many childhood challenges. This is one of the thorniest issues in the contemporary framework. Parents and teachers must be encouraged to avoid premature labeling and, often, medication. School policies must tighten against the current temptation to cushion against setbacks: there was no excuse for a pandemic-inspired measure, in some districts, that prohibited teachers from giving less than 50 points (on a scale of 100) even when students had turned in no work. More subtle recalibrations are essential as well. But this does not mean a return to the bad old days of neglect for serious mental health issues or a new stigma against needed therapy or a more punitive approach to schooling. Here too, like it or not, elements of the contemporary framework are not going away anytime soon, and too much nostalgia will waste time and misdirect effort.

Then, it is vital to remember the paradoxical aspects of contemporary childhood. There have been huge gains during recent decades that should not be jeopardized. Children who are better able to avoid teenage pregnancy or high alcohol consumption or dangerous driving are assets to themselves and to society as a whole. While contemporary gender patterns among children certainly raise some new issues, the balance, in promoting more opportunities for girls, is surely positive, compared to the situation in the 1950s. The greater tolerance for diversities that many contemporary children demonstrate, compared to generations past, is also a gain that should not be jeopardized.

The point is clear. Contemporary American childhood needs reformist attention from many angles, but it must continue to be built around some basic changes that show every sign of persistence, and around many features that are positively desirable. The need for appropriate balance is inescapable. The most compelling goal in dealing with contemporary childhood centers on a better adaptation to major change, not appealing to earlier models.

New Measures: The Moral Dimension

Several developments in contemporary American society have created issues for the moral education of children that are too rarely discussed. Most obviously, the decline in churchgoing and Sunday school participation creates a potential void. The commercial bombardment of children offers little by way of moral guideposts. The increasingly utilitarian cast of education and of young people's educational goals compared to patterns a half century ago suggests another limitation. The same applies to the demonstrable increase in children's alone-ness.

To address this problem, American society needs to create spaces and programs where personal and social development is fostered. One path involves curricular expansion in the schools, to add more ethical and philosophical components that encourage children to reflect on moral dilemmas and to develop their own reasoned beliefs about right and wrong. Art and literature programs can be leveraged to discuss values, dilemmas, and different cultural perspectives. Schools might also incorporate community service into educational programs, along with classroom instruction, providing a practical framework for discussing ethical issues while engaging with diverse community members. The obvious challenge, that this will take away classroom time, can be met with the obvious response: we need to be reconsidering classroom time anyway, for the present pattern is too narrowly focused and too test-dependent. The ethical dimension will offer a new range of opportunities for less structured learning.

Community centers can strengthen and expand programs that bring different generations together for storytelling and workshops. Efforts in the Netherlands to juxtapose children with the elderly have proved to benefit both groups. Mentorship programs, along the lines of Big Brothers and Big Sisters, pair young people with adults from various professions and backgrounds, providing not only career guidance but also ethical discussions informed by real-world experiences. Community center programs can also encourage interfaith and intercultural initiatives that foster dialogue and understanding across different traditions.

Efforts of this sort are vital to provide all children the opportunity to develop a well-rounded sense of morality and social responsibility, regardless of religious background, affiliation, or non-affiliation.

New Measures: Competence

Here's the most vital goal: find new or renewed ways to give children a greater opportunity to demonstrate competence and independence, with opportunities to take moderate risks, make mistakes, and learn in the process. Overprotective parenting practices and wider safetyism have demonstrably gone too far, resulting in a lack of resilience and self-efficacy in children and limiting the capacity ultimately to navigate the complexities of the adult world. Here is where some policy changes and crucial cultural adjustments must combine.

Many children do not want to be treated as fragile and completely dependent; many crave opportunities to do more to contribute to family and society and have their talents recognized. Providing the necessary scope in the contemporary context obviously involves some special challenges, like the need for extensive formal schooling, but they can be met. And some older devices can be reintroduced as well. Providing children with opportunities to contribute and shine will require changes in educational settings, family dynamics, community involvement, and public spaces.

In schools, test-structured learning must be reduced to allow more project activities, where children can engage with real-world problems. This approach also allows them to apply what they have learned in meaningful ways, fostering a sense of accomplishment and contribution. Schools can also empower students by involving them more extensively in decision-making processes in the classroom. Allowing children a say in teaching methods and evaluation processes can enhance their capacity for agency. The same applies to adding more service learning components to the curriculum, taking students into the community and developing a sense of social responsibility.[6]

At home, parents can do more to encourage independence and contribution. Assigning age-appropriate chores and taking the time to allow children to work into full competence are vital adjustments that have been needlessly neglected. From an early age children want to contribute to the family and they should be counted on to do so, learning crucial life skills in the process. From an early age also, children can be given opportunities for money management and saving. Parents can also do more to involve children in family decisions, such as planning vacations or managing schedules. This inclusion reinforces children's sense of importance within the family and builds negotiating skills.

The goal is not to turn children into premature adults but to give childhood itself a greater sense of purpose and meaning than contemporary patterns currently encourage. But the importance of opportunities for more independent play, ideally with groups of children of somewhat varying ages, are vital components of competence as well. Not only families but society more generally needs to adjust to seeing more children partially on their own, providing appropriate spaces—including outdoor spaces—accordingly. The days when well-meaning police scoop up children of suitable age playing on their own in a park, or doing some family shopping at a local store, on the assumption that they are being dangerously neglected, should be over. And we should not need to call more flexible parenting "free range"—it's just good parenting.[7]

Implementing these strategies allows families and society at large to help children feel more valued, competent, and involved, as well as able to overcome some setbacks and mistakes on their own. The result helps meet children's need to contribute and have their capabilities recognized while also enriching families, schools, and communities by harnessing the unique perspectives and talents that children can bring to bear.

The High Note

The greatest danger in citing the various adjustments that can and should be made in contemporary American childhood is that it risks enhancing the notion that dealing with children today is nothing but a joyless chore. That's not the case now and will not be with the adjustments in motion. A more relaxed parenting style will actually reward a decline in safetyism and anxious competitiveness. Teaching will benefit as well if there is more opportunity to help students explore and less compulsion simply to drill— and probably a somewhat happier student body as well. Part of the process of restoring higher priority to childhood involves greater recognition of the pleasures it can entail for all involved.

Joy can be a crucial part of contemporary children's experience as well, beyond the commercialized treats that too often pass for pleasure. One of the strengths of the Progressive vision a century ago was an effort to universalize an ideal in which childhood offered a time for excitement, discovery, and exploration. The specifics of the earlier twentieth century cannot be recaptured, and they were deeply flawed in any event. But the larger ideal remains valid.

There is much work to do to make contemporary American childhood a greater success and the nation itself a child-friendlier society. Progress can be measured through more widely shared opportunities, a reduction in some of the alarming rates of poverty, and a greater ability to compensate for some of the instabilities of family life. But the goal can be more ambitious still. Contemporary American society can give children more opportunities for real joy.

The American Child: The Transformation of Childhood Since World War II. Steven Mintz and Peter N. Stearns, Oxford University Press. © Oxford University Press 2025. DOI: 10.1093/9780197797112.003.0012

Endnotes

Preface

1. Important studies that verge on the one-factor approach—usually a fairly recent factor, along with a clear sense of declensions from the past—include Jean Twenge, *iGen: Why Today's Super-Connected Kids Are Growing Up Less Rebellious, More Tolerant, Less Happy—and Completely Unprepared for Adulthood* (New York: Atria, 2017) (which decries the impact of social media) and Abigail Shrier, *Bad Therapy: Why the Kids Aren't Growing Up* (New York: Sentinel, 2024) (a critique of the impact of therapeutic culture on children).

Chapter 1

1. Vivek Murthy, *Protecting Youth Mental Health* (Washington, DC: U.S. Surgeon General's Advisory, 2021), https://www.hhs.gov/sites/default/files/surgeon-general-youth-mental-health-advisory.pdf.
2. Lance Klaus et al., "History of Attention Deficit Hyperactivity Disorder," *ADHD Attention Deficit and Hyperactivity Disorders* (December 2010), https://pubmed.ncbi.nlm.nih.gov/21258430/.
3. John Holmes et al., "Youth Drinking in Decline: What Are the Implications for Public Health, Public Policy and Public Debate?," *International Journal of Drug Policy* 102 (2022), https://pubmed.ncbi.nlm.nih.gov/35131690/; Elizabeth Wildsmith et al., "The 30-Year Decline in Teen Birth Rates Has Accelerated Since 2010," *Child Trends* (December 2022), https://www.childtrends.org/blog/the-30-year-decline-in-teen-birth-rates-has-accelerated-since-2010.
4. This category is complex. Rates rose massively from 1975 to 1995, then dropped steadily until about 2007. They have since risen about 25 percent, clearly troubling, but remain below peak levels. Centers for Disease Control and Prevention, "QuickStats: Suicide Rates for Teens Aged 15–19 Years, by Sex—United States, 1975–2015," *Morbidity and Mortality Weekly Report*, August 4, 2017, https://www.cdc.gov/mmwr/volumes/66/wr/mm6630a6.htm?s_cid=mm6630a6_w.
5. Rami Benbenishty and Ron Avi Astor, *School Violence in Context* (New York: Oxford University Press, 2005); Rami Benbenishty, Ron Avi Astor, and Adam Roziner, "An Eighteen-Year Longitudinal Study of School Victimization and Weaponry in California Secondary Schools," *World Journal of Pediatrics* (March 2023), https://doi.org/10.1007/s12519-023-00714-w.
6. J. F. Sandberg and S. L. Hofferth, "Changes in Children's Time with Parents: United States, 1981–1997," *Demography* 38 (2001), https://doi.org/10.2307/3088356.
7. See, for example, the range of articles in the admirable *Journal of the History of Childhood and Youth*. But also see Paula Fass, *The End of American Childhood: A History of Parenting from the Frontier to the Managed Child* (Princeton, NJ: Princeton University Press, 2016); Paula Fass and Michael Grossberg, eds., *Reinventing Childhood After World War II* (Philadelphia: University of Pennsylvania Press, 2012); Pamela Riney-Kehrberg, *The Nature of Childhood: An Environmental History of Growing Up in America Since 1865* (Lawrence: University of Kansas Press, 2014); and Irwin Redlener, *The Future of Us: What the Dreams of Children Mean to Twenty-First-Century America* (New York: Columbia University Press, 2017).
8. C. Y. C. Chen, J. Byrne, and T. Velez, "Impact of the 2020 Pandemic of Covid-19 on Families with School-Aged Children in the United States: Roles of Income Level and Race," *Journal of Family Issues* 43 (2021), https://doi.org/10.1177/0192513X21994153; National Center for Educational Statistics, "More than 80 Percent of U.S. Public Schools Report Pandemic Has Negatively Impacted Student Behavior and Socio-Emotional Development," July 6, 2022, https://nces.ed.gov/whatsnew/press_releases/07_06_2022.asp.

9. Ashley Abramson, "Children's Mental Health Is in Crisis," *Monitor on Psychology* 53 (2022), https://www.apa.org/monitor/2022/01/special-childrens-mental-health.
10. Jean Twenge, *iGen: Why Today's Super-Connected Kids Are Growing Up Less Rebellious, More Tolerant, Less Happy—and Completely Unprepared for Adulthood* (New York: Atria, 2017); E. Kross et al., "Social Media and Well-Being: Pitfalls, Progress, and Next Steps," *Trends in Cognitive Sciences* (November 2020), https://pubmed.ncbi.nlm.nih.gov/33187873/.
11. Sharlene Hesse-Biber, *Am I Thin Enough Yet? The Cult of Thinness and the Commercialization of Identity* (New York: Oxford University Press, 2012).
12. Abraham Lincoln, "House Divided" speech, Springfield, IL, 1858.
13. Allan Horwitz, *Anxiety: A Short History* (Baltimore: Johns Hopkins University Press, 2013); Lee Rainee and Andre Perrin, "Key Findings About Americans' Declining Trust in Government and Each Other," Pew Research Center, July 22, 2019, https://www.pewresearch.org/short-reads/2019/07/22/key-findings-about-americans-declining-trust-in-government-and-each-other/; Barry Glassner, *The Culture of Fear: Why Americans Are Afraid of the Wrong Things* (New York: Basic Books, 1999); Robert Putnam, *Bowling Alone: Collapse and Revival of American Community* (New York: Simon & Schuster, 2000).

Chapter 2

1. Steven Mintz, *Huck's Raft: A History of American Childhood* (Cambridge, MA: Belknap Press of Harvard University Press, 2004); Paula S. Fass, *The End of American Childhood: A History of Parenting from Life on the Frontier to the Managed Child* (Princeton, NJ: Princeton University Press, 2016); Peter N. Stearns, *Childhood in World History* (4th ed., New York: Routledge, 2021).
2. Hugh Hindman, *Child Labor: An American History* (Amonk, NY: Routledge, 2002).
3. J. D. Hacker and Evan Roberts, "Fertility Decline in the United States, 1850-1930: New Evidence from Complete-Count Datasets," *American Demographic History* 138 (2019), https://www.ncbi.nlm.nih.gov/pmc/articles/PMC9255892/.
4. Peter N. Stearns, *Shame: A Brief History* (Urbana: University of Illinois Press, 2017).
5. Gary Cross, *Kids' Stuff: Toys and the Changing World of American Childhood* (Cambridge, MA: Harvard University Press, 1997).
6. Kriste Lindenmeyer, *A Right to Childhood: The U.S. Children's Bureau and Child Welfare, 1912-1946* (Urbana: University of Illinois Press, 2007).
7. Lloyd deMause, ed., *The History of Childhood: The Untold Story of Child Abuse* (Lanham, MD: Peter Bedrick Books, 1977), 1.
8. Steven Mintz, *Huck's Raft: A History of American Childhood* (Cambridge, MA: Belknap Press of Harvard University Press, 2004).
9. Gary Cross, *The Cute and the Cool: Wondrous Innocence and Modern American Children's Culture* (New York: Oxford University Press, 2004).
10. J. Engelmann, *A History of the Birth Control Movement in America* (Santa Barbara, CA: Praeger, 2011).
11. Phillip Rieff, *The Triumph of the Therapeutic: Uses of Faith After Freud* (Chicago: University of Chicago Press, 1966); Katie Wright, *Rise of the Therapeutic Society: Psychological Knowledge and the Contradictions of Cultural Change* (Washington, DC: New Academia, 2011); Allan Horwitz, *Anxiety: A Short History* (Baltimore: Johns Hopkins University Press, 2013); Lance Klaus et al., "Attention Deficit Disorder."
12. The application of the neologism "therapize" to children began in the 1990s. Ellen Barry, "Summer Camp: Sun, Swimming, Archery. And Therapy," *New York Times*, August 7, 2023, https://www.nytimes.com/2023/08/06/health/summer-camp-mental-health.html.
13. Daniel Bell, The Coming of Post-Industrial Society (New York: Basic Books, 1976); Walter Powell and Kaisa Snellman, "The Knowledge Economy," *Annual Review of Sociology* 30 (2004), http://dx.doi.org/10.1146/annurev.soc.29.010202.100037.
14. Jan Van Bevel and David Reher, "The Baby Boom and Its Causes. What We Know and What We Ought to Know," *Population and Development Review* 79 (2013), http://www.jstor.org/stable/41857595; Frank L. Sweetser and Paavo Piepponen, "Postwar Fertility Trends and Their Consequences in Finland and the United States," *Journal of Social History* 2 (1967), https://pubmed.ncbi.nlm.nih.gov/11632347/.
15. Census Bureau, "The U.S. Child Population Fell by One Million Between 2010 and 2020," *USA Facts*, September 30, 2021, https://usafacts.org/articles/the-us-child-population-shrank-by-

1-million-between-2010-and-2020/; George Masrick, "Childless Households Have Become the Norm," Harvard, Joint Center for Housing Studies, April 15, 2013, https://www.jchs.harvard.edu/blog/childless-households-have-become-the-norm.
16. U.S. Bureau of Labor Statistics, "Women in the Labor Force, 1970–2009," *TED: The Economics Daily*, January 5, 2011, https://www.bls.gov/opub/ted/2011/ted_20110105.htm; Kendra Cherry, "Parental Age and Child Development," *Very Well Family*, September 27, 2020, https://www.verywellfamily.com/parental-age-impact-child-development-4150443; Anne Morse, "Stable Fertility Rates 1990-2019 Mask Distinct Variations by Age," U.S. Census Bureau, April 6, 2022, https://www.census.gov/library/stories/2022/04/fertility-rates-declined-for-younger-women-increased-for-older-women.html.
17. Lindenmeyer, *Right to Childhood*; J. Michael and M. Goldsmith, "Reviving the White House Conference on Children," Child Welfare League of America, 2010, https://www.cwla.org/reviving-the-white-house-conference-on-children/.
18. J.A. Kushner, "The Fair Housing Amendments Acts of 1988: The Second Generation of Fair Housing," *Vanderbilt Law Review* 45 (1990); Matthew Desmond, *Evicted: Poverty and Profit in the American City* (New York: Crown, 2016).
19. K. Krisberg, "Thousands of Children and Teens Killed Annually by Guns in the U.S.," *The Nation's Health* 49 (1977); S, Mehta, "There's Only One Country That Hasn't Ratified the Convention on Children's Rights," *American Civil Liberties Union: Speak Freely* (November 3, 2014); C. Sesin, "Federal Spending on Children Falls to Lowest Levels in a Decade," NBC News, September 17, 2019.

Chapter 3

1. The first distinct reference to parents as helicopters seems to be Haim Ginnott, *Between Parents and Teenagers* (New York: Macmillan, 1969), and even though it only reached wide public attention later it was a fairly standard term in child-rearing literature by 1990. Estimates of incidence, by the twenty-first century, range from 10 to 41 percent of all American parents, and of course there are varying degrees of involvement. D. J. van Ingen et al., "Helicopter Parenting: The Effect of an Overbearing Caregiving Style on Peer Attachment and Self-Efficacy," *Journal of College Counseling* 18, no. 1 (2015), 215–20, https://doi.org/10.1002/j.2161-1882.2015.00065.x. Dave Cornell, "15 Helicopter Parenting Examples," HelpfulProfessor.com, January 3, 2024, https://helpfulprofessor.com/helicopter-parenting-examples/.
2. Vanessa LoBue, "Why Helicopter Parenting Fosters Failure," *Psychology Today*, July 12, 2020, https://www.psychologytoday.com/us/blog/the-baby-scientist/202007/why-helicopter-parenting-fosters-failure.
3. Rachel Flynn, N. J. Shaman, and D. L. Redleaf, "The Unintended Consequences of 'Lack of Supervision' Child Neglect Laws," Society for Research on Child Development, *Social Policy Report* 36, no. 1 (2023) 1–38, https://srcd.onlinelibrary.wiley.com/doi/full/10.1002/sop2.27.
4. Lenore Skenazy, *Free-Range Kids: How Parents and Teachers Can Let Go* (San Francisco: Jossy-Bass, 2021).
5. Duane Alwin, "From Obedience to Autonomy: Changes in Traits Desired in Children, 1924–1978," *The Public Opinion Quarterly* 52 (1988), http://www.jstor.org/stable/2749110; T. Caplow et al., *All Faithful People: Change and Continuity in Middletown's Religion* (Minneapolis: University of Minnesota Press, 1983); Alex Inkeles, "Social Change and Social Character: The Role of Parental Mediation," *Journal of Social Issues* 11 (1984), doi:10.1111/j.1540-4560.1983.tb00183.x.
6. Pamela Druckman, *Bringing Up Bebe: One American Mother Discovers the Wisdom of French Parenting* (New York: Penguin, 2019).
7. Steven Mintz, *Huck's Raft: A History of American Childhood* (Cambridge, MA: Belknap Press of Harvard University Press, 2004).
8. Lydia Maria Child, *The Mother's Book* (Boston: Carter, Henlon, 1831), 32.
9. New England Association of Farmers, Mechanics and Other Workingmen, Child Labor Petition, 1832.
10. E. A. Rotundo, *American Manhood* (New York: Hachette, 1993).
11. Child, *Mother's Book*, 29; see also T. S.. Arthur, *Mother's Book* (Philadelphia, 1856: Classic Reprints), 289–90.
12. Felix Adler, *The Moral Instruction of Children* (New York: D. Appleton & Co., 1892: repr. Independent Publishing, 1955); Child, *Mother's Book*, 6–10.

13. Adler, *Moral Instruction*.
14. D. F. Lincoln, *School and Industrial Hygiene* (Philadelphia: P. Blakiston, 1880); John Keating, ed., *Cyclopedia of the Diseases of Children*, v. 3 (Philadelphia: P. Blakiston, 1890).
15. Viviana Zelizer, *Pricing the Priceless Child* (Princeton, NJ: Princeton University Press, 1994).
16. Ida Tarbell, "Who Is to Blame for Child Killing?," *Collier's* 70 (October 7, 1922), 12, https://search-ebscohost-com.mutex.gmu.edu/login.aspx?direct=true&db=rgr&AN=522035832&site=ehost-live; Joel Tarr and Mark Tebeau, "Managing Danger in the Home Environment," *Journal of Social History* (1996), doi:10.1353/jsh/29.4.797. The comparative intensity of the American safety approach shows up in many areas involving children, from trail markers and railings to some features of car seat regulations (particularly the back-seat-until-age-twelve requirement). However, crucial limitations in this approach also demand attention, a point to which we will return in dealing with the fragility/nonchalance dichotomy.
17. Jane Addams, *Spirit of Youth and the City Streets* (1907; repr. Urbana: University of Illinois Press, 2001).
18. Steven Starker, *Evil Influences: Crusades Against the Mass Media* (New Brunswick, NJ: Rutgers University Press, 1989).
19. Brian P. Gill and Steven L. Schlossman, "Villain or Savior? The American Discourse on Homework, 1850-2003," *Theory into Practice* 43 (2004), http://www.jstor.org/stable/3701518.
20. G. Stanley Hall, "A Case Study of Fear," *American Journal of Psychology* 8, no. 2 (1897), 147–246, https://doi.org/10.2307/1410940; Alice Birney, *Childhood* (New York: F.A. Stokes Co., 1904; repub. University of California Libraries, 2019), 24–8.
21. Winnifred de Kok, *Guiding Your Child Through the Formative Years* (New York: Emerson Books, 1935), 76.
22. Birney, *Childhood*; Allan Fromme, *Children in the Family* (New York: Open Library, 1937), 101. See also Ruth Spin, "What to Do When Your Child Is Afraid," *Parents Magazine* 2 (1927), 25–7, https://archive.org/details/sim_parents_1927-03_2_3/pag e/24/mode/2up.
23. Benjamin Spock, *The Common Sense Book of Baby and Child Care* (New York: Duell, Sloane, 1945), 196–7; John Watson, *Psychological Care of Infant and Child* (New York: W.W. Norton, 1928), 45–68; Carl Renz and Mildred Renz, *Big Problems on Little Shoulders* (New York: MacMillan, 1934), 24–28.
24. Sybil Foster, "A Study of the Personality Makeup and Social Setting of Fifty Jealous Children," *Mental Hygiene* 11 (1927), 533–71; D. M. Levy, "Rivalry Between Children of the Same Family," *Child Study* 12 (1934), 233.
25. D. H. Thom, *Child Management* (Washington, DC: Children's Bureau, 1935), 14; Lynn Chalmer, "When Children Ask About Death," *Parents Magazine* 7 (1932); Peter Slater, *Children in the New England Mind: In Death and in Life* (Hamden, CT: Archon, 1977); Peter N. Stearns, *Revolutions in Sorrow: The American Experience of Death in a Global Context* (New York: Westview, 2016), 89–127.
26. Hence earnest advice to the tune of "never let your children go to bed sad" or "avoid unpleasant incidents like the plague; they shake the fabric of happiness to its foundations." Dorry Metcalfe, *Bringing Up Children* (New York: Macmillan, 1947), 62–3; M. V. O'Shea, *The Parent's Library: Faults of Children and Youth* (Chicago: Leopold's Classic, 1920).
27. Spock, *The Common Sense Book*; Michael Zuckerman, "Dr. Spock: The Confidence Man," in *The Family in History*, ed. Zuckerman and Charles Rosenberg (Philadelphia: University of Pennsylvania Press, 1975).
28. J. G. Fine and C. Sung, "Neuroscience of Child and Adolescent Mental Development," *Journal of Counseling Psychology* 61, no. 4 (2014), 521-527, https://www.researchgate.net/publication/266623348_Neuroscience_of_Child_and_Adolescent_Health_Development.
29. Wilson Orthodontics, "Why So Many Kids and Adults Need Orthodontic Treatment Today," January 2, 2012, https://wilson-ortho.com/why-do-many-kids-and-adults-need-orthodontic-treatment-today/. Explanations of why the need for treatment is rising so fast tend to be rather vague, emphasizing improved techniques and better information about the sources of tooth troubles later in life, but also the apparent results of human evolution and, possibly, population mixing in the United States.
30. Matthew Smith, *Hyperactive: The Controversial History of ADHD* (London: Reaktion Books, 2012).
31. Russell Heimlich, "Most Parents Expect Their Children to Attend College," Pew Research Center, February 27, 2012, https://www.pewresearch.org/short-reads/2012/02/27/most-parents-expect-their-children-to-attend-college/.

32. Linsey Black, Emily Terlizzi, and Anjel Vahratian, "Organized Sports Participation Among Children Aged 6–17 Years," *National Center for Health Statistics Data Brief* #441, August 2022, https://www.cdc.gov/nchs/products/databriefs/db441.htm.
33. Ruthann Clay and Peter Stearns, "Revisiting the Fearful Parent: The Crucial Decade," *Journal of the History of Children and Youth* (2018), https://doi.org/10.1353/hcy.2018.0033.
34. Lynne Edmondson and Laura Dreuth Zeman, "Making School Bully Laws Matter," *Reclaiming Children and Youth* 20 (2011), https://eric.ed.gov/?id=EJ932136; on the tremendous surge of commentary on bullying, Google Ngram (American English).
35. Jonathan Haidt and Greg Lukianoff, *The Coddling of the American Mind* (New York: Penguin, 2018).
36. "School Bus History," https://www.trackschoolbus.com/school-bus-history/. Note, however, that when it comes to driver's licenses, Americans are less stringent, another example of the kind of inconsistency discussed later, but also a reflection of urgent needs in the heavily suburban context.
37. In the United States in the late 1940s, 60 percent of children were toilet trained by eighteen months—a distant memory. Jacqueline Howard, "How the World Potty Trains," CNN Health, November 8, 2017, https://www.cnn.com/2017/10/31/health/potty-training-parenting-without-borders-explainer. This is a development, and comparative context, that deserves more attention than it has received from childhood historians.
38. "Play Date Etiquette Explained," CBS News, August 20, 2009, https://www.cbsnews.com/news/play-date-etiquette-explained/.
39. It seems clear that many American parents go about preparing for chores in the wrong way: they start too late, and then convey impatience with the ways kids go about things—both turning off what is a common childish eagerness to help. Lynn White and David Brinkerhoff, "Children's Work in the Family," *Journal of Marriage and the Family* 42, no. 4 (1981), 789–98, https://doi.org/10.2307/351336;Sampson Blair, "Children's Participation in Household Labor," *Journal of Youth and Adolescence* 21, no. 2 (1992), 241–58, https://doi.org/10.1007/bf01537339.
40. Caroline Hoxby, "The Changing Selectivity of American Colleges," *Journal of Economic Perspectives* 23 (2009), 95–118, https://www.aeaweb.org/articles?id=10.1257/jep.23.4.95. The increase in college aspirations was striking: in the mid-1950s, 15 percent of the relevant age group was heading to college, but by 1943 this had soared to 43 percent. College slots actually expanded accordingly, but competitive anxiety undoubtedly increased.
41. Jianjun Wang, Betty Greathouse, and V. M. Falcinella, "An Empirical Assessment of Self-Esteem Enhancement in a High School Challenge Service Learning Program," *Education* 119 (1998), 99–105, https://link.gale.com/apps/doc/A53415404/OVIC?u=viva_gmu&sid=bookmark-OVIC&xid=38cd1c95; William Cutler, *Parents and Schools: The 150-Year Struggle for Control in American Education* (Chicago: University of Chicago Press, 2000).
42. Jenny Reichert and James Richardson, "Decline of a Moral Panic," *Nova Religio* 16 (2012), 47–63, https://doi.org/10.1525/nr.2012.16.2.47; Paula Fass, *Kidnapped: Child Abduction in America* (New York: Oxford University Press, 1997).
43. Jean Twenge, "Age of Anxiety? The Birth Cohort Change in Anxiety and Neuroticism, 1952–1993," *Journal of Personality and Social Psychology* 79 (2000), 1007–21, https://www.apa.org/pubs/journals/releases/psp7961007.pdf.
44. Stephen Farrone et al., "The Worldwide Prevalence of ADHD: Is It an American Condition?," *World Psychiatry* 2 (2007), 104–13, https://www.ncbi.nlm.nih.gov/pmc/articles/PMC1525089/; Melissa Danielson et al., "Prevalence of Parent-Reported ADHD Diagnoses and Associated Treatment Among U.S. Children and Adolescents," *Journal of Clinical Child and Adolescent Psychology* 47, no. 2 (2018), 199–212, https://pubmed.ncbi.nlm.nih.gov/29363986/.
45. Peter N. Stearns, "Student Anxiety and Its Impact: A Recent American History," *History of Education Quarterly* (2023), doi:10.1017/heq.2023.10; Laura Weiler, "Are Students in the US More Likely to Have an Anxiety Disorder than European Students?," *Chasing the Storm: The Student News of Imagine Prep Surprises*, December 7, 2021, https://chasingthestorm.org/6494/features/are-students-in-the-us-more-likely-to-have-an-anxiety-disorder-than-european-students/.
46. It also remains telling that the United States is the only nation not to have signed the Convention on the Rights of the Child, though several factors are involved here. M. A. Mason, "The U.S. and the International Children's Rights Crusade: Leader or Laggard?," *Journal of Social History* (2005), http://www.jstor.org/stable/3790484; Amy Rothschild, "Is America

Holding Out on Protecting Children's Rights?," *The Atlantic*, May 2, 2017, https://www.the-atlantic.com/education/archive/2017/05/holding-out-on-childrens-rights/524652/. It is also revealing that while many American schools now grant older students some mental health days, they continue to monitor student newspapers and performances quite closely.

47. The need for focused comparative work on the modern history of childhood is obvious; the few existing works mainly center on juxtaposing Western and other patterns, rather than dealing with variations within Western society. Peter N. Stearns, *Childhood in World History*, 4th ed. (New York: Routledge, 2022).

48. Julie C. Garlen, "Interrogating Innocence: 'Childhood' as Exclusionary Social Practice," *Childhood* 26, no. 1 (2018) https://doi.org/10.1177/0907568218811484, and "The End of Innocence: School and Schooling for a Post-Pandemic World," *Journal of Teaching and Learning* 15, no. 2 (2021), https://doi.org/10.22329/jtl.v15i2.6724.

49. Within the broader comparative domain, work on different approaches to children's competence in modern history would be highly desirable and represents a real opportunity for some collaborative effort. The same applies to the related issue of comparative rates of psychological distress, from ADHD to the current differentials in reported levels of significant anxiety. On safety, see Dennis Adeloye et al., "Global and Regional Childs Deaths Due to Injury," *Journal of Global Health* 8 (2018), https://www.ncbi.nlm.nih.gov/pmc/articles/PMC6317703/.

50. Lenore Skenazy, *Free Range Kids: How Parents and Teachers Can Let Go and Let Grow* (New York: Wiley, 2021); Stearns, "Student Anxiety"; Allan Horwitz, *Anxiety: A Short History* (Baltimore: Johns Hopkins University Press, 2013).

51. Neil Montgomery, "The Negative Impact of Helicopter Parenting on Personality," in Poster Session Presented at the Annual Meeting of the Association of Psychological Science, Boston, May 2010.

52. Jean Twenge, *iGen: Why Today's Super-Connected Kids Are Growing Up Less Rebellious, More Tolerant, Less Happy—and Completely Unprepared for Adulthood* (New York: Atria, 2017); Gary Cross, *Machines of Youth: America's Car Obsession* (Chicago: University of Chicago Press, 2018).

53. Twenge, *iGen*.

Chapter 4

1. Rob Henderson, *Troubled: A Memoir of Foster Care, Family, and Social Class* (New York: Gallery Books, 2024).
2. Michelle Obama, *Becoming* (New York: Crown, 2018).
3. Samira Ahmed, *Love, Hate and Other Filters* (New York: Soho Teen, 2018).
4. Staceyann Chin, *The Other Side of Paradise: A Memoir* (New York: Scribner, 2009).
5. Thi Bui, *The Best We Could Do: An Illustrated Memoir* (New York: Abrams ComicArts, 2018).
6. Valeria Luiselli, *Tell Me How It Ends: An Essay in Forty Questions* (Minneapolis: Coffee House Press, 2018).
7. US Bureau of the Census, 1990 Census of Population and Housing, Summary Population and Housing Characteristics (CPH-1-1) Table 1. 1970 Census, Characteristics of the Population, US Summary, Table 52. 1980 Census, General Population Characteristics, US Summary, Table 41. Current Population Reports, Series P-25, No. 311, Estimates of the Population of the United States by Single Years of Age, Color, and Sex, 1900 to 1959, pp. 22–3, 42–3. Current Population Reports, Series P-25, No. 917, Preliminary Estimates of the Population of the United States by Age, Sex, and Race: 1970 to 1981, Table 2. Current Population Reports, Series P-25, No. 985, Estimates of the Population of the United States by Age, Sex, and Race: 1980 to 1985, Table 2. Current Population Reports, Series P-25, No. 985, Projections of the Population of the United States by Age, Sex, and Race Hispanic Origin: 1993 to 2050, Table 2; Donald J. Hernandez and Katherine Darke, "Socioeconomic and Demographic Risk Factors and Resources Among Children in Immigrant and Native-Born Families: 1910, 1960, and 1990," in *Children of Immigrants: Health, Adjustment, and Public Assistance*, ed. Hernandez (Washington, DC: National Academies Press, 1999), 19–125, https://www.ncbi.nlm.nih.gov/books/NBK224436/. Office of Juvenile Justice and Delinquency Prevention, "Youth (0 to 17) Population Profile Detailed by Age, Sex, and Race/Ethnicity," https://ojjdp.ojp.gov/statistical-briefing-book/population/faqs/qa01104. Also see Child Population Statistics, https://aspe.hhs.gov/sites/default/files/private/pdf/172181/pf1.pdf.
8. David Dinkins quoted in "The Mosaic Thing," *New York Times*, January 3, 1990, sec. A, p. 18, https://www.nytimes.com/1990/01/03/opinion/the-mosaic-thing.html.

9. Rakesh Kochhar and Stella Sechopoulos, "How the American Middle Class Has Changed in the Past Five Decades," Pew Research Center, April 20, 2022, https://www.pewresearch.org/short-reads/2022/04/20/how-the-american-middle-class-has-changed-in-the-past-five-decades/.
10. Richard V. Reeves, Katherine Guyot, and Eleanor Krause, "Defining the Middle Class: Cash, Credentials, or Culture?," Brookings, May 7, 2018, https://www.brookings.edu/articles/defining-the-middle-class-cash-credentials-or-culture.
11. Abinash Mohanty, "Dynamics of Economic Well-Being: Poverty, 2013–2016," Current Population Reports, August 2021, P70BR-172, https://www.census.gov/content/dam/Census/library/publications/2021/demo/p70br-172.pdf.
12. Sean F. Reardon, "No Rich Child Left Behind," *New York Times*, April 27, 2013, SR1, https://archive.nytimes.com/opinionator.blogs.nytimes.com/2013/04/27/no-rich-child-left-behind/.
13. Paul Tough, *How Children Succeed: Grit, Curiosity and the Hidden Power of Character* (New York: Houghton Mifflin, 2012).
14. Annette Lareau, *Unequal Childhoods: Class, Race, and Family Life*, 2nd ed. (Berkeley: University of California Press, 2011).
15. Daniel S. Levine, "Schools Resegregate After Being Freed from Judicial Oversight," Stanford Graduate School of Education, December 5, 2012, https://ed.stanford.edu/news/schools-resegregate-after-being-freed-judicial-oversight.
16. U.S. Bureau of the Census, "Census Bureau Releases New Estimates on America's Families and Living Arrangements," November 17, 2022, https://www.census.gov/newsroom/press-releases/2022/americas-families-and-living-arrangements.html.
17. Emily Badger, Claire Cain Miller, and Alicia Parlapiano, "The Americans Most Threatened by Eviction: Young Children," *New York Times*, October 2, 2023, https://www.nytimes.com/2023/10/02/upshot/evictions-children-american-renters.html.
18. Hein de Haas, *How Migration Really Works: The Facts About the Most Divisive Issue in Politics* (New York: Basic Books, 2023).
19. Amy Hsin and Yu Xie, "Explaining Asian Americans' Academic Advantage over Whites," *PNAS* 111, no. 23 (2014), 8416–21, https://www.pnas.org/doi/full/10.1073/pnas.1406402111.
20. Kay S. Hymowitz, "Brooklyn's Chinese Pioneers: Hardworking Fujianese Immigrants Use the Borough as a Launching Pad to the Middle Class," City Journal, Spring 2014, https://www.city-journal.org/article/brooklyns-chinese-pioneers.
21. ChangHwan Kim and Andrew Taeho Kim, "Is Hyper-Selectivity a Root of Asian American Children's Success?," *Social Science Research* 113 (July 2023), https://www.sciencedirect.com/science/article/pii/S0049089X23000418; Todd L. Pittinsky, "Backtalk: Learning from the Other Achievement Gap," *Phi Delta Kappan* 98, no. 5 (2017), https://journals.sagepub.com/doi/abs/10.1177/0031721717690376?journalCode=pdka.
22. University of California – San Diego, "Is There a 'Tiger Mother' Effect? Asian Students Study Twice as Many Hours, Analysis Finds," Science Daily, May 8, 2011, https://www.sciencedaily.com/releases/2011/05/110505103345.htm.
23. Kathy Seal, "Asian-American Parenting and Academic Success," Pacific Standard, June 14, 2017, https://psmag.com/education/asian-american-parenting-and-academic-success-26053; National Center for Education Statistics, "Status and Trends in the Education of Racial and Ethnic Minorities," https://nces.ed.gov/pubs2010/2010015/figures/figure_19_1.asp; Hsin and Yu Xie, "Asian Americans' Academic Advantage."
24. Vivian Louie, *Compelled to Excel: Immigration, Education and Opportunity Among Chinese Americans* (Stanford, CA: Stanford University Press, 2004).
25. Asian Americans make up 5.7 percent of the US population but comprise 42 percent of the students at MIT, 40 percent at Caltech, 38 percent at UC San Diego, 36 percent at UC Irvine, 35 percent at Berkeley, 30 percent at Carnegie Mellon, 28 percent at UCLA, and 25 percent at Harvard.
26. Avigna Ramachandran, "The Case for Greater Asian-American Representation in Athletics," February 14, 2020, https://www.aycevote.org/post/the-case-for-greater-asian-american-representation-in-athletics; Robert T. Teranishi, "Asian American and Pacific Islander Students and the Institutions That Serve Them," *Change: The Magazine of Higher Learning* 44, no. 2 (2012), 16–22, https://eric.ed.gov/?id=EJ960016.
27. Jeffrey M. Jones, "LGBT Identification in U.S. Ticks Up to 7.1 Percent," Gallup, February 17, 2022, https://news.gallup.com/poll/389792/lgbt-identification-ticks-up.aspx.

Chapter 5

1. Taya May, "Why Don't Kids Want to Go to School?," Quora, https://www.quora.com/Why-dont-kids-want-to-go-to-school/answer/Taya-May?no_redirect=1; Martha Ruth, "Why Do Kids Think School Is Bad?," Quora, https://www.quora.com/Why-do-kids-think-that-school-is-bad/answer/Martha-Ruth-2?no_redirect=1.
2. Thomas Snyder, ed., *120 Years of American Education: A Statistical Portrait* (Washington, DC: Center for Educational Statistics, 1993).
3. Alexander Astin et al., *The American Freshman: Thirty-Five Year Trends* (Los Angeles: American Council on Education, 2002).
4. United States National Commission on Excellence in Education. *A Nation at Risk: The Imperative for Educational Reform*. The National Commission on Excellence in Education, 1983, 1.
5. For an overview, William Reese, *America's Public Schools: From the Common School to "No Child Left Behind"* (Baltimore: Johns Hopkins University Press, 2005).
6. Peter N. Stearns, *Schools and Students in Industrial Society: Japan and the West, 1870–1940* (Boston: Bedford, 1998).
7. Brian Gill and Steven Schlossman, "Villain or Savior? American Views on Homework 1850–2003," *Theory Into Practice* 43 (2004), http://www.jstor.org/stable/3701518.
8. Urban Institute, "Which Students Receive a Greater Share of School Funding?," Washington, April 25, 2022, https://apps.urban.org/features/school-funding-trends/; but see the study by Adam Tynes, "Think Again: Is Educational Funding in American Schools Still Unequal?," Thomas Fordham Institute, July 11, 2023, https://fordhaminstitute.org/national/research/think-again-education-funding-america-still-unequal. On the problem of growing inequality, Sean F. Reardon, *Whither Opportunity? Rising Inequality, Schools, and Children's Life Chances* (New York: Russell Sage, 2011); Jonathan Kozol, *An End to Inequality: Breaking Down the Walls of Apartheid in American Education* (New York: The New Press, 2024).
9. Sherman Dorn, "Origins of the 'Dropout Problem,'" *History of Education Quarterly* 33 (1993), doi:10.2307/368197.
10. Snyder, *120 Years*.
11. Caroline Hoxby, "The Changing Selectivity of American Colleges," *Journal of Economic Perspectives* 23 (2009), https://www.aeaweb.org/articles?id=10.1257/jep.23.4.95.
12. Snyder, *120 Years*.
13. Robert Pittman, Roy Cox, and Guy Burchfiel, "The Extended School Year: Implications for Student Achievement," *Journal of Experimental Education* 54 (1986), http://www.jstor.org/stable/20151654.
14. Deborah Powell et al., "Impact of No Child Left Behind on Rural Schools," *Rural Educator* 31 (2009), https://doi.org/10.35608/ruraled.v31i1.439; Dawn Ramsburg, "No-Recess Policies Being Implemented in US Schools," *Parent News* 4 (1998); National Commission on Excellence in Education, *A Nation At Risk* (Washington, DC: National Commission, 1983), https://www.reaganfoundation.org/media/130020/a-nation-at-risk-report.pdf.
15. Ramsburg, "No-Recess."
16. Christopher Berry and Martin West, "Growing Pains: The School Consolidation Movement and Student Outcomes," *Journal of Law, Economics and Organization* 26 (2010), http://www.jstor.org/stable/25620048.
17. Sarah A. Cordes, Christopher Rick, and Amy Ellen Schwartz, "Do Long Bus Rides Drive Down Academic Outcomes?," *Educational Evaluation and Policy Analysis* 44 (2020), https://www.edworkingpapers.com/ai21-504.
18. David Deming and Susan Dynarski, "The Lengthening of Childhood," *Journal of Economic Perspectives* 22 (2008), https://www.aeaweb.org/articles?id=10.1257/jep.22.3.71.
19. Mark DeGuerin, "Average Class Sizes for Every U.S. State," *Insider*, August 20, 2019, https://www.insider.com/states-with-the-best-and-worst-public-education-systems-2019-8.
20. Astin et al., *American Freshman*; Gill and Schlossman, "Villain or Savior?"; Brian Gill and Steven Schlossman, "'A Nation at Rest': The American Way of Homework," *Educational Evaluation and Policy Analysis* 25, no. 3 (2003), 319–337, http://hss.cmu.edu/history/docs/schlossman/A-Nation-at-Rest.pdf.
21. Gill and Schlossman, "Villain or Savior?", 178.
22. Irwin Sarason, "Test Anxiety, General Anxiety, and Intellectual Performance," *Journal of Counseling Psychology* 21, no. 6 (1957), 485–490, https://doi.org/10.1037/h0043012; Peter N. Stearns, "Student Anxiety and Its Impact: A Recent American History," *History of Education Quarterly* 63, no. 2 (2023), 271–297, https://doi.org/10.1017/heq.2023.10.

23. Michael Johanek, *A Faithful Mirror: Reflections on the College Board and Education in America* (New York: College Board, 2001).
24. Mark DeGuerin, "Here's How the SAT Has Changed over the Past 90 Years and Where It Might Be Heading," *Insider*, August 9, 2019, https://www.insider.com/how-the-sat-has-changed-over-the-past-90-years-2019-8; Alexis Redding, "Extreme Pressure: The Negative Consequences of Achievement Culture for Students During the Elite Admissions Process," *Journal of College Admissions* 32 (2013), https://www.academia.edu/4935394.
25. George J. Allen, "The Behavioral Treatment of Test Anxiety: Recent Research and Future Trends," *Behavior Therapy* 3, no. 2 (1972), 253–262, https://www.sciencedirect.com/science/article/abs/pii/S000578947280087X.
26. "The Learning Network, "Dress Codes, Anti-Bias Training, Standardized Tests and Smiles: Our Favorite Student Comments of the Week," *New York Times*, April 26, 2018, https://www.nytimes.com/2018/04/26/learning/dress-codes-anti-bias-training-standardized-tests-and-smiles-our-favorite-student-comments-of-the-week.html.
27. National Commission, *Nation at Risk*; Peter Taubman, *Teaching by Numbers: Deconstructing the Discourse of Standards and Accountability* (New York: Routledge, 2009).
28. Taubman, *Teaching by Numbers*; Frederick Hess and Michael McShane, eds., *Common Core Meets Education Reform: What It All Means for Politics, Policy, and the Future of Schooling* (New York: Teachers College Press, 2013).
29. Dan Goldhaber and Roddy Theobald, "Teacher Attrition and Mobility in the Pandemic," *Education Evaluation and Policy Analysis* 45, no. 4 (2022), 1–6, https://journals.sagepub.com/doi/10.3102/01623737221139285.
30. D. L. Farnsworth, *Mental Health in College and University* (Cambridge, MA: Harvard University Press, 1963).
31. Michael Weishan, "The Real Gentleman's C," Franklin Delano Roosevelt Foundation, *FDR Suite*, June 30, 2014, https://fdrfoundation.org/the-real-gentlemans-c/.
32. Hoxby, "Changing Selectivity."
33. David Lang, "Class Rank, GPA, and Valedictorians: How High Schools Rank Students," *American Secondary Education* 35 (2007), http://www.jstor.org/stable/41406287.
34. Johanek, *Faithful Mirror*.
35. Louis Goldman, "Betrayal of the Gatekeepers: Grade Inflation," *Journal of General Education* 37, no. 2 (1985), 97–121, http://www.jstor.org/stable/27797025; Harvey Mansfield, "Grade Inflation: It's Time to Face the Facts," *Chronicle of Higher Education* 47 (2001), https://www.chronicle.com/article/grade-inflation-its-time-to-face-the-facts/; Peggy Perkins, "Grade Inflation: A Consideration of Additional Causes," *Journal of Instructional Psychology* 22, no. 2 (1979), 163–165.
36. John Reynolds et al., "Have Adolescents Become Too Ambitious? High School Seniors' Educational and Occupational Plans, 1976–2000," *Social Problems* 53 (2006), https://doi.org/10.1525/sp.2006.53.2.186.
37. Astin et al., *American Freshman*.
38. Astin et al., *American Freshman*; Victor Saenz et al., *First in My Family: A Profile of First-Generation College Students at Four-Year Institutions Since 1971* (Berkeley, CA: American Council on Education, 2007).
39. Jane Hoggman, "Chronicling Email Pitches from Colleges to High School Sophomores," *Journal of College Admissions* 221 (2013), 3; Edwin Fiske, "How College Admissions Came to Be Hawked in the Marketplace," *Chronicle of Higher Education* 55, no. 5 (2008), A112, https://eric.ed.gov/?id=EJ814581.
40. Hoxby, "Changing Selectivity."
41. Redding, "Extreme Pressure"; Julie Vultaggio and Stephen Friedfeld, "Stresses in College Choice: Applications and Decision-Making," *Journal of College Admissions* 32 (2013), 7-12; Jeffrey Selingo, *Who Gets in and Why: A Year Inside College Admissions* (New York: Scribners, 2020).
42. Lang, "Class Rank."
43. Scott Jaschik, "For-Profit High School Recruits Students with Guarantee on Admission to Top College," *Insider Higher Ed*, May 28, 2018, https://www.insidehighered.com/admissions/article/2018/05/29/profit-high-school-recruits-students-guarantee-admission-top-colleges.
44. Ray Rist, "Student Social Class and Teacher Expectations: The Self-Fulfilling Prophecy in Ghetto Education," *Harvard Educational Review* 40 (1970), https://faculty.washington.edu/rsoder/EDUC305/310RistHarvardEdReview.pdf.
45. S. Melman, S. Little, and K. Akin-Little, "Adolescent Overscheduling," *High School Journal* 90 (2007), https://www.jstor.org/stable/40364197; On the distinctive American role for

extracurriculars, see Alexander Astin, Robert Panos, and John Creager, "National Norms for Entering College Freshmen," *ACE Research Reports* 2 (1967), https://files.eric.ed.gov/fulltext/ED011393.pdf.

46. Rebecca Onion, "The Teacher Would Suddenly Yell 'Drop,'" *Slate*, March 13, 2018, https://slate.com/human-interest/2018/03/are-duck-and-cover-school-drills-from-the-nuclear-era-a-useful-parallel-to-active-shooter-drills.html; G. Diamond and J. Bachman, "High School Seniors and the Nuclear Threat, 1975–1984," *International Journal of Mental Health* 15 (1986), https://www.jstor.org/stable/41344423.

47. Mai Ellsherief et al., "Impacts of School Shooter Drills," *Humanities and Social Sciences Communications*, December 8, 2021, https://www.nature.com/articles/s41599-021-00993-6.

48. Elizabeth Gershoff and Sarah Font, "Corporal Punish in US Schools: Prevalence, Disparities in Use, and Status in State and Federal Policy," Society for Research in Child Development, *Social Policy Report*, 30 (2016), https://www.ncbi.nlm.nih.gov/pmc/articles/PMC5766273/.

49. American Psychological Association, "Are Zero Tolerance Policies Effective in the Schools?," *American Psychologist* 63 (2008), https://www.apa.org/pubs/reports/zero-tolerance; Christina Samuels, "70,000 Students with Disabilities Secluded, Restrained in Schools," *Education Week*, May 16, 2017, https://www.edweek.org/leadership/70-000-students-with-disabilities-secluded-restrained-in-school/2017/05.

50. Laura Gardner, "Rules of Engagement," *Brandeis Magazine*, Summer 2014, https://www.brandeis.edu/magazine/2014/summer/featured-stories/parietals.html.

51. "Field Trips in Decline amid More Standardized Testing," *Columbus Dispatch*, October 13, 2012, https://www.dispatch.com/story/news/education/2012/10/13/school-field-trips-in-decline/24213810007/.

52. Rachel Dunifon and Lori Kowalski-Jones, "The Influence of Participation in the National School Lunch Program and Food Insecurity in Child Well-Being," *Social Service Review* 77 (2003), https://doi.org/10.1086/345705; Susan Levine, *School Lunch Politics and the Surprising History of America's Favorite Welfare Program* (Princeton, NJ: Princeton University Press, 2010).

53. Paul Tough, "Americans Are Losing Their Faith in Higher Education. Whose Fault Is That?," *New York Times*, September 5, 2023.

54. Christopher Kearney, et al., "School Attendance and School Absenteeism: A Primer for the Past, Present and Theory for the Future," *Frontiers of Education* 7 (2022), https://www.frontiersin.org/journals/education/articles/10.3389/feduc.2022.1044608/full; Suzanne Blake, "America Has a School Attendance Crisis," *Newsweek*, January 9, 2024, https://www.newsweek.com/absentee-student-problem-pandemic-america-falling-behind-1859222.

55. Libby Stanford, "Educators Feel Growing Pressure for Students to Perform Well on Standardized Tests," *Education Week*, September 1, 2023.

56. Thanks to Ruthie Clay for these observations.

57. Brita Belli, "National Survey: Student Feelings About High School Are Mostly Negative," *Yale News*, January 30, 2020, https://news.yale.edu/2020/01/30/national-survey-students-feelings-about-high-school-are-mostly-negative; Yale Center for Emotional Intelligence, "How Do U.S. High School Students Feel at School? School Report," 2020, https://narrative4.com/wp-content/uploads/2022/05/Yale-Emotion-Revolution-Study.pdf. The Yale survey, taken in 2019, involved interviews with about 20,000 students.

58. See, for example, N. Kallova, "Happiness as an Aim of Education," *Human Affairs*, April 22, 2021.

Chapter 6

1. Judith Aulette, ed., *The Changing American Family*, 3rd ed. (Boston: Allyn and Bacon, 2009); Theresa Ciabattari, *Sociology of Families: Change, Continuity, Diversity* (Los Angeles: Sage, 2021); Nicole Benokraitis, *Marriages and Families: Changes, Choices and Constraints*, 9th ed. (Upper Saddle River, NJ: Prentice Hall, 2018); Deborah Chambers and Pablo Garcia, *A Sociology of Family Life: Change and Diversity in Intimate Relations* (Cambridge: Cambridge University Press, 2022). For a particularly gloomy assessment, David Popenoe, "The American Family in Decline," *Journal of Marriage and the Family* 55 (1993), https://doi.org/10.2307/353333. See also Orlando Thornton and Linda Demaro, "Four Decades of Trends in Attitudes Toward Family Issues in the United States: The 1960s to the 1990s," *Journal of Marriage and the Family* 66 (2004), https://www.jstor.org/stable/3599811.

2. Steven Mintz and Susan Kellogg, *Domestic Revolutions: A Social History of American Family Life* (New York: Free Press, 1988), 177–203; Stephanie Coontz, "'Leave It to Beaver' and 'Ozzie and Harriet': American Families in the 1950s," in Coontz, *Undoing Place?* (New York: Routledge, 2020).
3. Against overdoing the instability theme, it is worth noting that by the twenty-first century American children were far less likely than their counterparts in the past to experience the death of a parent. Only 4.3 percent of kids suffered that jolt before they were eighteen by 2019 (though some estimates range a bit higher), well below the figure a century before. But a good bit of this change occurred before the later twentieth century. G. Kliman, "Death: Some Implications for Child Development and Child Analysis," *Advances in Thanatology* 4 (1980).
4. George Chauncey, *Why Marriage? The History Shaping Today's Debate over Gay Equality* (New York: Basic Books, 2005).
5. Stephanie Coontz, *Marriage, A History* (New York: Viking, 2006).
6. Anna Brown, "Growing Share of Childless Adults in U.S. Don't Expect to Ever Have Children," Pew Research Center, November 19, 2021, https://www.pewresearch.org/short-reads/2021/11/19/growing-share-of-childless-adults-in-u-s-dont-expect-to-ever-have-children/.
7. Michael Young and Peter Willmott, *The Symmetrical Family* (New York: Pantheon, 1971).
8. Ramesh Ponnuru, "An Emerging Culture War: No Kids," *Washington Post*, December 19, 2023; Karen Kicak, "How I Used to Write Jokes About How Parenting Is Terrible; Then I Had My Daughter," *New York Times*, December 24, 2023.
9. Scott South and Stewart Tolnay, eds., *The Changing American Family: Sociological and Demographic Perspectives* (New York: Routledge, 2019); David Allyn, *Make Love, Not War: The Sexual Revolution: An Unfettered History* (Boston: Taylor and Francis, 2000).
10. W. Ombelet and J. Van Robays, "Artificial Insemination History: Hurdles and Milestones," *Facts, Views and Vision in ObGyn* 7 (2015), https://www.ncbi.nlm.nih.gov/pmc/articles/PMC4498171/.
11. Rachel Arocho, Elizabeth Lozano, and Carolyn Halpern, "Estimates of Donated Sperm Use in the United States: National Survey of Family Growth, 1995–2017," *National Library of Medicine*, July 29, 2019, https://www.ncbi.nlm.nih.gov/pmc/articles/PMC6765402/.
12. Stephanie Kramer, "U.S. Has World's Highest Rate of Children Living in Single-Parent Households," Pew Research Center, December 12, 2019, https://www.pewresearch.org/short-reads/2019/12/12/u-s-children-more-likely-than-children-in-other-countries-to-live-with-just-one-parent/.
13. Mintz and Kellogg, *Domestic Revolutions*, 203–238.
14. Judith Wallerstein and Joan Kelley, *Surviving the Breakup: How Children and Parents Cope with Divorce* (New York: Basic Books, 1980); Vance Packard, *Our Endangered Children: Growing Up in a Changing World* (Boston: Little, Brown, 1983).
15. Andrew J. Cherlin, *Marriage, Divorce, Remarriage* (Cambridge, MA: Harvard University Press, 1992).
16. Lee Rainwater and William Yancey, *The Moynihan Report and the Politics of Controversy* (Cambridge, MA: Harvard University Press, 1967); Andrew Billingsley, *Black Families in White America* (New York, 1968); R. Farley and A. J. Hermalin, "Family Stability: A Comparison of Trends Between Blacks and Whites," *American Sociological Review* 36 (1971), https://doi.org/10.2307/2093502.
17. Wendy Wang, "The U.S. Divorce Rate Has Hit a 50-Year Low," *Institute for Family Studies*, November 10, 2020, https://ifstudies.org/blog/the-us-divorce-rate-has-hit-a-50-year-low.
18. Daniel Meyer, Marcia Carlson, and Md Moshi Ul Alam, "Increases in Shared Custody After Divorce in the United States," *Demographic Research* 46 (2022), https://www.demographic-research.org/articles/volume/46/38.
19. Susan Brown, *Families in America* (Berkeley: University of California Press, 2017); Susan Brown, "Family Structure and Child Well-Being: The Significance of Parental Cohabitation," *Journal of Marriage and the Family* 66 (2008), https://www.jstor.org/stable/3599842.
20. U.S. Department of Health and Human Services, Children's Bureau, "Trends in Foster Care and Adoption," Washington, DC, 2022, https://www.acf.hhs.gov/cb/report/trends-foster-care-adoption; Rosalie Zimmerman, *Foster Care in Retrospect* (New Orleans: Tulane University Studies in Social Welfare, 1982).
21. Carl Finer, "Adoption: By the Numbers," *The Imprint: Youth and Family News*, February 23, 2017, https://imprintnews.org/report/adoption-by-the-numbers/24973.

22. K. Kumar, "The Blended Family Life Cycle," *Journal of Divorce and Remarriage* 58 (2017), https://psycnet.apa.org/record/2017-08627-003.
23. Melissa Kearney, *The Two-Parent Privilege: How Americans Stopped Getting Married and Started Falling Behind* (Chicago: University of Chicago Press, 2023).
24. Madison Troyer, "Fifty Ways the American Family Has Changed in the Last 50 Years," *Stacker*, April 8, 2019, https://stacker.com/family/50-ways-american-family-has-changed-last-50-years; Kearney, *Two-Parent*; Brown, "Family Structure."
25. Kearney, *Two-Parent*.
26. Stefanie DeLuca, Holly Wood, and Peter Rosenblatt, "Why Poor Families Move (and Where They Go): Reactive Mobility and Residential Decisions," *City and Community* 18 (2019), https://doi.org/10.1111/cico.12386. Over the decades since the 1970s American families overall have moved less than they once did. But residential changes within the inner city are frequent, mainly reflecting landlord actions, violence, or plumbing or other problems—rarely providing opportunities for careful selection of optimal schools or neighborhoods. Children in poverty, and particularly children of color, are now four times more likely to move five or more times than their better-off counterparts, with obvious implications for health and schooling.
27. Kearney, *Two-Parent*; Brown, "Family Structure"; Ciabattari, *Sociology of Families*.
28. Maria Gayatari and Mardiana Puspilsaro, "The Impact of Covid-19 Pandemic on Family Well-Being: A Literature Review," *The Journal of the Family*, October 5, 2022, https://www.ncbi.nlm.nih.gov/pmc/articles/PMC9535451/.
29. Joseph Hotz and Matthew Wiswall, "Child Care and Child Care Policy," *American Academy of Political and Social Science* 686 (2019), https://doi.org/10.1177/0002716219884078.
30. Thomas J. Arno, "Does Head Start Make a Difference?," *American Economic Review* 85 (1995).
31. Joseph Hotz and Mo Xiao, "The Impact of Regulations on the Supply and Quality in Child Care Markets," *American Economic Review* 101 (2011), https://www.aeaweb.org/articles?id=10.1257/aer.101.5.1775; Hortz and Wiswall, "Child Care."
32. Mintz and Kellogg, *Domestic Revolutions*; Sheila Kamerman and Alfred Kahn, "The Day-Care Debate: A Wider View," *Public Interest* 54 (1979), https://www.nationalaffairs.com/public_interest/detail/the-day-care-debate-a-wider-view.
33. Hotz and Xiao, "Impact."
34. Douglass Besharov and Douglass Call, "Head Start Falls Further Behind," *New York Times*, February 8, 2011, https://www.nytimes.com/2009/02/08/opinion/08besharov.html.
35. Sam Cook, "The Decline of the Classic Extended Family and the Rise of the Privatized Nuclear Family," *Revise Sociology*, April 25, 2011; Mintz and Kellogg, *Domestic Revolutions*, 218. On the impact of even earlier suburbanization, see Richard Sennett, *Families Against the City: Middle-Class Homes of Industrial Chicago, 1872–1890* (Cambridge, MA: Harvard University Press, 1984).
36. Department of Education, National Center for Education Statistics, *Early Childhood Participation Program Participation* (Washington, DC: Department of Education, 2019), https://nces.ed.gov/pubs2020/2020075REV.pdf.
37. Xiang Zhou and Z. E. Taylor, "Differentiating the Impact of Family and Friend Support for Single Mothers in Parenting and Internalizing Symptoms," *Journal of Affective Disorders* 8 (2022), https://doi.org/10.1016/j.jadr.2022.100319.
38. Paola Scommegna, "More U.S. Children Raised by Grandparents," *Population Reference Bureau*, March 26, 2012, https://www.prb.org/resources/more-u-s-children-raised-by-grandparents/.
39. "Reunion Research and Statistics," *Reunions Magazine*, March 31, 2017, https://reunionsmag.com/reunion-research-statistics/.
40. Becky Mansfield, "Why Cousins Are the Best," *Your Modern Family*, January 23, 2023, https://www.yourmodernfamily.com/cousins/. What little study there is of American cousins centers on the marriage among fourth cousins, which persisted surprisingly strongly into the mid-nineteenth century and then disappeared fairly quickly. This is very interesting, but it does not help with the assessment of twenty-first-century childhood. Steph Yin, "When Did Americans Stop Marrying Their Cousins?," *New York Times*, March 1, 2018, https://www.nytimes.com/2018/03/01/science/cousins-marriage-family-tree.html.
41. Madonna Meyer and Amra Kandis, "Grandparenting in the United States," *Innovation in Aging* 1 (2017), https://pubmed.ncbi.nlm.nih.gov/30480118/; Kiley Hurst, "More Than Half

of Americans Live Within an Hour of Extended Family," *Pew Research Report*, May 18, 2022, https://www.pewresearch.org/short-reads/2022/05/18/more-than-half-of-americans-live-within-an-hour-of-extended-family/; Maria Monserud, "Continuity and Change in Grandchildren's Closeness to Grandparents," *Marriage and Family Review* 46 (2010), https://www.ncbi.nlm.nih.gov/pmc/articles/PMC3041964/.
42. Murray Strauss, "Prevalence, Societal Causes and Trends in Corporal Punishment by Parents in World Perspective," *Law and Contemporary Problems* 73 (2010), https://www.jstor.org/stable/25766385.
43. An early twenty-first-century survey thus asked parents in Chicago and Taiwan to respond to the following proposition: "a pre-schooler should be shamed if he or she does not follow social rules"; 43 percent of the Taiwanese responded affirmatively, but literally no Chicago parent agreed. Yin Wang and Jeanne Tsai, "Cultural Models of Guilt and Shame," in *The Self-Conscious Emotions: Theory and Research*, eds. J. Tracy, R. Robins, and J. Tangney (New York: ,Guilford Press, 2007).
44. Troyer, "Fifty Ways."
45. J. F. Sandberg and S. L. Hofferth, "Changes in Children's Time with Parents: United States, 1981–1995," *Demography* 38 (2001), https://doi.org/10.2307/3088356; Dotti Sani and J. Treas, "Educational Gradients in Parents' Child-Care Time Across Countries, 1969–2010," *Journal of Marriage and the Family* 78 (2016), https://archive.org/details/sani602561.
46. Anna Jones, "The Parents Who Track Their Children," *Family Tree*, November 7, 2021, https://www.bbc.com/worklife/article/20211105-the-parents-who-track-their-children. Some estimates of parents who track their children are below 20 percent; some of the variance reflects different evaluations of regular versus occasional use.
47. Peter N. Stearns, "Happy Children: A Modern Emotional Commitment," *Frontiers in Psychology*, September 6, 2019, https://www.frontiersin.org/articles/10.3389/fpsyg.2019.02025/full.
48. Robin Berman, *Permission to Parent* (New York: HarperCollins, 2015) and "Unhappiness: The Key to Raising Unhappy Kids," in Editors, "The Misguided Desire of Wanting Our Kids to be Happy," *Goop*, May 26, 2016, https://goop.com/wellness/parenthood/the-misguided-desire-of-wanting-our-kids-to-be-happy/.
49. Berman, "Unhappiness."
50. Donna Bee Gates, *I Want It Now: Childhood in a Material World* (London: Macmillan, 2007). The consumerism and entertainment theme is explored more fully below, in chapter 7.
51. Peter N. Stearns, *Anxious Parents: A History of Modern Childrearing in America* (New York: New York University Press, 2004).
52. Clara De Vincenzi et al., "Consequences of Covid-19 on Remote Work," *Journal of Environmental Research and Public Health*, September 6, 2022, https://pubmed.ncbi.nlm.nih.gov/36141948/.
53. Jeff Diamant and Elizabeth Sciupac, "10 Key Findings About the Religious Lives of U.S. Teens and Their Parents," *Pew Research Report*, September 10, 2020, https://www.pewresearch.org/short-reads/2020/09/10/10-key-findings-about-the-religious-lives-of-u-s-teens-and-their-parents/.
54. Google Ngram, American English, 1900–present, "dysfunctional family."
55. V. J. Felitti et al., "Relationship of Childhood Abuse and Household Dysfunction to Many of the Leading Causes of Death in Adults: The Adverse Childhood Experiences (ACE) Study," *American Journal of Preventative Medicine* 14 (1998), https://pubmed.ncbi.nlm.nih.gov/9635069/. Note that while this and later surveys did include some teenagers, the focus was more on young adults recalling their childhoods.
56. M. T. Merrick et al., "Prevalence of Adverse Childhood Experiences from the 2011–2014 Behavioral Risk Factor Surveillance System in 23 States," *JAMA Pediatrics* 172 (2018), https://jamanetwork.com/journals/jamapediatrics/fullarticle/2702204. This study particularly highlights differences in rates depending on race and income. See also S. R. Dube et al., "The Impact of Adverse Childhood Experiences on Health Problems: Evidence from Four Birth Cohorts Dating Back to 1900," *Preventative Medicine* 37 (2003), https://pubmed.ncbi.nlm.nih.gov/12914833/; M. Dong et al., "The Interrelatedness of Multiple Forms of Childhood Abuse, Neglect and Household Dysfunction," *Child Abuse and Neglect* 28 (2004), https://pubmed.ncbi.nlm.nih.gov/15261471/; and M. Metzler et al., "Adverse Childhood Experiences and Life Opportunities: Shifting the Narrative," *Children and Youth Services Review* 72 (2017), https://psycnet.apa.org/record/2017-02960-003.

57. A clear symptom of the changing standards for family evaluation centers on the apparent rise of disputes between young adults and their older parents about the quality of earlier childhood, with a growing number of the former deciding—correctly or not—that they had been inadequately parented and not infrequently opting for estrangement in response, to the bewilderment of their seniors. Joshua Coleman, *Rules of Estrangement: Why Adult Children Cut Ties and How to Heal the Conflict* (Chatsworth, CA: Penguin Random House, 2021).
58. S. R. Dube et al., "Growing Up with Parental Alcohol Abuse, Neglect and Household Dysfunction," *Child Abuse and Neglect* 25 (2001), https://pubmed.ncbi.nlm.nih.gov/11814159/; "Mad Men and the Evolution of the Drinking Culture," *Inspire Malibu*, October 13, 2015, https://www.inspiremalibu.com/blog/alcohol-addiction/mad-men-the-evolution-of-the-drinking-culture/.
59. Alfred Kinsey et al., *Sexual Behavior of the Human Female* (Philadelphia: W.B. Saunders, 1953).
60. Jennifer Glass, Robin Simon, and Matthew Andersson, "Parenthood and Happiness: Effects of Work-Family Reconciliation Policies in 22 OECD Countries," *American Journal of Sociology* 122 (2016), https://www.ncbi.nlm.nih.gov/pmc/articles/PMC5222535/. Predictably, however, some other American polls point in other directions: Colyn Ritter, "Survey Finds Parents More Hopeful, Satisfied, than Those Without Children," *Engage*, May 10, 2023, https://www.edchoice.org/engage/survey-finds-parents-more-hopeful-satisfied-than-those-without-children/. Most well-being studies, similarly, find parenting a positive correlate. The comparative gap, and the evidence of declining satisfaction levels, remain important, even without definitive judgments of relative happiness.
61. Stearns, *Anxious Parents*.
62. Glass, Simon, and Andersson, "Parenthood."
63. Paul Amato, "The Consequences of Divorce for Parents and Children," *Journal of Marriage and the Family* 62 (2000), https://www.jstor.org/stable/1566735; J. Pedro-Carroll, *Putting Children First: Proven Parenting Strategies for Helping Children Thrive Through Divorce* (New York: Avery/Penguin, 2010).
64. Sara McLanahan, Laura Tach, and Daniel Schneider, "The Causal Effects of Father Absence," *Annual Review of Sociology* (2013), https://www.ncbi.nlm.nih.gov/pmc/articles/PMC3904543/.
65. Chambers and Garcia, *Sociology of Family Life*.
66. Johns Hopkins All Children's Hospital, "How Well Do Parents and Kids Get Along?," *Time for Kids*, May 2022, https://kidshealth.org/media/kidspoll/ParentChildRelationships.html.

Chapter 7

1. Cara Bafile, "Is This 'It' for Tag?," *Education World*, October 8, 2007, https://www.education-world.com/a_admin/admin/admin498.shtml; Lucy Schouten, "Bans on Tag: Are School Children Getting the Right Playtime?," *Christian Science Monitor*, September 26, 2015, https://www.csmonitor.com/USA/Society/2015/0926/Ban-on-Tag-Are-school-children-getting-the-right-playtime.
2. Schouten, "Bans."
3. Brian Sutton-Smith, "Does Play Prepare for the Future?," in *Toys, Play and Child Development*, ed. Jeffrey Goldstein (Cambridge: Cambridge University Press, 1994), 130–146.
4. Rodney Carlisle, *Encyclopedia of Play in Today's Society* (Newbury Park, CA: Sage, 2009).
5. Matthew Wills, "Losing Our Marbles," JSTOR Daily, June 25, 2018, https://daily.jstor.org/losing-our-marbles/.
6. National Parks and Recreation Association, "Children in Nature: Improving Health by Reconnecting Youth with Outdoor Activity," 2010, https://www.nrpa.org/uploadedFiles/nrpa.org/Advocacy/Children-in-Nature.pdf; L. R. Larson, G. T. Green, and H. K. Cordell, "Children's Time Outdoors: Implications of the National Kids Survey," *Journal of Parks and Recreation* 29 (2011); L. R. Larson et al., "Screen Time and Connections to Nature: Troubling Trends Among Rural Youth?," *Environmental Behavior* 51 (2018), https://scholarworks.umass.edu/cgi/viewcontent.cgi?referer=&httpsredir=1&article=1030&context=nerr. By 2023 the impact of global warming presented yet another limitation on outdoor play during crucial months that was likely to loom larger over time.
7. Lisa Morton, *Trick or Treat: A History of Halloween* (Chicago: University of Chicago Press, 2012).
8. Steven Mintz, *Huck's Raft: A History of American Childhood* (Cambridge, MA: Harvard University Press, 2004), 347–48; Howard Chudacoff, *Children at Play: An American History* (New York: New York University Press, 2007), 154–181.

9. "Play Date Etiquette Explained," CBS News, August 25, 2009, https://www.cbsnews.com/news/play-date-etiquette-explained/; Google Ngram, "Play Date," *American English*, 1900ff.
10. Alexis Madrigal, "Chuck E. Cheese's Silicon Valley Startup," *Atlantic*, December 15, 2009, https://www.theatlantic.com/technology/archive/2013/07/chuck-e-cheeses-silicon-valley-startup-the-origins-of-the-best-pizza-chain-ever/277869/.
11. Chudacoff, *Children at Play*; Jason Reid, *Get Out of My Room! A History of Teen Bedrooms in America* (Chicago: University of Chicago Press, 2016).
12. Chudacoff, *Children at Play*.
13. Benjamin McArthur, "The Chicago Playground Movement," *Social Service Review* 49 (1975), https://www.jstor.org/stable/30015251.
14. Brian Sutton-Smith, *Toys as Culture* (New York: Gardner, 1986); Gary Cross, *Kids' Stuff: Toys and the Changing World of the American Child* (Cambridge, MA: Harvard University Press, 1997) and *The Cute and the Cool: Wondrous Innocence and Modern American Children's Culture* (New York: Oxford University Press, 2004).
15. The term "wish list," rarely used before 1960, began a rapid ascent in American language usage from the late 1970s onward. Google Ngram, "wish list," *American English*, 1900ff.
16. Peter Gray, "The Decline of Play and the Rise of Psychopathology in Children and Adolescents," *American Journal of Play* 3 (2011), https://files.eric.ed.gov/fulltext/EJ985541.pdf; Joe Frost, *History of Children's Play and Play Environments* (New York: Routledge, 2010).
17. Sandra Hofferth and John Sandberg, "Changes in American Children's Time, 1981–1997," in *Children in the Millenium, Where Have We Come From? Where Are We Going?*, eds. Timothy Owens and Sandra Hofferth (Amsterdam: Elsevier, 2001), 193–232.
18. Rhonda Clements, "An Investigation of the Status of Children's Play," *Contemporary Issues in Early Childhood* 5 (2004), https://eric.ed.gov/?id=EJ1051197; Gray, "Decline of Play"; see also Doris Fromberg and Doris Bergen, eds., *Play from Birth to Twelve and Beyond* (New York: Routledge, 1998).
19. Bill Maxwell, "Child's Play: A Thing of the Past," *St. Petersburg Times*, November 15, 1998; Bruno Bettelheim, "The Importance of Play," *Atlantic*, March 1987, https://www.theatlantic.com/magazine/archive/1987/03/the-importance-of-play/305129/.
20. E. Miller and J. Almon, *Crisis in the Kindergarten: Why Children Need to Play in School* (College Park: University of Maryland Press, 2008).
21. Sally Bieser et al., "An Investigation of Play: From the Voices of Fifth- and Sixth-Grade Talented and Gifted Students," *Gifted Child Quarterly*, June 20, 2012, https://eric.ed.gov/?id=EJ995869.
22. Maggie Davis, "Down the Rabbit Hole: 18 Percent of Disney Goers Have Racked Up Debt but Few Have Regrets," Lending Tree, November 15, 2022, https://www.lendingtree.com/debt-consolidation/disney-debt-survey/.
23. Sean Gregory, "How Kids' Sports Became a $15 Billion Industry," *Time*, August 24, 2017, https://time.com/4913687/how-kids-sports-became-15-billion-industry/.
24. Gary Fine, *With the Boys: Little League Baseball and Preadolescent Culture* (Chicago: University of Chicago Press, 1987).
25. Project Play, "Youth Sports Facts, Participation Rates," *State of Play*, 2022, https://projectplay.org/youth-sports/facts/participation-rates.
26. The group now known as Women and Girls Soccer, initially based in Washington, DC, held its first tournament in 1975. It now hosts over 300 teams in the Northern Virginia region.
27. Hilary Levey Friedman, "When Did Competitive Sports Take Over American Childhood?," *Atlantic*, September 20, 2013, https://www.theatlantic.com/education/archive/2013/09/when-did-competitive-sports-take-over-american-childhood/279868/ and *Playing to Win: Children in a Competitive Culture* (Berkeley: University of California Press, 2013); Jacob Bogage, "Youth Sports Study: Declining Participation, Rising Costs, Unqualified Coaches, *Washington Post*, September 6, 2013, https://www.washingtonpost.com/news/recruiting-insider/wp/2017/09/06/youth-sports-study-declining-participation-rising-costs-and-unqualified-coaches/.
28. Eda LeShan, "Are We Making Our Lives Too Full?," *New York Times*, August 7, 1960.
29. Friedman, *Playing to Win*.
30. Friedman, "When Did Competitive Sports..."
31. Katie Melville, "The Overscheduled Child: Are Our Kids Too Busy?," *Chris Kresser Podcast*, August 14, 2020, https://chriskresser.com/overscheduled-child/.
32. Kenneth Elpus and Carl Abril, "Who Enrolls in High School Music?," *Journal of Research in Music Education* 67, no. 3 (2019), 322–338, https://doi.org/10.1177/0022429419862837.

33. Chudacoff, *Children at Play*; Sydney Stern and Ted Schoenbaum, *Toyland: The High Stakes Game of the Toy Industry* (New York: Birch Lane Press, 1990); Stephen Kline, *Out of the Garden: Children's Toys, TV, and Children's Culture in the Age of Marketing* (London: Verso, 1993).
34. Gray, "Decline of Play"; see also Marcy Guddemi, Tom Jambor, and Robin Moore, "Advocacy for the Child's Right to Play," in *Play from Birth to Twelve*, eds. Doris Fromberg and Doris Bergen, *Play from Birth to Twelve and Beyond* (New York: Routledge, 1998), 519–529. Peter Gray, David F. Lancy, and David F. Bjorklund, "Decline in Independent Activity as a Cause of Decline in Children's Mental Well-Being: Summary of the Evidence," *Journal of Pediatrics* 260 (2023), 1–8, https://www.jpeds.com/article/S0022-3476(23)00111-7/abstract, concludes "that if children are to grow up well-adjusted, they need ever-increasing opportunities for independent activity, including self-directed play." For the recent assessment of impact on mental health, see Gray, Lancy, and Bjork, "Decline in Independent Activity." For the impact on adult fun, see Karen Heller, "Fun Is Dead," *Washington Post*, December 23, 2023, https://www.washingtonpost.com/style/of-interest/2023/12/23/fun-is-dead/.
35. Chudacoff, *Children at Play*.
36. Hal Herzog, "Why Kids with Pets Are Better Off," *Psychology Today*, June 12, 2017, https://www.psychologytoday.com/us/blog/animals-and-us/201707/why-kids-pets-are-better; Katherine Grier, *Pets in America: A History* (Chapel Hill: University of North Carolina Press, 2007).
37. A fourth concern has been mentioned that warrants some attention: the progressive preemption of children's imagination by store-bought toys, comic books, and television themes, and more recently electronic games and social media, not to mention reading blockbusters like Harry Potter. On the other hand children often prove inventive in adapting the materials they are presented with. Barbie dolls and their carefully themed costumes are often put to uses in girls' play, for example, far from the calculations of their manufacturer. Howard Chudacoff describes how kids even make television sets into imagined cities. See also the following chapter.
38. Alvin Rosenfeld and Nicole Wise, *The Overscheduled Child: Avoiding the Hyper-Parenting Trap* (New York: Macmillan, 2001).
39. Jean Twenge, *iGen: Why Today's Super-Connected Kids are Growing Up Less Rebellious, More Tolerant, Less Happy—and Completely Unprepared for Adulthood* (New York: Atria, 2017), appendices.
40. Rachel Dunifon, Paula Fomby, and Kelly Musick, "Siblings and Children's Time Use in the United States," *Demographic Research* 37 (2017), https://www.demographic-research.org/volumes/vol37/49/37-49.pdf.
41. Jean Twenge et al., "Worldwide Increases in Adolescent Loneliness," *Journal of Adolescence* 93, no. 1 (2021), 257–269, https://doi.org/10.1016/j.adolescence.2021.06.006; Mintz, *Huck's Raft*; Chudacoff, *Children at Play*. The history of modern children's loneliness is underdeveloped. See Katie Barclay, Elaine Chalus, and Deborah Simonton, eds., *The Routledge History of Loneliness* (London: Routledge, 2023), particularly the chapter on only children in England by Alice Violett. Recent work by social psychologists like Twenge, immensely valuable, focuses on the undeniable impact of social media but leaves open the issue of whether overreliance on the media causes loneliness in many children (particularly younger teenage girls) or results from it. The larger recent history of children's play strongly suggests the latter.
42. Emily Willingham, "People Have Been Having Less Sex—Whether They're Teenagers or 40-Somethings," *Scientific American*, January 3, 2022, https://www.scientificamerican.com/article/people-have-been-having-less-sex-whether-theyre-teenagers-or-40-somethings/.
43. For early comments, see Laurence Reece, "The Play Needs of Children Aged 6 to 12," *Marriage and Family Living* 16, no. 2 (1954), 131–134, https://www.jstor.org/stable/347769;); Dorothy Barclay, "Children's Hour: Adults Keep Out," *New York Times Magazine*, September 17, 1961, 86, https://www.nytimes.com/1961/09/17/archives/childrens-hour-adults-keep-out.html. See also Frances Horwith, "Don't Rob Them of Their Childhood," *Today's Education* 54 (1954).
44. Gray, "Decline of Play"; the Clinton quote is from an article in Steven Cohen, ed., *The Games We Played: A Celebration of Childhood and Imagination* (New York: Simon & Schuster, 2001).

Chapter 8

1. Jean Pelser, "Tween Taste Is Expensive These Days,. Blame social media," *Washington Post*, January 14, 2024, https://www.washingtonpost.com/business/2024/01/14/trends-tweens-tiktok-social-media-skin-care/.

2. Ann Carrns, "Average Weekly Allowances? It's Now $30, a New Survey Finds," *New York Times*, October 17, 2019, https://www.nytimes.com/2019/10/04/your-money/weekly-allowance-average.html.
3. Kathleen McDonnell, *Honey, We Lost the Kids: Re-Thinking Childhood in the Multimedia Age*, revised ed. (Toronto: Second Story Books, 2005); David Elkind, *The Hurried Child: Growing Up Too Fast Too Soon*, 25th anniversary ed. (New York: Perseus Books, 2009).
4. Kathleen McDonnell, *Kid Culture: Children & Adults & Popular Culture* ((Toronto: Second Story Books, 1994).
5. William A. Corsaro, *We're Friends, Right? Inside Kids' Cultures* (Washington, DC: Joseph Henry Press, 2003); William A. Corsaro, *Friendship and Peer Culture in the Early Years* (Norwood, NJ: Ablex Publishing Corporation, 1985); William A. Corsaro, *The Sociology of Childhood* (Newbury Park, CA: Pine Forge Press, 1997); Barrie Thorne, *Gender Play: Girls and Boys in School* (New Brunswick, NJ: Rutgers University Press, 1993); Gary Alan Fine, *With the Boys: Little League Baseball and Preadolescent Culture* (Chicago: University of Chicago Press, 1987).
6. Ron Kovic, *Born on the Fourth of July* (New York: McGraw-Hill, 1976).
7. Homer H. Hickam Jr., *Rocket Boys: A Memoir* (New York: Delacorte Press, 1998).
8. Susan Allen Toth, *Blooming: A Small-Town Girlhood* (Boston: Little, Brown, 1981).
9. Wini Breines, *Young, White, and Miserable: Growing Up Female in the Fifties* (Chicago: University of Chicago Press, 2001).
10. Ruth J. Simmons, *Up Home: One Girl's Journey* (New York: Random House, 2023).
11. Adriana Barbero and Jeremy Earp, *Media Education Foundation Study Guide: Consuming Kids* (Northampton, MA: Media Education Foundation, 2008), 5, https://www.mediaed.org/discussion-guides/Consuming-Kids-Discussion-Guide.pdf.
12. Neil Browne et al., "Commercializing Children: Laws and Regulations Affecting Advertisements Directed at Children in France, Spain and Sweden," Economics Faculty Publications (Bowling Green University) 17 (2018), https://papers.ssrn.com/sol3/papers.cfm?abstract_id=3518109.
13. Peter Gray, "The Play Deficit," Aeon, September 18, 2013, https://aeon.co/essays/children-today-are-suffering-a-severe-deficit-of-play; Revising the Children's Shelf, "The Case of Disappearing Nursery Rhymes," March 15, 2014, https://revisitingthechildrensshelf.com/2014/03/15/the-case-of-the-missing-nursery-rhymes/.
14. Emily A. Vogels, Risa Gelles-Watnick, and Navid Massarat, "Teens, Social Media and Technology 2022," Pew Research Center, August 10, 2022, https://www.pewresearch.org/internet/2022/08/10/teens-social-media-and-technology-2022/.
15. Karen Gilchrist, "Don't Want to Give Your Kid a Smartphone? Here Are Some Alternatives," CNBC, November 25, 2022, https://www.cnbc.com/2022/11/25/how-to-know-when-to-give-a-child-a-smartphone-what-are-the-alternatives.html.
16. Stephen Kline, *Out of the Garden: Toys, TV, and Children's Culture in the Age of Marketing* (London: Verso, 1995).
17. James Paul Gee, *What Video Games Have to Teach Us About Learning and Literacy*, 2nd revised ed. (New York: Palgrave Macmillan, 2007); Gerard Jones, *Killing Monsters: Why Children Need Fantasy, Super Heroes, and Make-Believe Violence* (New York: Basic Books, 2002); Steven Johnson, *Everything Bad Is Good for You: How Today's Popular Culture Is Actually Making Us Smarter* (New York: Riverhead, 2003).
18. Henry Jenkins, "Children's Culture," n.d., http://web.mit.edu/cms/People/henry3/children.htm, and Henry Jenkins, "Complete Freedom of Movement: Video Games as Gendered Play Spaces," n.d., http://web.mit.edu/cms/People/henry3/pub/complete.html.
19. Jenkins, "Children's Culture" and "Complete Freedom of Movement."

Chapter 9

1. Joan Rothschild, *The Dream of the Perfect Child* (Bloomington: Indiana University Press, 2005).
2. Peter N. Stearns, *Anxious Parents: A History of Modern Childrearing in America* (New York: New York University Press, 2003).
3. Nick Haslam, Jesse S. Y. Tse, and Simon De Deyne, "Concept Creep and Psychiatrization," *Frontiers in Sociology* 6 (2021), https://www.frontiersin.org/articles/10.3389/fsoc.2021.806147/full.
4. Ethan Watters, *Crazy Like Us: The Globalization of the American Psyche* (New York: Simon & Schuster, 2010).

5. Ruth E. Taylor, "Death of Neurasthenia and Its Psychological Reincarnation," *British Journal of Psychiatry* 179, no. 6 (2018), https://www.cambridge.org/core/journals/the-british-journal-of-psychiatry/article/death-of-neurasthenia-and-its-psychological-reincarnation/CBF3F9183ED6368E940BB0F0AB327482.
6. Matthew Smith, *Hyperactive: The Controversial History of ADHD* (London: Reaktion Books Ltd., 2012); Matthew Smith, *Another Person's Poison: A History of Food Allergy* (New York: Columbia University Press, 2015); John Donvan and Caren Zucker, *In a Different Key: The Story of Autism* (New York: Crown Publishers, 2016); Steve Silberman, *NeuroTribes: The Legacy of Autism and the Future of Neurodiversity* (New York: Penguin Random House, 2015).
7. Nick Haslam, "Concept Creep: Psychology's Expanding Concepts of Harm and Pathology," Social Science Research Network, November 14, 2015, http://papers.ssrn.com/sol3/papers.cfm?abstract_id=2690955.
8. Ethan Watters, "American Culture and A.D.H.D.," *New York Times*, October 13, 2011, http://www.nytimes.com/roomfordebate/2011/10/12/are-americans-more-prone-to-adhd/american-culture-and-adhd.
9. National Center for Education Statistics, "Students with Disabilities," accessed August 16, 2023, https://nces.ed.gov/fastfacts/display.asp?id=60; National Center for Education Statistics, "A Majority of College Students with Disabilities Do Not Inform School, New NCES Data Show," April 26, 2022, https://nces.ed.gov/whatsnew/press_releases/4_26_2022.asp.
10. Colleen Eren, "The Problem with Disabling," *Discourse*, July 13, 2023, https://www.discoursemagazine.com/culture-and-society/2023/07/13/the-problem-with-disabling/.
11. Centers for Disease Control and Prevention, *Childhood Obesity Facts*, accessed August 3, 2016, https://www.cdc.gov/healthyschools/obesity/facts.htm; Centers for Disease Control and Prevention, *Childhood Obesity Causes & Consequences*, accessed August 3, 2016, http://www.cdc.gov/obesity/childhood/causes.html; On moral panics and childhood, see Frank Furedi, *Paranoid Parenting: Why Ignoring the Experts May Be Best for Your Child* (Chicago: Chicago Review Press, 2002); Steven Mintz, *Huck's Raft: A History of American Childhood* (Cambridge, MA: Belknap Press of Harvard University Press, 2004), 335–71.
12. Tina Moffat, The "'Childhood Obesity Epidemic': Health Crisis or Social Construction?," *Medical Anthropology Quarterly* 24, no. 1 (2010), 1–21.
13. Ashley W. Kranjac and Dinko Kranjac, "Child Obesity Moderates the Association Between Poverty and Academic Achievement," *Psychology in the Schools*, February 10, 2021, https://onlinelibrary.wiley.com/doi/abs/10.1002/pits.22497.
14. R. Rogers et al., "The Relationship Between Childhood Obesity, Low Socioeconomic Status, and Race/Ethnicity: Lessons from Massachusetts," *Child Obesity* 11, no. 6 (2015), 691–95; Taylor F. Eagle et al., "Understanding Childhood Obesity in America: Linkages Between Household Income, Community Resources, and Children's Behaviors," *American Heart Journal* 163, no. 5 (2012), 836–43.
15. Erik Melén et al., "Allergies to Food and Airborne Allergens in Children and Adolescents: Role of Epigenetics in a Changing Environment," *Lancet Child Adolescent Health* 6 (2022), 810–19, https://pubmed.ncbi.nlm.nih.gov/35985346/.
16. Melén et al., "Allergies."
17. Ruby Pawankar et al., "White Book on Allergy: Executive Summary, Update 2013" World Allergy Organization, 2013, https://allergypaais.org/wp-content/themes/twentytwentyone/pdf/ExecSummary-2013-v6-hires.pdf; Luciana Kase Tanno and Pascal Demoly, "Food Allergy in the World Health Organization's International Classification of Diseases (ICD)-11," *Pediatric Allergy and Immunology*, 33, no. 11 (November 16, 2022), https://onlinelibrary.wiley.com/doi/full/10.1111/pai.13882; American Academy of Allergy, Asthma, and Immunology, "Allergy Statistics," accessed August 16, 2023, https://www.aaaai.org/about/news/for-media/allergy-statistics; Matthew Smith, "The Hives and the Hive-Nots," *Literary Review*, June 2023, 21, https://literaryreview.co.uk/the-hives-and-the-hive-nots.
18. Smith, "Hives and Hives Not."
19. Karin Zetterqvist Nelson and Bengt Sandin, "The Politics of Reading and Writing Problems: Changing Definitions in Swedish Schooling During the Twentieth Century," *History of Education* 34, no. 2 (2005), 189–205.
20. Zetterqvist Nelson and Sandin, "Politics of Reading and Writing Problems."
21. Julian G. Elliott and Elena L. Grigorenko, *The Dyslexia Debate* (Cambridge: Cambridge University Press, 2014); Julian Elliott and Rod Nicolson, *Dyslexia: Developing the Debate* (London: Bloomsbury Academic, 2016).

22. Centers for Disease Control and Prevention, "Data and Statistics About ADHD," accessed August 16, 2023, https://www.cdc.gov/ncbddd/adhd/data.html.
23. CDC, "Data and Statistics About ADHD."
24. CDC, "Data and Statistics About ADHD"; Matthew Smith, "The ADHD Increase in Context," *A Short History of Mental Health* blog, *Psychology Today*, accessed August 3, 2016, https://www.psychologytoday.com/blog/short-history-mental-health/201304/the-adhd-increase-in-context. Matthew Smith, "The History of Hyperactivity," *A Short History of Mental Health* blog, *Psychology Today*, accessed August 3, 2016, https://www.psychologytoday.com/blog/short-history-mental-health/201301/the-history-hyperactivity. Matthew Smith, "What's in a Name?," *A Short History of Mental Health* blog, *Psychology Today*, accessed August 3, 2016, https://www.psychologytoday.com/blog/short-history-mental-health/201208/whats-in-name
25. Matthew Smith, "The Hyperactive State: ADHD in Its Historical Context," in *(De)Medicalising Misery II*, eds. Ewen Speed, Joanna Moncrieff, and Mark Rapley (New York: Palgrave Macmillan, 2014), 89–104.
26. Matthew Smith, "Rethinking Methylphenidate in Childhood ADHD," *A Short History of Mental Health* blog, *Psychology Today*, accessed August 3, 2016, https://www.psychologytoday.com/blog/short-history-mental-health/201601/rethinking-methylphenidate-in-childhood-adhd. Matthew Smith, *An Alternative History of Hyperactivity: Food Additives and the Feingold Diet* (New Brunswick, NJ: Rutgers University Press, 2011).
27. Geoffrey H. Donovan et al., "Association Between Exposure to the Natural Environment, Rurality, and Attention-Deficit Hyperactivity Disorder in Children in New Zealand: A Linkage Study," *Lancet: Planetary Health* 3 (May 2019), https://www.thelancet.com/journals/lanplh/article/PIIS2542-5196(19)30070-1/fulltext; Richard Louv, *Last Child in the Woods: Saving Our Children from Nature-Deficit Disorder* (New York: Algonquin Books of Chapel Hill, 2008).
28. The fifth edition of the *Diagnostic and Statistical Manual of Mental Disorders (DSM-5)*, issued in 2013, eliminated Asperger syndrome as a separate disorder and folded it into autism spectrum disorder. Asperger syndrome was not removed from the World Health Organization's 10th revision of the *International Statistical Classification of Diseases and Related Health Problems*, which was originally published in 1992. *DSM-4* distinguished autism and Asperger syndrome, holding that autism typically involved delays in cognitive and language development.

Chapter 10

1. Centers for Disease Control and Prevention, "Anxiety and Depression in Children: Get the Facts," *Children's Mental Health*, March 8, 2023, https://www.cdc.gov/childrensmentalhealth/features/anxiety-depression-children.html; R. H. Bitsko et al., "Epidemiology and Impact of Health Care Provider-Diagnosed Anxiety and Depression Among United States Children," *Journal of Developmental and Behavioral Pediatrics* 39 (2018), https://www.ncbi.nlm.nih.gov/pmc/articles/PMC6003874/.
2. John Duffy, *Parenting the New Teen in the Age of Anxiety* (Coral Gables, FL: Mango Publishing, 2018). See also Peter N. Stearns, "Student Anxiety and Its Impact: A Contemporary American History," *History of Education Quarterly* (Spring 2023), doi:10.1017/heq.2023.10.
3. Bitsko et al., "Epidemiology"; Jessica Bryant and Lyss Welding, "College Student Mental Health Statistics," *Best Colleges*, February 15, 2023, https://www.bestcolleges.com/research/college-student-mental-health-statistics/.
4. C. G. Last and S. Perrin, "Anxiety Disorders in African-American and White Children," *Journal of Abnormal Child Psychology* 21 (1993), https://doi.org/10.1007/BF00911313; Arlene T. Gordon-Hollingsworth et al., "Anxiety Disorders in Caucasian and African-American Children: A Comparison of Clinical Characteristics, Treatment Process Variables, and Treatment Outcomes," *Child Psychiatry and Human Development* 46 (2015), https://www.ncbi.nlm.nih.gov/pmc/articles/PMC4390415/.
5. B. Henker, C. Wharton, and R. O'Neill, "Worldly and Workday Worries: Contemporary Concerns of Children and Young Adolescents," *Journal of Abnormal Child Psychology* 23 (1995), https://pubmed.ncbi.nlm.nih.gov/8609308/; thanks to Nina Keisu for data from the Public Health Agency of Sweden, from 2022.
6. Christine Gross-Loh, *Parenting Without Borders* (New York: Penguin Random House, 2014); Sally Weale, "Levels of Distress and Illness Among UK Students 'Alarmingly' High," *Guardian*, March 4, 2019, https://www.theguardian.com/education/2019/mar/05/levels-of-distress-and-illness-among-students-in-uk-alarmingly-high.

7. Rollo May, *Meaning of Anxiety* (New York: Ronald Press, 1950; rev. ed., 1977).
8. Stearns, "Student Anxiety."
9. Allan Horwitz, *Anxiety: A Short History* (Baltimore: Johns Hopkins University Press, 2013); W. H. Auden, *The Age of Anxiety* (Princeton, NJ: Princeton University Press, 1950).
10. Andrea Tone, *Age of Anxiety: America's Turbulent Affair with Tranquillizers* (New York: Basic Books, 2008); David Hertzberg, *Happy Pills in America: from Milltown to Prozac* (Baltimore: Johns Hopkins University Press, 2019).
11. Horwitz, *Anxiety*.
12. Stearns, "Student Anxiety."
13. Norman Gysbers, "Remembering the Past, Shaping the Future: A History of School Counseling," (Alexandria, VA: American School Counselor Association 2010); Roger Aubrey, "The Historical Development of Guidance and Counseling and Implications for the Future," *Personnel and Guidance Journal* 55, no. 6 (1977), 288–294 https://eric.ed.gov/?id=EJ154748; Joshua Watson, "Managing College Stress: The Role of College Counselors," *Journal of College Counseling* 15, no. 1 (2012), 3–4, https://doi.org/10.1002/j.2161-1882.2012.00001.x.
14. Charles Reifler and Myron Liptzin, "Epidemiological Studies of College Mental Health," *Archives of General Psychiatry* 20 (1968), https://jamanetwork.com/journals/jamapsychiatry/article-abstract/489954; William Smith, Norris Hansell, and Joseph English, "Psychiatric Disorder in a College Population," *Archives of General Psychiatry* 15 (1963), https://jamanetwork.com/journals/jamapsychiatry/article-abstract/488405; Graham Blaine and Charles McArthur, eds., *The Emotional Problems of College Students*, 2nd ed. (New York: Appleton-Century, 1971).
15. Irwin Sarason, "Test Anxiety and the Intellectual Performance of College Students," *Journal of Behavioral Psychology* 52 (1961), https://doi.org/10.1037/h0049095; George J. Allen, "The Behavioral Treatment of Test Anxiety: Recent Research and Future Trends," *Behavior Therapy* 3 (1972), https://doi.org/10.1016/S0005-7894(72)80087-X; R. W. Svinn, "The STABS, a Measure of Test Anxiety for Behavior Therapy," *Behavior Research and Therapy* (1972), https://doi.org/10.1016/0005-7967(69)90018-7.
16. R. B. Cattell, *Handbook for the IPAT Anxiety Scale* (Champaign, IL: Institute for Personality and Ability Testing, 1957); A. Castaneda, B. McCandless, and D. Palermo, "The Children's Form of the Manifest Anxiety Scale," *Child Development* 22 (1956), https://pubmed.ncbi.nlm.nih.gov/13356330/.
17. Jean Twenge, "The Age of Anxiety? Birth Cohort Change in Anxiety and Neuroticism, 1963–1993," *Journal of Personality and Social Psychology* 79 (1999), https://www.apa.org/pubs/journals/releases/psp7961007.pdf.
18. Twenge, "Age of Anxiety"; Stearns, "Student Anxiety."
19. D. L. Farnsworth, *Mental Health in College and University* (Cambridge, MA: Harvard University Press, 1963); R. M. Rust, "The Epidemiology of Mental Health in College," *Journal of Psychology* 49 (1960), https://doi.org/10.1080/00223980.1960.9916406; R. Sutton-Smith et al., "Historical Changes in the Freedom with Which Children Express Themselves on Personality Inventories," *Journal of Genetic Psychology* 99 (1961), https://pubmed.ncbi.nlm.nih.gov/13918569/; Reifler and Liptzin "Epidemiological Studies"; Max Siegel, ed., *The Counseling of College Students* (New York: Free Press, 1968); Benjamin Ayres and Michelle Barrow, *Anxiety in College Students* (New York: Nova Science, 2009).
20. Siegel, ed., *Counseling*; S. B. Karh, "Dimensions of Manifest Anxiety and Their Relationship to College Achievement," *Journal of Counseling and Clinical Psychology* 15 (1970), https://api.semanticscholar.org/CorpusID:144348990.
21. Kathy Ybanez-Llorente, "Addressing Anxiety in School Settings: Information for Counselors," *American Counseling Association Vistas Online* (2014), https://padletuploads.blob.core.windows.net/prod/203351970/efb2d40badc7d7752c6e68d85be0d109/Addressing_Anxiety_in_Schools.pdf; for an early statement in the school context, see S. B. Campbell, "Developmental Issues in Childhood Anxiety," in *Anxiety Disorders of Childhood*, ed. R. Gittelman (New York: Springer, 1986), 53–79; W. K. Silverman, A. M. La Greca, and S. Wasserstein, "What Do Children Worry About? Worries and Their Relation to Anxiety," *Child Development* 66, no. 3 (1995), 671–686, https://pubmed.ncbi.nlm.nih.gov/7789194/.
22. Ybanez-Llorente, "Addressing Anxiety."
23. Twenge, "Age of Anxiety."
24. Twenge, "Age of Anxiety"; Stearns, "Student Anxiety."

25. Brian D'Onofrio and Robert Emery, "Parental Divorce or Separation and Children's Mental Health," *World Psychiatry* 18 (2019), https://pubmed.ncbi.nlm.nih.gov/30600636/; Jochen Hardt et al., "Anxiety and Depression as an Effect of Birth Order or Being an Only Child," *Insights: Depression, Anxiety*, September 2017, https://www.heighpubs.org/hda/ida-aid1003.php.
26. Jeffrey Selingo, *Who Gets In, and Why* (New York: Scribner, 2020).
27. J. D. Hunt and D. Eisenberg, "Mental Health Problems and Help-Seeking Behavior Among College Students," *Journal of Adolescent Health* 46 (2019), https://pubmed.ncbi.nlm.nih.gov/20123251/.
28. Silke Luttenberger, Sigrid Wimmer, and Manuela Paechter, "Spotlight on Math Anxiety," *Psychological Research and Behavior Management* 11 (2018), https://www.ncbi.nlm.nih.gov/pmc/articles/PMC6087017/; D. R. Hopko et al., "The Abbreviated Math Anxiety Scale (AMAS): Construction, Validity, and Reliability," *Assessment* 10 (2003), https://pubmed.ncbi.nlm.nih.gov/12801189/. For a chart on the striking rise in reference to math and English anxiety, see Google Ngrams, American English, 1950–present.
29. Horwitz, *Anxiety*; Jonathan Engel, *American Therapy: A History of Psychotherapy in the United States* (New York: Gotham Books, 2006); T. LeMoyne and T. Buchanan, "Does 'Hovering' Matter? Helicopter Parenting and Its Effect on Well-Being," *Sociological Spectrum* 31 (2011), https://doi.org/10.1080/02732173.2011.574038.
30. Hunt and Eisenberg, "Mental Health Problems."
31. Payton Jones, So Yeon Park, and G. T. Lefevor, "Contemporary College Student Anxiety: The Role of Academic Distress, Financial Distress, and Support," *Journal of College Counseling* 21 (2019), https://doi.org/10.1002/jocc.12107.
32. Stearns, "Student Anxiety."
33. Betul Keles, Niall McCrea, and Annmarie Graelish, "A Systematic Review: The Influence of Social Media on Depression, Anxiety and Psychological Distress in Adolescents," *International Journal of Adolescence and Youth* 25 (2020), https://doi.org/10.1080/02673843.2019.1590851; Claire McCarthy, "Anxiety in Teens Is Rising: What's Going On?," *American Academy of Pediatrics Healthy Children,* November 20, 2019, https://www.healthychildren.org/English/health-issues/conditions/emotional-problems/Pages/Anxiety-Disorders.aspx.
34. McCarthy, "Anxiety in Teens."
35. Robert Graff, G. D. MacLean, and Andrew Loving, "Group Reactive Inhibitions and Reciprocal Inhibitions Therapy with Anxious College Students," *Journal of Counseling and Psychology* 18 (1971), https://doi.org/10.1037/h0031516; George Allen, "The Behavioral Treatment of Test Anxiety: Recent Research and Future Trends," *Behavior Therapy* 3 (1972), https://doi.org/10.1016/S0005-7894(72)80087-X; Richard Cornish and Josiah Dilley, "Comparison of Three Methods of Reducing Test Anxiety," *Journal of Counseling Psychology* 20 (1973), https://doi.org/10.1037/h0035172.
36. Joshua Watson, "Managing College Stress: The Role of College Counselors," *Journal of College Counseling* 15 (2012), https://doi.org/10.1002/j.2161-1882.2012.00001.x. The number of counselors feeling overwhelmed by the level of student demand doubled already between 1985 and 2002, by which point 83 percent of all centers were reporting major increases in severe anxiety disorders over the previous five years; Martha Anne Kitzrow, "Mental Health Needs of Today's College Students," *National Association of Personnel Administrators Journal* 41 (2003), https://doi.org/10.2202/1949-6605.1310.
37. K. Rickels, "Drug Use in Outpatient Treatment," *American Journal of Psychiatry* 125 (1968), https://pubmed.ncbi.nlm.nih.gov/4865730/; Tori DeAngelis, "Anxiety Among Kids Is on the Rise: Wider Access to CBT May Provide Needed Solutions," *Monitor on Psychology* 10 (2022), https://www.apa.org/monitor/2022/10/child-anxiety-treatment.
38. DeAngelis, "Anxiety."
39. Ybanez-Llorente, "Addressing Anxiety."
40. Jill Castellano, "Pet Therapy Is a Nearly Cost-Free Anxiety Reducer on College Campuses," *Forbes*, July 6, 2015, https://www.forbes.com/sites/jillcastellano/2015/07/06/pet-therapy-is-a-nearly-cost-free-anxiety-reducer-on-college-campuses/?sh=54cde9207c59.
41. Some modifications reflected principled reconsideration of educational practices: see Josh Eyler, "The Problem with Grades," *Teaching in Higher Education*, February 17, 2022, https://teachinginhighered.com/podcast/the-problem-with-grades/. But it would be interesting to have a wider sense of ad hoc adjustments, like abolishing exams, shortening papers, and accepting work whenever it arrived, and the wider results.

Chapter 11

1. Ariana Prothero, "More Schools Are Offering Mental Health Days," *Education Week*, January 19, 2023, https://www.edweek.org/leadership/more-schools-are-offering-student-mental-health-days-heres-what-you-need-to-know/2023/01.
2. Prothero, "More Schools."
3. Julianna Horowitz and Nikki Graf, "Most U.S. Teens See Anxiety and Depression as Major Problems Among Their Peers," *Pew Research Reports*, February 20, 2019, https://www.pewresearch.org/social-trends/2019/02/20/most-u-s-teens-see-anxiety-and-depression-as-a-major-problem-among-their-peers/.
4. Centers for Disease Control and Prevention, "Childhood Obesity Facts," May 17, 2022, https://www.cdc.gov/obesity/data/childhood.html.
5. R. M. Ghandour et al., "Prevalence and Treatment of Depression, Anxiety and Conduct Problems in U.S. Children," *Journal of Pediatrics* (2018), https://www.jpeds.com/article/S0022-3476(18)31292-7/fulltext.
6. Ghandour et al., "Prevalence and Treatment."
7. Ryan McBain et al., "Growth and Distribution of Child Psychiatrists in the United States, 2007–2015," *Pediatrics* 144 (2019), https://www.ncbi.nlm.nih.gov/pmc/articles/PMC6889947/.
8. Peter Gray, David Lancy, and David Bjorklund, "Decline in Independent Activity as a Cause of Decline in Children's Mental Well-Being: Summary of the Evidence," *Journal of Pediatrics* 260 (February 2023), https://pubmed.ncbi.nlm.nih.gov/36841510/.
9. The comparative challenge is tantalizing in dealing with causation. For example, explanations that rely on social media must account for the fact that American children are not particularly distinctive in their usage rates and habits, compared with a number of other affluent societies, but their rates of distress, though not unique, are measurably more severe. Damian Radcliffe, "How Do Teens and Tweens in the UK and the USA Use Media and Technology?," *Medium*, December 29, 2015. https://medium.com/damian-radcliffe/how-do-teens-and-tweens-in-the-uk-and-usa-use-media-and-technology-6-key-trends-e15f1a75f8c8.
10. For a particularly vigorous attack on the effects of therapy and "over-medicalization" on children generally, see Abigail Shrier, *Bad Therapy: Why the Kids Aren't Growing Up* (New York: Penguin Random House, 2024).
11. Kelly Kelleher and Jack Stevens, "Evolution of Children's Mental Health Services in Primary Care," *Academy of Pediatrics* 94 (2009), https://www.ncbi.nlm.nih.gov/pmc/articles/PMC2699251/.
12. Karin Nelson and Bengt Sandin, "The Politics of Reading and Writing: Changing Definitions in Swedish Schooling During the Twentieth Century," *History of Education* 34 (2005), https://doi.org/10.1080/0046760042000338764.
13. Sheryl Kataoka, Lily Zhang, and Kenneth Wells, "Unmet Need for Mental Health Care Among U.S. Children: Variation by Ethnicity and Insurance Status," *American Journal of Psychiatry* (2002), https://doi.org/10.1176/appi.ajp.159.9.1548.
14. Lyss Welding, "Students with Disabilities in Higher Education: Facts and Statistics," *Best Colleges*, March 29, 2023, https://www.bestcolleges.com/research/students-with-disabilities-higher-education-statistics/; for the statement on the persistence of disability, see National Center for Learning Disabilities, "Transitioning to Life After High School," *Our Research*, January 27, 2017, https://www.ncld.org/research/state-of-learning-disabilities/transitioning-to-life-after-high-school/.
15. Jana Koci and Stewart Donaldson, *Well-Being and Success for University Students* (New York: Routledge, 2024).
16. Noah Smith, "How Happy Is America?," Reading Eagle, August 11, 2021, https://www.readingeagle.com/2021/08/11/noah-smith-how-happy-is-america/.

Chapter 12

1. Grace Abbott, *The Child and the State* (Chicago: University of Chicago Press, 1938).
2. Jonathan Haidt, *The Anxious Generation: How the Great Rewiring of Childhood Is Causing an Epidemic of Mental Illness* (New York: Penguin/Random House, 2024).
3. J. C. C. Miller and N. Irwin, "The Radically Simple New Approach to Helping Families: Send Money," *New York Times*, February 9, 2021, https://www.nytimes.com/2021/02/09/upshot/biden-stimulus-plan-families.html; Angel Vahraton and R. B. Johnson, "Maternity Leave Benefits in the United States: Today's Economic Climate Underlines Deficiencies," *Birth* 36,

no. 3 (2009), 177–179, https://doi.org/10.1111/j.1523-536X.2009.00330.x; United Health Foundation, "America's Health Rankings: International Comparisons," *Annual Report*, 2018, https://www.americashealthrankings.org/learn/reports/2018-annual-report; Children's Defense Fund, "Child Poverty," in *The State of America's Children, 2023* (Washington, DC: Children's Defense Fund, 2023), https://www.childrensdefense.org/tools-and-resources/the-state-of-americas-children/soac-child-poverty/.
4. Robert Putnam and S. Garrett, *The Upswing: How Americans Came Together a Century Ago and How We Can Do It Again* (New York: Simon & Schuster, 2020); Anthony M. Platt, *The Child Savers: The Invention of Delinquency* (New Brunswick, NJ: Rutgers University Press, 2009); Kriste Lindenmeyer, *A Right to Childhood: The U.S. Children's Bureau and Child Welfare, 1912–1946* (Urbana: University of Illinois Press, 2007).
5. T. Toch, "PARENTS: The Plight of the PTA," *New York Times*, January 7, 2001, https://www.nytimes.com/2001/01/07/education/parents-the-plight-of-the-pta.html.
6. Steven Mintz, "American Childhood as a Social and Cultural Construct," in *Families as They Really Are*, eds. Barbara Risman, Kristi Howe, and Virginia Muller (New York: W.W. Norton, 2024), 78–93.
7. Lenore Skenazy, *Free-Range Kids: How Parents and Teachers Can Let Go and Let Grow* (New York: Wiley, 2021).

Suggestions for Further Reading

A new childhood emerged over the past half century that differs decisively from the kinds of childhood that characterized the early post-World War II era. For a useful overview of the transformation of American childhood from the colonial era to the early twenty-first century, see Steven Mintz, *Huck's Raft: A History of American Childhood* (Cambridge, MA: Harvard University Press, 2004).

Studies that trace the developments that have reshaped childhood in the United States—cultural, demographic, economic, educational, and familial—since World War II include Paula S. Fass, *Children of a New World: Society, Culture, and Globalization* (New York: New York University Press, 2006) and *The End of American Childhood: A History of Parenting from Life on the Frontier to the Managed Child* (Princeton, NJ: Princeton University Press, 2016); and two essay collections, Paula S. Fass and Michael Grossberg, eds., *Reinventing Childhood After World War II* (Philadelphia: University of Pennsylvania Press, 2014); and Timothy Owens and Sandra Hofferth, eds., *Children in the Millennium; Where Have We Come From? Where Are We Going?* (Leeds, UK: JAI Press, 2002).

Recent changes in family structure and familial dynamics are well studied in Andrew J. Cherlin, *Labor's Love Lost: The Rise and Fall of the Working-Class Family in America* (New York: Russell Sage Foundation, 2014) and *The Marriage-Go-Round: The State of Marriage and the Family in America Today* (New York: Vintage, 2010); and Philip N. Cohen, *Enduring Bonds: Inequality, Marriage, Parenting, and Everything Else That Makes Families Great and Terrible* (Berkeley: University of California Press, 2018) and *The Family: Diversity, Inequality, and Social Change*, 2nd ed. (New York: W.W. Norton & Company, 2021).

Regarding diversity and inequality in children's lives, an especially important study is Annette Larau, *Unequal Childhoods: Class, Race and Family*, 2nd ed. (Berkeley: University of California Press, 2011).

Shifting cultural attitudes toward children are traced in Katie Wright, *Rise of the Therapeutic Society: Psychological Knowledge and the Contradictions of Cultural Change* (Washington, DC: New Academia, 2011); Pamela Druckman, *Bringing Up Bebe: One American Mother Discovers the Wisdom of French Parenting* (New York: Penguin, 2019); Viviana Zelizer, *Pricing the Priceless Child* (Princeton, NJ: Princeton University Press, 1994); and Vance Packard, *Our Endangered Children: Growing Up in a Changing World* (Boston: Little, Brown, 1983).

On changes in parental and societal attitudes toward education, schooling practices and policies, and children's everyday school experiences, see William Reese, *America's Public Schools: From the Common School to "No Child Left Behind"* (Baltimore: Johns Hopkins University Press, 2005); Peter Taubman, *Teaching by Numbers: Deconstructing the Discourses of Standards and Accountability* (New York: Routledge, 2009); Jonathan Kozol, *An End to Inequality: Breaking Down the Walls of Apartheid Education in America* (New York: New Press, 2024); Jeffrey Selingo, *Who Gets in and Why: A Year Inside College Admissions* (New York: Simon & Schuster, 2020).

On the history of children's play, see Jeffrey Goldstein, ed., *Toys, Play and Child Development* (Cambridge: Cambridge University Press, 1994); Howard Chudacoff, *Children at Play: An American History* (New York: New York University Press, 2007); Peter Gray, "The Decline of Play and the Rise of Psychopathology in Children and Adolescents," *American*

Journal of Play 3, no. 4 (2011), 443–463; E. Miller and J. Almon, *Crisis in the Kindergarten: Why Children Need to Play in School* (College Park: University of Maryland Press, 2008); Alice Rosenfeld and Nicole Wise, *The Overscheduled Child: Avoiding the Hyper-Parenting Trap* (New York: Macmillan, 2001); Gary Alan Fine, *With the Boys: Little League Baseball and Preadolescence* (Chicago: University of Chicago Press, 1987).

On children's peer cultures and social worlds, see William A. Corsaro and Judson E. Everitt, *The Sociology of Childhood* (Thousand Oaks, CA: Sage Publications, 2024) and Madeleine Leonard, *The Sociology of Children, Childhood and Generation* (Thousand Oaks, CA: Sage Publications, 2015).

On children's cultural worlds, Stephen Kline, *Out of the Garden: Toys, TV and Children's Culture in the Age of Marketing* (London: Verso, 1995): Kathleen Honey, *We Lost the Kids: Re-Thinking Childhood in the Multimedia Age*, rev. ed. (Toronto: Second Story Books, 2005) and *Kid Culture* (Toronto: Second Story Books, 1994); Gerard Jones, *Killing Monsters: Why Children Need Fantasies, Super-Heroes and Make-Believe Violence* (New York: Basic Books, 2002). On video game playing, see James Paul Gee, *What Video Games Have to Teach Us About Learning and Literacy* (New York: Palgrave Macmillan, 2007).

On consumerism and children, valuable studies include Gary Cross, *Kid's Stuff: Toys and the Changing World of American Childhood* (Cambridge, MA: Harvard University Press, 1997) and *The Cute and the Cool: Wondrous Innocence and Modern American Children* (New York: Oxford University Press, 2004); Donna Dee Gates, *I Want It Now: Children in a Material World* (London: Macmillan, 2007); and Sydney Stern and Ted Schoenhaus, *Toyland: The High-Stakes Game of the Toy Industry* (New York: Birch Lane Press, 1991).

On the special problems facing boys, see Gary Cross, *Men to Boys: The Making of Modern Immaturity* (New York: Columbia University Press, 2008); Kay S. Hymowitz, *Manning Up: How the Rise of Women Has Turned Men into Boys* (New York: Basic Books, 2012); and Richard V. Reeves, *Of Boys and Men: Why the Modern Male Is Struggling, Why It Matters, and What to Do About It* (London: Swift Press, 2022). A particularly influential examination of issues facing girls is Mary Pipher and Sara Pipher Gilliam, *Reviving Ophelia 25th Anniversary Edition: Saving the Selves of Adolescent Girls* (New York: Riverhead Books, 2019).

On shifts in parenting and child-rearing practices, see Peter N. Stearns, *Anxious Parents: A History of Modern Childrearing in America* (New York: New York University Press, 2004).

Regarding physical and other organic disabilities in children, see Joan Rothschild, *The Dream of the Perfect Child* (Bloomington: Indiana University Press, 2005). Important studies on the "new" disorders and disabilities of childhood include Jean Twenge, "'Age of Anxiety': The Birth Cohort Change in Anxiety and Neuroticism, 1952–1993," *Journal of Personality and Social Psychology* 79 (2000), 1007–21; Matthew Smith, *Hyperactive: The Controversial History of ADHD* (London: Reaktion Books, 2012); Caren Zucker, *In a Different Way: The Story of Autism* (New York: Crown Publishers, 2014); Frank Furedi, *Paranoid Parenting: Why Ignoring the Experts May Be Best for Your Child* (Chicago: Chicago Review Press, 2002); Julian Elliott and Elena Grigorenko, *The Dyslexia Debate* (Cambridge: Cambridge University Press, 2014); John Duffy, *Parenting in the Age of Anxiety* (Coral Gables, FL: Mango Publishing, 2018); and David Herzberg, *Happy Pills in America from Milltown to Prozac* (Baltimore: Johns Hopkins University Press, 2019).

Many popular and psychologically and sociologically informed studies treat the story of post-World War II American childhood as a history of decline. Examples include David Elkind, *The Harried Child: Growing Up Too Fast, Too Soon* (New York: Penguin Books, 2009); Madeline Levine, *The Price of Privilege: How Parental Pressure and Material Advantage Are Creating a Generation of Disconnected and Unhappy Kids* (New York: HarperCollins, 2009); Margaret Nelson, *Parenting Out of Control: Anxious Parents in Uncertain Times* (New York: New York University Press, 2010); Vance Packard, *Our Endangered Children: Growing Up in a Changing World* (Boston: Little, Brown, 1983); and Neil Postman, *The Disappearance of Childhood* (New York: Vintage, 1982).

Studies that focus on the mental health struggles of adolescents and pre-adolescents and the recent sense of a crisis of childhood include Jonathan Haidt, *The Anxious Generation: How the Great Rewiring of Childhood Is Causing an Epidemic of Mental Illness* (New York: Penguin, 2024); Greg Lukianoff and Jonathan Haidt, *The Coddling of the American Mind: How Good Intentions and Bad Ideas Are Setting Up a Generation for Failure* (New York: Penguin, 2018); and Jean M. Twenge, *Generations: The Real Differences Between Gen Z, Millennials, Gen X, Boomers, and Silents—and What They Mean for America's Future* (New York: Atria Books, 2023), *iGen: Why Today's Super-Connected Kids Are Growing Up Less Rebellious, More Tolerant, Less Happy—and Completely Unprepared for Adulthood—and What That Means for the Rest of Us* (New York: Atria Books, 2017), and *Generation Me - Revised and Updated: Why Today's Young Americans Are More Confident, Assertive, Entitled—and More Miserable Than Ever Before* (New York: Atria Books, 2006); and Jean M. Twenge and W. Keith Campbell, *The Narcissism Epidemic: Living in the Age of Entitlement* (New York: Atria Books, 2009).

A number of recent studies offer a variety of prescriptions for improving children's lives. These include Richard Louv, *Last Child in the Woods: Saving Our Children from Nature-Deficit Disorder* (Chapel Hill, NC: Algonquin Books, 2008) and Lenore Skenazy, *Free-Range Kids: How Parents and Teachers Can Let Go and Let Grow*, 2nd ed. (Hoboken, NJ: Jossey-Bass, 2021).

Index

Since the index has been created to work across multiple formats, indexed terms for which a page range is given (e.g., 52–53, 66–70, etc.) may occasionally appear only on some, but not all of the pages within the range.

Academic Achievement and Inequality 55–59, 61–62, 86–88
Academic Competition 100–101, 104–106, 221–222
ADHD / Attention Deficit Disorder 1–2, 6, 14, 33, 41–42, 189, 196–197, 199–200, 208–210, 227, 229–230
Adoption and Foster Care 123–124
Adult Anxiety and Children 213, 222
Adult Supervision and Overscheduling 145, 148–150, 154, 158–159, 164
Adultification of Childhood 11, 170
Advance Placement (AP) Courses 101
Advertising and Commercialization of Childhood 10, 169–170, 172–173, 181–184, 244
After-School Activities and Programs. 106, 154
Ahmed, Samira 48
Allergies 197, 205–206, 227, 229–230
  Environmental factors and 205
Amusement Parks and Family Vacations 155
Anxiety in Children 1, 4–6, 41–42, 83, 96, 98–99, 212–226
  causes of 219–223
  in historical perspective 214–215
  United States vs. other countries 213
Asian American Childhoods 74–76
Assimilation and Multiculturalism 70–71
Autism Spectrum Disorder 196–197, 210–211, 229–230

Baby Boom and Its Impacts 15–16, 32, 86, 93–94
Bike Riding, Decline of 147
Bilingualism 54, 71
Birth Control and Family Planning 118–119
Birthdays and Birthday Parties 150
Black Childhoods 68–70
Blended Families and Step-Families 121, 124–125

Body Image Issues and Cosmetics Marketing 5, 169–170
Boredom in Students 82, 98–99
Breines, Wini 180–181
Bui, Thi 49
Bullying and Cyberbullying 35–36

Civic and Political Advocacy by Children 18
Child Care and Day Care 126–129
Child Labor 9, 19, 23–24, 26–28
Child Mortality 10
Child Poverty and Concentrated Poverty 57–58
Child Policy and Child Rights 10–11, 17–19, 43, 56–57
Child Welfare Programs 56–57
Childhood Autonomy 192–193
Childhood Disorders
  emergence of 227–229
  numbers and Rates 229–230
  causation challenge 230–232
  responses to 232–236
Childhood Happiness 1–2, 10
Childhood Inequality 240–241
Childhood Innocence and Romanticization 3, 24–25, 27–28
Childhood Mental Health and Therapy 232–235, 248–250
Childhood Vulnerability (Historical Emergence) 20–28, 32
Children and Moral Education 247–248
Children of Immigrants 72–74
Children's Changing Leisure Patterns 22–23, 34, 38–39, 45–46, 153–154
Children's Competence and Independence 22–23, 34, 38–39, 45–46, 248–250
Children's Consumerism and Toy Culture 10, 17, 172, 181–182
Children's Emotional Wellbeing 29–31, 135–136, 142–143

Children's Media and Digital Culture 172, 185–186, 188–192
Children's Mental Health Awareness 224, 232–233
Children's Play and Games 144–146, 151–154, 162–168
Childfree Movement 118–119
Chin, Staceyann 49
Chores 38
Cohabitation and Marriage Trends 117, 122–123, 125
College Admissions and Testing Requirements (SAT/ACT) 96–97, 100–101, 104–105, 110–111
Colonization of Children's Imagination 184–186
College Students and Mental Health 217–218, 229–230
Commercialization of Childhood 238, 244
Commercialization of Children's Play and Toys 10, 28, 146–147, 152, 163, 169–170, 181–184
Competition Among Students 104–106
Concentrated Poverty and Residential Segregation 58
Concept Creep (Disability Categories) 198–199
Corporate Exploitation of Childhood 238, 244
Cultural Critiques of Children's Culture 174–175
Cultural Differences in Therapeutic Emphasis 231–233

Demographic Shifts and Childhood 16, 171, 188–189
Depression in Children and Adolescents 229–230
Diagnosis Difficulties (New Disorders) 227, 231–232
Disability Accommodation Trends 235–236
Discipline, Corporal Punishment, and Zero-Tolerance Policies 108–109
Disney and Commercialization of Childhood 10
Divorce Trends and Family Stability 14, 120–122
Diversity in Childhood and Family Structures 50–51, 53–55, 62–64
Dropouts (Educational) 88–89
Dyslexia 196–197, 199, 206–208

Economic Changes and Impact on Childhood 15, 55–59

Education and Mental Health 221–222, 245–246
Education and Inequality 2, 4, 9, 15, 17, 21, 34, 39–40, 54–56, 59, 62, 81–88
Electronic Entertainment and Screen Time 5, 145, 147, 153–155, 167, 172, 188–192
Emotional Fragility and Psychological Vulnerabilities 29–31, 41–42
Extended Family and Grandparental Care 73–74, 129–132
Extracurricular Activities (General Trends) 106

Family Life and Changing Structures 2, 62–64, 117–126, 137–139
Family Structure Changes and Anxiety 220–221
Fear and Safety Concerns in Childhood 30, 34, 36, 144–145, 147–148, 154
Fertility Problems and Assisted Reproduction 119–120
Food Marketing and Childhood Obesity 203–204
Fragile Child Hypothesis 20–23, 32, 43–46
Free-Range Parenting 21, 45

Gay and Lesbian Parenting 117, 119–120
Gender and Childhood 64–68, 157, 159
Gender Identity and Sexual Orientation 77–78
Global Comparisons on Anxiety 213
Golden Age of Childhood: Myths and Realities 170–172, 177–179
Grade Inflation and the Importance of Grades 100–102
Grandparents' Role 130–132

Haidt, Jonathan 169, 242
Halloween, Transformation of 148
Helicopter Parenting 20, 32, 39, 136
and anxiety 219, 238
Henderson, Rob 48
Hickam, Homer 179
Historical Memory, Nostalgia, and Childhood 11–12, 170–172, 177–178, 193–194
Historical Perspective on Childhood. 3–6, 151–152
Homework and Educational Pressures 28–29, 39–40, 94–95
Hopscotch, Jump Rope, Simon Says 147
Household Pets and Children's Emotional Development 164
Housing Costs, Discrimination, and Outdoor Play 1, 56, 171, 178

INDEX 281

Inequality
  academic achievement and 55–59, 61–62, 86–88
  economic inequalities 55–59, 173, 181
  in access to mental health services 233–234
  in access to media and toys 173, 192–193
  in education 86–88
Informal Outdoor Play (Loss of) 145–146, 152–154
Injury, Safety Concerns, and "Safetyism," 36, 144–145, 147–148, 154
Intersectionality in Childhood Studies 52–53

Juvenile Delinquency Fears 13

Kovic, Ron 178–179

Latchkey Kids and Changing After-School Experiences 2, 154
Learning Disabilities and Disorders 115, 196–197, 199–200, 206–208
Length of School Day and Year 90
Loneliness in Children and Adolescents 1, 4–5, 165–166
Luiselli, Valeria 49–50

Marriage and Family Trends 117, 122–123
Media Literacy and Regulation 244
Medicalization of Childhood and Mental Health Trends 29–30, 32–33, 196–198, 200, 211
Memoirs and Autobiographies About Childhood 178–181
Mental Health Disorders 227–229, 231–232, 243
Mental Health Days for Students 225, 241, 246
Middle-Class Parenting Trends and Children's Culture 22–23, 43–44, 173, 192–193
Moral Panics and Childhood 34, 40
Music Participation and Music Education 161–162

Neighborhood Play, Decline of 145–146, 153–154
New Disorders of Childhood 196–201, 227–229
No Child Left Behind and Educational Testing Trends 84–85, 98–99

Obama, Michelle 48
Obesity among Children 203–204, 229
Organized Children's Sports and Travel Teams 156–160

Parental Attitudes Toward Play and Structured Leisure 144–146, 151, 158, 162–163
Parental Roles and Expectations 84, 100–101, 106
Parenting Styles 132–137
Partisanship and Childhood Policies 242–244
Pathologization of Children's Behavior 4, 40–41
Peer Relations and Identity Formation 176–177
Pharmaceuticals and Mental Health 215, 225
Physical Education and Health Concerns 91–92, 95
Play Dates and Sleepovers 149–150
Play Theory and Critics of Play Decline 163–164, 167–168
Play, Decline and Transformation 2, 37–38, 144–146, 151–154, 162–168, 173, 176, 178, 188–189
Playgrounds and Changes in Physical Space 148
Political Debates Over Childhood Issues 4–5
Positive Psychology and Wellbeing Initiatives 235
Post-Pandemic Trends in Childhood and Schooling 111–113
Privatization of Childhood 173, 192
Psychologization of Childhood 197, 211
Public Policy and Childhood Inequality 56–57

Race, Class, and Anxiety Patterns 213
Race, Structural Racism, and Childhood 68–70
Reading Disabilities and Dyslexia 196–197, 199, 206–208
Reading for Pleasure, Decline of 147
Recess Loss and Lunch Reductions 91–92, 110–111
Regulation of Children's Environment 244–245
Religion and Families 137
Resistance and Subversion in Children's Culture 175, 177
Romanticization of Childhood and Innocence 3

Safety Measures in Schools 225–226, 235
Safetyism and "Safety First" Culture 36, 144–145, 147–148, 154
School Counseling Expansion 219, 232–233
School Diversity and Structural Changes 86–87, 92–93

282 INDEX

School Shootings, Security, and Lockdowns 107, 223
Screen Time, Social Media, and Electronic Play 5, 17, 45, 188–192, 223
Sexual Activity, Decline Among Teens 166–167
Sibling Relations and Rivalry 13, 31–33
Simmons, Ruth, J. 181
Smith, Matthew 206, 208–209
Social Class and Access to Play and Activities 151, 155–156, 159, 164
Social Class and Family Structure Differences 57–58, 123–124, 128, 141
Socialization and After-School Friendships 151, 154, 164
Societal Anxieties and Children 222
Socioeconomic Divisions and Inequality 4, 55–59, 173, 181, 192–193, 204
Specialized Summer Camps 155–156
Spock, Dr. Benjamin 30, 32–33
Standardized Testing and Student Stress 96–100
Structured Leisure vs. Free Play 146, 151, 158
Student Counseling Services Expansion 232–233
Student Fragility and Mental Health Expectations 232–233, 235–236

Student Perceptions of School and Education 81, 103–106, 114–115

Tag, Hide-and-Seek, Kick-the-Can Decline 144–146
Technology's Impact on Children and Childhood 5, 172, 188–192
Test Anxiety 216, 221–222
Therapeutic Culture Growth 231–234
Therapy, Expansion of Access and Limits 224–226, 232–235
Toy Commercialization 152
Travel Sports Teams and Competition Intensification 157–159
Twenge, Jean 169, 217, 219–221

Unstructured Outdoor Play, Loss Of 144–146, 151–154

Violence in Media and Play 170, 178, 190
Visual, Technological, and Media Literacy 191

Wellbeing Centers and Prevention Efforts 235
Work and Children (Historical Views) 9, 13
Working Mothers and Family Change 2

Youth Culture and Mental Health 1, 3–5